MANAGING WATER-RELATED CONFLICTS:

THE ENGINEER'S ROLE

Proceedings of the Engineering Foundation Conference

co-sponsored by the
Committee on Social and Environmental Objectives
   of the Water Resources Planning and Management Division
   of the American Society of Civil Engineers
Institute for Water Resources, U.S. Army Corps of Engineers
National Science Foundation
Universities Council on Water Resources

Sheraton Santa Barbara
Santa Barbara, California
November 5-10, 1989

Edited by Warren Viessman, Jr. and Ernest T. Smerdon

Published by the
American Society of Civil Engineers
345 East 47th Street
New York, New York 10017-2398

ABSTRACT

The problems facing water resources planners and managers are extensive. The major challenge is finding the key to cooperative rather than divisive approaches to water resources management. In order to accomplish this, the engineer must understand not only the technological aspects of water management, but also the social aspects. This proceedings is concerned with helping the engineer to better understand the area of conflict management and what his role might be in managing water conflicts. Such topics as analytical aids to conflict management, innovative compensation arrangements, a water supply planning model, alternative dispute resolution, and the changing role of the engineer are discussed. With this type of information, an engineer will be able to participate in the resolution of the differing public, agency, and governmental views concerning the area of water resources management.

Library of Congress Cataloging-in-Publication Data

Engineering Foundation (U.S.). Conference (1989: Santa Barbara, Calif.)
    Managing water-related conflicts: the engineer's role: proceedings of the Engineering Foundation Conference, Sheraton Santa Barbara, Santa Barbara, California, November 5-10, 1989/co-sponsored by the Committee on Social and Environmental Objectives of the Water Resources Planning and Managment Division of the American Society of Civil Engineers . . . [et al.]; edited by Warren Viessman, Jr. and Ernest T. Smerdon.
    p. cm.
    ISBN 0-87262-744-6
    1. Water resources development—Social aspects—United States—Congresses. 2. Water resources development—United States—Planning—Congresses. 3. Water rights—United States—Congresses. I. Viessman, Warren. II. Smerdon, Ernest T. III. American Society of Civil Engineers. Water Resources Planning and Management Division. Committee on Social and Environmental Objectives.
IV. Title.
HD1694.A5E53   1989   89-78366
333.91'17'0973—dc20   CIP

AN INTRODUCTION TO THE CONFERENCE PROCEEDINGS

Warren Viessman, Jr.*
Ernest T. Smerdon**
Conference Co-Chairmen, Members, ASCE

The problems facing water resources planners and managers are extensive. They have both technologic and social dimensions. A major challenge is finding the key to cooperative rather than divisive approaches to managing the Nation's waters. The technologic capability for solving water-related problems is vast but its potential will be far from realized if it is not exercised within the realities of prevailing political and social systems.

Water management problems embrace the ever-changing goals of society and they challenge our technologic capabilities. They have dimensions of risk, uncertainty, and society's preferences. In particular, they are heavily associated with extreme events—floods and droughts. They cannot be solved in the technologic arena alone. Optimal engineering approaches may be, and often are, politically and socially infeasible. The engineers role must increasingly embrace a blend of social and technological comprehension. Engineers must be society-wise as well as technology-wise. Technologic talents will have to be focused so they will be respected and accepted by those who are in the decision making arena. Engineers and other technologists must learn how to function in the context of practical realities and to communicate effectively with those who are charged with the responsibility for determining our courses of action. To this end:

- more direct involvement of engineering practitioners in forums for addressing water management conflicts should be encouraged;
- engineers must be provided specific educational opportunities related to conflict management practices;
- engineers must be prepared to more effectively acquaint decision makers with options for dealing with critical periods of varying frequency;
- analyses of how conflicts have been dealt with in the past, successfully and unsuccessfully, need better identification and documentation so they can be used effectively as instructional vehicles; and
- curricula related to water resources planning and engineering should be proposed to more fully address subjects such as conflict management, dealing with critical events, decision making processes, working with the public and governmental bodies, policy analysis, and vehicles for fostering interactive (public-agency-decision maker) approaches to water resources problem solving.

* Department of Environmental Engineering Sciences, University of Florida, Gainesville, Florida 32611-2013
** College of Engineering and Mines, University of Arizona, Tucson, Arizona 85721

Water resources planning and management processes must address, up-front, potential conflicts of interest and incorporate mechanisms for dealing with them that have a high probability of being accepted by all of those having a stake in the issue of concern. The ability to implement water resources plans will depend heavily on our skills in identifying and managing conflicting public, agency, and governmental views. And unless engineering expertise is introduced more effectively in the arenas where conflicts are dealt with the outcomes of these forums will almost certainly be technologically deficient. Accordingly, strategies are needed to facilitate:

- understanding by water resources engineers, planners and managers of the importance of identifying conflict potentials in advance so that the prevention of conflicts rather than a need to resolve them might be the order;
- the incorporation of conflict management techniques in water resources planning and management processes;
- coordinating critical period strategies with those appropriate to normal conditions; and
- to enhance the ability of scientists and engineers to deal with various publics regarding water management plans and proposals so that a cooperative rather than a combative arena is the result.

Accordingly, the Engineering Foundation Conference that produced these proceedings was designed to develop workable engineering strategies for dealing with conflicts and to present those findings in a useful and tutorial documentary form.

Each of the papers included in the proceedings has been accepted for publication by the Proceedings Editors. All papers are eligible for discussion in the Water Resources Planning and Management Division Journal. All papers are eligible for ASCE awards.

CONFERENCE STEERING COMMITTEE

1 Dr. Warren Viessman, Fr., Chairman   (Chairman)
Dept. of Environmental Engineering
217 Black Hall
University of Florida
Gainesville, Florida 32611

2. Dr. Ernest T. Smerdon, Dean   (Co-Chairman)
College of Engineering and Mines
Office of the Dean
Civil Engineering Building #72
Tucson, Arizona 85721

3. Dr. Harold J. Day
University of Wisconsin—Green Bay
SEC, EJ 317
Green Bay, Wisconsin 54302

4. Dr. Claire Welty
Department of Civil and
  Architectural Engineering
Drexel University
32nd and Chestnut Street
Philadelphia, Pennsylvania 19104

5. Mr. Kyle E. Schilling
U.S. Army Corps of Engineers
Institute for Water Resources
Casey Building
Fort Belvoir, Virginia 22060

6. Dr. Jerome Delli Priscoli
U.S. Army Corps of Engineers
Institute for Water Resources
Fort Belvoir, Virginia 22060

7. Ms. Suzanne G. Orenstein
Senior Associate
The Conservation Foundation
1250 24th Street, N.W.
Washington, D.C. 20037

CONTENTS

INTRODUCTION III
    Warren Viessman, Jr. and Ernest T. Smerdon

PART I—BACKGROUND

Institutional Aspects of Managing Conflicts 1
    Frank Gregg

Dealing With Critical Periods (Floods and Droughts) 15
    Walter M. Grayman

Analytical Aids to Conflict Management 23
    Daniel P. Loucks

The Role of Negotiation in Managing Water Conflicts 38
    Gail Bingham and Suzanne G. Orenstein

Expanding the Role of the Engineer in
Conflict Management 54
    Ernest T. Smerdon

PART II—INSTITUTIONS FOR MANAGING CONFLICTS

From Hot-Tub to War: Alternative Dispute Resolution in
the U.S. Corps of Engineers 70
    Jerome Delli Priscoli

Innovation Compensation Arrangements for Resolving
Water Transfer Conflicts 94
    William E. Cox and Leonard A. Shabman

Institutional Aspects of Water Dispute Resolution 110
    William B. Lord

PART III—CRITICAL PERIOD CONSIDERATIONS

Negotiating Water Supply Management Agreements
for the National Capitol Region 116
    Robert S. McGarry

Platte River Conflict Resolution 131
    Ann S. Bleed

Water Supply Planning Model for Southwest Florida 141
    James P. Heaney

PART IV—ANALYTICAL AIDS TO CONFLICT MANAGEMENT

Disputes Surrounding 404 Permitting in Colorado 156
    Merle S. Lefkoff

The Changing Role of the Engineer in Interstate
Water Disputes: From Designer to Manager 170
    Charles T. DuMars

Linked Models for Indian Water Rights Disputes 180
    William B. Lord, Mary G. Wallace,
    and Rose M. Shillito

PART V—THE ROLE OF NEGOTIATION IN CONFLICT MANAGEMENT

Dispute Resolution Experiences: the Engineer's Role 194
    Charles L. Lancaster

Utilizing Negotiations to Resolve Complex
Environmental Disputes 208
    Chris Moore

Managing Conflict Over a Dam Safety Problem 223
    Curtis A. Brown

PART VI—THE ENGINEER'S ROLE IN CONFLICT MANAGEMENT

Conflict Management and the Urban/Rural Watershed 238
    Harold J. Day

Conflict: A Stimulant for Action 245
    Jonathan W. Bulkley

A Social Scientist's Viewpoint on Conflict Management 261
    Madge O. Ertel

PART VII—WORK GROUP REPORTS

Institutional Structures 266

Analytical Aids 273

Managing Water related Conflicts Using Negotiation 280

List of Participants 289

Subject Index 291

Author Index 293

Institutional Aspects of Managing Conflicts

Frank Gregg[1]

Abstract

Resolution of conflicts in water resources management takes place within the context of complex institutional arrangements. Understanding institutions enhances prospects for devising effective conflict management strategies.

For purposes of analysis, one of the more illuminating ways of defining institutions is as a set of written and unwritten rules that order relationships among actors in a network formed out of shared interests in a particular set of values (resources are values).

Investigators on a study in progress on institutional responses to changing water policy environments have chosen to adopt this concept of rules as the distinguishing feature of institutions, and a specific structure of rules as the framework for analysis of specific institutions.

The investigators have drawn theories from several literatures to explain relationships between the form and content of rules and the actions of actors in institutional networks. The method adopted for case studies differentiates among water resource issues types, among positions of actors in the issue types, and

----

[1]Professor, School of Renewable Natural Resources, University of Arizona, Tucson, AZ, 85721. The research described in this paper is supported by the U.S. Geological Survey, Department of the Interior, under U.S.G.S. Award Number 14-08-0001-G1639. The views and conclusions contained in this document are those of the authors and should not be interpreted as necessarily representing the official policies, either express or implied, of the United States government.

1

among incentives provided by differing categories of tools as key variables in actors' responses to rules.

The rules which order relationships within an institution are shaped in part by interactions among participants, but are strongly affected by the endowments which actors bring to the institution, such as wealth, position in community, command of information and technical resources, property interests in the natural resources at issue, and public policies and administrative practices.

The capacity of organizations within networks may be particularly vulnerable to constraints placed upon them by myths, symbols, desired images, and deeply held belief systems of professions and organizational fields.

Hypotheses about the connection between actors, rules and institutional outputs have not yet been tested in case studies for explanatory power or utility. The investigators expect that the ongoing research will ultimately provide improved methods for diagnosis of water resource institutional situations as a step toward improved capability in institutional design.

Introduction

My purpose in this paper is to direct attention early in the conference to those institutional and organizational characteristics that influence capacities for managing conflict.

Assessing the capacity of institutions to lead or participate effectively in technically, economically, and socially responsible conflict resolution requires a body of theory and method for institutional analysis and design. The burden of this paper draws from work in progress on a study of "Institutional Response to a Changing Water Policy Environment", supported by a grant from the U. S. Geological Survey, for which Steve Born of the University of Wisconsin and Helen Ingram, Bill Lord, Marvin Waterstone and I of the University of Arizona are principal investigators. My fellow investigators, of course, are not to be held responsible for my interpretations of what we have studied or learned to date.

I will define a few key terms, and outline concepts from several bodies of literature. The concept of rules is adopted as the primary basis for characterizing and differentiating institutions. A structure of rules is summarized below. A format for organizing data collection in increments suitable for analysis is outlined. A discussion of variables which affect institutional responses to inputs follows. Concluding sections summarize characteristics of institutions and organizations which may facilitate or constrain institutional capacity in conflict management, but the utility of the paper for this conference will rest primarily on its value in outlining an analytical approach to assessing and enhancing institutional capacity.

Definitions and Concepts

"Institution" as used in this paper refers to a set of rules which order relationships among actors in a network that functions over time as an arena for the pursuit of diverse interests in a defined set of values -- in our case, in values associated with use of water and related resources. The definition is an amalgamation derived from political sociology (Knoke, 1989) and public choice (Ostrom, 1987).

"Rules" refers to factors which structure relationships and incentives of participants in an institution, and shape outcomes of their interactions. Rules include factors which a) determine who is permitted to participate in what positions under what conditions of selection and tenure, exercising what degree of authority over what scope of actions; b) specify the conditions under which decisions are made and actions ordered and executed; c) specify channels for and control of information and its use in making decisions; and d) determine patterns of distribution of benefits and costs. The inspiration and much of the vocabulary and methodology relating to rules comes from Ostrom (1989, 1987), but a number of interpretations of the structure of rules and the use of rules in analysis may be inconsistent with Dr. Ostrom's specific application of them.

"Organizations," as distinguished from institutions, are collectives in which goals, strategies, positions, roles and rewards are determined by an internal authority structure. Organizations may be actors within an institutional network, usually as members of coalitions of advocates seeking to influence the allocation of the values and costs at issue. (Sabatier, 1987a, 1987b; Milward and Wamsley, 1985).

The approach outlined here assumes that the incentives and actions of individuals and collectives with common interests in a defined set of values may be understood by examining:

-- the nature of the water resource issues in terms of kinds and conditions of use and effects on other uses and users (common pool issues, externalities, public goods issues);

-- the structure and incentives of various positions in various water resource issue types (for example, generators as distinct from bearers of externalities), and the consequent formation of coalitions of like interests which include those occupying similar positions;

-- the initial distribution of endowments among participants (wealth, power, position, relevant property interests and the current form and content of law, policy and administrative practices);

-- the rules (including rules arising from the initial distribution of endowments) which establish relative positions of power and thereby order relationships among participants in their continuing interactions with respect to the resource values at issue.

The neoclassical assumption of informed self-interest is recognized as a pervasive determinant of behavior. The self-interest of actors and coalitions may, however, include preferences for outcomes not readily measurable in economic terms, such as policies or actions leading to preservation of intrinsic environmental values or sustainability as a constraint on current levels and patterns of resource use (Livingston, 1989).

We also recognize behavioral motivations which expand upon the neo-classical model of the rational, utility-maximizing individual. Value driven constraints on "rational" behavior imposed by what organization theorists describe as the "institutional objectives" of "organizational fields" are recognized as potentially significant factors affecting institutional capacity for conflict management (DiMaggio and Powell, 1983).

Framework for Analysis

A structure of rules which may be used to examine and explain the actions of actors within a network is taken from Ostrom (1989, 1987). After some tinkering with Ostrom's terminology, we adopted the following structure:

a) <u>Scope rules</u>, which define the range of actions and outcomes which can be affected by the actors occupying positions in the network.

b) <u>Boundary rules</u>, which specify who is and who is not recognized as a participant -- and who makes the in/out decisions.

c) <u>Position rules,</u> which govern the structure of positions, and control the selection and tenure of participants occupying various positions.

d) <u>Authority rules</u>, which specify the authority and scope of action vested in positions.

e) <u>Rules of decision and action</u> ("aggregation rules") in Dr. Ostrom's taxonomy) which specify the conditions under which decisions are made and actions taken.

f) <u>Information rules</u>, which specify information channels and conditions of access, and specify how information in support of various points of view is processed.

g) <u>Payoff rules</u>, which prescribe how benefits and costs of decisions and actions are to be distributed among participants.

It is important for understanding institutions as rules to reemphasize that the rules which establish peck orders among participants and positions are determined largely by the initial distribution of endowments. In addition to wealth, access to and control of information, technical capability and position in economic and political communities, the initial endowments distribution may also include specific property interests, including appropriative water rights, permits and licenses, leases, contracts, and other rights in the resources at issue. The specific provisions of public policy and administrative requirements and practices for implementing public policy may be key elements of rules with powerful effects on relationships and outcomes within a given rule set.

Initial endowments are also pivotal in considering actions to change the rules, most particularly those specified by public policies and programs.

With a structure of rules defined, an important first step in exploring a specific case is to describe the broad social, political and economic context which affects the environment of the case under study. To the extent that these broad contextual factors affect the range of choice involved in the case situation, they may become targets for analysis and potential change.

Ignoring contextual factors may fail to reveal the source and content of rules affecting relationships among participants, and may artificially constrain the relevant range of alternatives for closing gaps, thus frustrating prospects for conflict resolution. The contextual background should, of course, characterize the natural resource systems involved and delineate the relevant history of resource use and management.

With the rules structure as a framework for organizing data, steps in building an information base for a case analysis include:

1) Establish <u>the nature and intensity of demand</u> for use of water and related resources, and <u>gaps between existing and desired conditions</u> perceived by various groupings of interests. Classify the nature of issues/gaps as common pool resource issues, externalities, or public goods issues (from the vocabulary of environmental economics).

2) Delineate the <u>network of individuals, groups and organizations</u> in the context of scope, boundary, position and authority rules. Actors will include contending parties at interest, administrators of relevant public programs, and policy-makers regularly involved in the field of interest.

3) Classify participants into <u>coalitions with shared interests</u>, and specify the objectives of the coalitions. Actors in policy-making and administrative positions may function as members of advocacy coalitions, or as policy entrepreneurs and brokers operating across coalition boundaries. (Wamsley, 1985).

4) Examine and describe <u>initial endowments for pursuing objectives</u> held by participants. Classify the <u>key components of public policy and implementation measures</u> according to the nature of instruments specified -- incentives, both positive and negative; information, both technical and exhortatory; and coercive (Dahl and Lindblom, 1976). Treat the form and content of initial resources as elements of scope, position, authority, decision and action, information and payoff rules.

5) Examine and describe the <u>possible strategies</u>

<u>available to various classes of participants</u> for
pursuing their objectives, with appropriate
consideration of the nature of the water resource
issues, the positions of actors in those issues, their
preferences for the content of rules and tools, and the
political environment (Ingram and Schneider, 1988;
Schneider, 1989).

Behavioral Assumptions

A critical assumption underlying dynamics of
institutional change -- the roots of conflict -- is that
actors (individuals, groups, organizations) with similar
interests in closing a perceived gap between existing
and desired conditions will form into coalitions to
advocate their interests. Coalitions will form into
networks composed of the range of actors and interests
seeking to influence allocation of the values at issue.
Coalitions will include those actors in policy-making
and policy-implementing bodies who share objectives and
interests of specific coalitions. As noted earlier,
policy-makers, administrators and others may also occupy
positions as brokers in networks.

Coalitions of organizations and individuals may be
used as surrogates for examination of behavior of
individual participants (Sabatier, 1987, Wamsley, 1985).
(There may be problems with this assumption in CPR
situations, where individual appropriators are the key
actors).

Coalition behavior may be expected to arise from
combinations of institutional and technical objectives
as noted earlier (DiMaggio and Powell), the former
embracing the symbols, norms, desired images, shared
belief systems and long-term strategies of the actors
involved, and the latter their self-interests in the
resource values at issue in neoclassical economic terms.

Methods of Analysis

Analysis takes the form of examining the behavior
of participants occupying various positions in various
water resource issue types in response to differing
rules (including the properties of tools specified for
policy implementation) as reflected in relationships
among actors and the outcomes of their interactions.

The water resources issue typology distinguishes
among kinds and conditions of use and consequent effects
on resource systems and other users, existing or
potential. Key features of the typology:

a) <u>common pool resource issues</u> (CPRs), in which unrestricted access to a renewable or nonrenewable resource undermines incentive for any individual user to conserve;

b) <u>externalities</u>, (both spatial and temporal) in which uses of a resource by one or more classes of users affect the value of the resource for other uses and users;

c) <u>public goods issues</u> in which use by one or more categories of users does not diminish utility for others, but in which benefits are so widely disbursed as to discourage investment in maintaining resource stock or quality.

The typology of actors' positions in issue types has not yet been rigorously addressed, but will surely include generators and bearers of externalities, holders and non-holders of rights in a CPR, and those who interpret and administer the rules of resource allocation and use in all issue types.

For purposes of assessing conflict management capacity of institutions, a typology of conflict situations is important. One such typology is described by Bill Lord in discussion notes prepared for this conference.

The typology of tools -- incentives, information, coercion -- seems adequate for most situations; a fourth category to recognize public development/management as an authority rule/tool may be particularly relevant to the natural resources field.

The use of rules as a framework for specifying and analyzing hypotheses and variables for analysis is illustrated in the following paragraphs:

In a CPR situation, boundary rules must include all actors who hold rights to the use of the resource. If this is not the case, lack of incentive for management will confirm the tragedy of the commons.

Generators of externalities will prefer rules which shift the costs of externalities to others, and goals and tools for implementation which leave to the generators decisions about levels and means of externality abatement. Bearers of externalities (including intergenerational externalities) will prefer rules which specify standards to be achieved, means of achievement, and allocation of costs to generators.

Dominant actors and coalitions of actors will seek autonomy for securing their interests in scope, boundary, position, authority, and decision and action rules. Less powerful actors will seek rules which enhance prospects for modifying outcomes otherwise determined by the initial distribution of endowments (Wamsley). Brokers will tend toward inclusiveness in boundary and related scope rules.

Restrictive scope and authority rules relative to the range of actors' interests in resource values will stimulate demand for change in external rules, most obviously through changes in laws, regulations and budget allocations, but also through litigation and other forms of extra-institutional conflict management.

Conversely, scope and authority rules responsive to the range of interests in resource values will encourage participation in the network as an arena for conflict resolution, and will enhance institutional capacity for conflict management.

Even with respectable data for specifying institutional characteristics according to the structure of rules there is reason for caution in assuming that the results of analysis will be fully explanatory. For purposes of assessing institutional capacity for conflict management, the effects of institutional as distinct from technical objectives may prove both critical and difficult.

In a technical environment, actors (organizations and individuals) may be expected to concentrate energies on economic (broadly defined) objectives, and behavior may be expected to approximate that of the rational person with full information pursuing self-interest through informed choice. Symbolic and strategic (institutional) considerations lead to elaboration of norms and rules to which individual organizations are expected to conform if they are to receive support and legitimacy, and may constrain the exercise of "normal" self-interested behavior (Powell, 1989).

Rules which can be made rational in economic terms may be expected to produce "rational" results in technical situations, facilitating opportunities for bargaining. Fees, fines, pricing policies, mandated goals achievable through flexible means, research support and technical assistance may be combined in useful ways. On the other hand, deeply held convictions about what Sabatier calls core belief systems (1987) and other "institutional" imperatives may constrain or proscribe negotiation or bargaining even where the immediate self-interests of conflicting parties are not irreconcilable. As a general proposition, the rules governing the content of these institutional objectives are outside the scope of the institution, and often of public policy-making bodies as well.

Concluding Observations

Institutions will not always respond predictably to variations in types of water resource issues, positions in issue types and networks, and configurations of rules. Interests contending for outcomes can, if inspired to do so, confound the designs of policy-makers, administrators and institutional scholars and architects.

The general approach outlined in this paper may be useful, however, as:

-- a checklist of factors to be examined in trying to understand the structure of specific cases;

-- a checklist and format for collecting and arraying data for case studies, and for comparison across cases;

-- a system for diagnosis of situations-- typologies of water resource issues, the structure and objectives of actors and positions, the structure of rules -- which should narrow the range of uncertainty in considering alternatives for the design of institutions.

Beyond interpretations of institutional analysis literature and of the ongoing institutional analysis research project, some less formal opinions and observations directly on the conference theme may be in order.

Arguably, the essence of capability for pursuing non-confrontational approaches to conflict resolution is respect: the appearance and the fact of respect for different philosophical assumptions and value structures in considering range and priority of permissible actions. Decisions can be made and implemented without effective regard for differing value structures, but may foster an environment hostile to timely decision-making in which such technical factors as engineering feasibility, efficiency (however defined) and ecological sustainability are heavily weighted.

Societies, at least democratic societies, treasure their philosophical differences as a measure of freedom and as a primary source of social innovation. Politics is the appropriate arena for responding to value differences within the scope of public policy. But institutional environments for dealing with natural resources conflicts are often constrained by factors which appear to arise from profound differences, but which may in fact be less lofty in origin and more amenable to change.

The processes of professional education tend to mark students with the value systems and concepts of professionalism favored by faculties, including the minority of reductionist specialists, apologists for the interests of major client groups, and defenders of professional orthodoxies which are a hallmark of the academic landscape. In fact, a common experience on leaving the academy is shock induced by the intransigence of a world which is perceived as undervaluing professional imperatives in the conduct of public and private affairs. Renewed emphasis in many excellent colleges and universities on "general education" as distinguished from training offers hope for improvement; many educators in professional schools welcome the trend as the half-lives of technological and scientific states of the art decline.

In the arena of institutional design, a number of factors well within the reach of possibility are available as steps toward conflict management capacity.

One is the professional composition of natural resources institutions, and the roles available to professionals of diverse backgrounds.

In the public land arena, Congress recognized the biases and limitations of unidimensional professional staffs by requiring that land use plans be formulated by interdisciplinary teams. The teams work against a mandate that requires full consideration of alternative methods as well as objectives of management. It seems fair to suggest that the agencies' responses to this mandate has been constrained by core concepts of the dominant professions, particularly sustained yield of renewable resources for a range of consumptive and nonconsumptive uses, achieved through utilization and management programs carried out in accordance with accepted professional practices.

A bias toward sustained production of a diverse range of goods and services is a useful, indeed desirable, bias for professional stewards of public land (and water) resources. The core professional concepts are irrelevant,however, to those who place a premium on the values of rare and endangered species, species diversity generally, and relatively undisturbed natural systems in a technologically obtrusive society. Those who stress priorities for these values see even the best of professional practice as destructive of scarce and valuable resources such as old-growth Douglas fir stands (in land management) and wild river reaches with generous and protected flows (in water resources).

Liberalized professional education and professional diversity in institutions will help improve communications across gaps between professions and value structures. So will flexibility in the range of actions which may be taken in a particular situation in response to conflicting preferences. The federal public land agencies are generally in better position to respond to diversity and to broker or cooperate in negotiation of conflict than most water resources agencies. Their statutory authorities recognize a wide range of uses as legitimate, and authorize a wide range of actions in response. In the water resources field, responsibilities are typically divided among three or more levels of government and the private sector, with further divisions between quality and quantity; between adequacy and excess (floods) and surface and ground water on the quantity side; between polluting constituents and sources on the quality side.

As society's commitment to water quality reduces the risk of dominance by traditional water development interests (a condition that may have been achieved some years ago in many states), integration of quality and quantity and surface and ground water responsibilities becomes more attractive. Interests relatively content with the status quo as well as the high costs of institutional innovation are formidable constraints. The effort may not be worthwhile at the federal level, but there are benefits to be realized from movement toward state, local and special district water resources organizations which are obligated to serve wide sectors of interests and are equipped to do so.

To summarize: diversity in mission and professional mix, reasonable dependability in access to resources to meet responsibilities, openness to meaningful participation by interests representing differing value structures as well as immediate outcomes, flexibility in the range of authorities and tools, delegation of authority under appropriate rules of accountability -- all built on a core of technical competence and high ethical standards -- are attributes of institutional, and organizational, capability in conflict management.

REFERENCES

Dahl, Robert and Charles Lindblom. 1976. Politics,
    Economics and Welfare (Chicago: University of
    Chicago Press, 1976).

Derthick, Martha. 1989. "How to Think about
    Federalism: Advice to Policymakers," paper
    prepared for the Institutional Analysis Seminar,
    School of Renewable Natural Resources,University
    of Arizona, 1989.

DiMaggio, Paul J. and Walter W. Powell. 1983. "The
    Iron Cage Revisited: Institutional Isomorphism
    and Collective Rationality in Organizational
    Fields," American Sociology Review, 48:147-60.

Ingram, Helen M. and Anne Schneider. 1988. "Improving
    Implementation Through Policy Design: Framing
    Smarter Statutes," paper prepared for the Annual
    Meeting of the American Political Science
    Association, September 3, 1988.

Knoke, David. 1989. "The Political Sociology
    Approach to Institutional Analysis," paper
    prepared for the Institutional Analysis Seminar,
    School of Renewable Natural Resources, University
    of Arizona, 1989.

Livingston, Marie. 1989. "Normative and Positive
    Aspects of Institutional Economics: The
    Implications for Water Policy," paper prepared
    for the Institutional Analysis Seminar, School of
    Renewable Natural Resources, University of
    Arizona, 1989.

Milward, H. Brinton and Gary L. Wamsley. 1985.
    "Policy Subsystems, Networks and the Tools of
    Public Management," in Policy Implementation in
    Federal and Unitary Systems, Kenneth Hanf and
    Theo A.J. Toonen, eds. (Dordrecht: Martinus
    Nishoff Publishers, 1985).

Ostrom, Elinor. 1989. "Public Choice, Institutional
    Analysis and Water Resources," paper prepared for
    the Institutional Analysis Seminar, School of
    Renewable Natural Resources, University of
    Arizona, 1989.

_____. 1986. "A Method of Institutional
    Analysis," in Guidance, Control and Evaluation in
    the Public Sector, F. X. Kaufman, G. Mahone and
    V. Ostrom, eds. (Berlin: Walter de Gruyter,
    1986).

_____. 1986. "An Agenda for the Study of
    Institutions," Public Choice 48:3-25.

Powell, Walter W. 1989. "The New Institutionalism in
    Organizational Analysis," paper prepared for the
    Institutional Analysis Seminar, School of
    Renewable Natural Resources, University of
    Arizona, 1989.

Sabatier, Paul A. 1987. "Top-down and Bottom-up
    Approaches to Implementation Research: A
    Critical Appraisal and Suggested Synthesis,"
    Journal of Public Policy 6:21-48.

_____. 1987. "Knowledge, Policy-Oriented
    Learning, and Policy Change: An Advocacy
    Coalition Framework," Knowledge, Creation,
    Diffusion, Utilization 8:4, 649-692.

Schneider, Anne L. 1989. "Policy Design: Elements,
    Premises, and Strategies," paper prepared for
    the Institutional Analysis Seminar, School of
    Renewable Natural Resources, University of
    Arizona, 1989.

Wamsley, Gary L. 1985. "Policy Subsystems as a Unit
    of Analysis in Implementation Studies: A
    Struggle for Theoretical Synthesis," in Policy
    Implementation in Federal and Unitary Systems,
    Kenneth Hanf and Theo A. J. Toonen, eds.
    (Dodrecht: Martinus Nishoff Publishers, 1985).

DEALING WITH CRITICAL PERIODS (FLOODS AND DROUGHTS)

Walter M. Grayman, Member, ASCE[1]

Abstract

Hydrologic conditions provide the setting for conflicts in water resources. The most commonly recognized hydrologic setting is extreme events: floods and droughts. Such events may be characterized by the magnitude of the extreme event, the duration, the recurrence interval, the relationship to development and mitigation plans, seasonal impacts, and other factors. However, conflicts in water resources are not just limited to extreme events. Other hydrologic and human induced factors which can provide a setting for conflicts include spatial and temporal imbalances in water availability, long term variations in hydrology, catastrophic events, and competing uses for water.

Introduction

It is said that when Hollywood recognizes and popularizes an issue then that issue has truly reached the center stage of life. *China Syndrome* detailed the dangers and potential abuse associated with the construction and operation of nuclear power plants and was later validated by the accidents at Three Mile Island and Chernobyl. Many movies have dealt with pertinent issues such as drugs, war, politics, Wall Street dealings, the cold war and a plethora of other relevant topics.

---

[1] Owner, W.M. Grayman Consulting Engineer, 730 Avon Fields Lane, Cincinnati, Ohio 45229

The field of water resources - and more specifically, conflict resolution in water resources - has had its share of treatment in the cinema. *Chinatown* describes the issues associated with water rights and water shortages in the Los Angeles area in the 1930's and the sometimes bloody conflicts that resulted over this limited resource. *The River* deals with the full gamut of flooding, river development and the conflict between a poor, stubborn farmer and a greedy, wealthy land owner who must obtain water in order to fully develop his land holdings. *The Milagro Bean Field War* is a recent film describing the conflict over water between a group of poor natives in the Southwest and a wealthy land developer. In the true tradition of art imitating life, these movies show examples of the wide diversity of hydrologic, economic and institutional conditions that lead to conflicts in water resources.

Hydrologic Settings for Conflicts

Hydrologic conditions provide the settings for conflicts in water resources. If we all lived by a pool of water of infinite size, of perfect quality, and under our complete control then the cause for conflicts involving water would be minimal. However, such a pool does not exist and we are finding that even those situations in nature that we perceived to approach such a utopian condition in at least some dimensions, such as oceans (as infinite sinks for our wastes) and remote pristine lakes (as scenic and recreation areas and water supply sources free of detrimental impacts from man) are truly not infinite pools and serious conflicts can arise over these water resources.

Classically, the two extremal events, floods and droughts, have been viewed as the hydrologic setting for potential conflicts in water resources. Biblical references such as the 40 day flood of Noah's time and the 7 year drought foretold by Joseph represent very early occurrences of such extremal events. However, with the increasing use of our earth's resources by man and the increasing complexity of interactions between man and the environment, it is becoming clear that there are a vastly wider range of hydrologically related settings that can easily spur conflicts related to our water resources.

In this paper, the range of hydrologically related and frequently, man induced, events and circumstances that can lead to conflicts will be explored. The dimensions of these conflicts will be enumerated leading to a broad taxonomy of circumstances that may spawn conflicts in water resources.

Extremal Events: Floods and Droughts

Floods are generally characterized by the magnitude of the flow and the frequency with which such a magnitude is expected to occur. We are all familiar with the traditional plot of recurrence intervals as shown in Figure 1. In this particular plot, the recurrence interval of annual peak flows are shown. For example, an annual peak flow of 3600 cfs is expected to occur once every two year, while a flow of 4900 cfs is expected to occur once every 10 years and a flow of 6400 cfs once every 100 years. Such plots are constructed based on historical data and implicitly assume that there are no forces of nature or man affecting the underlying probabilistic distribution of floods.

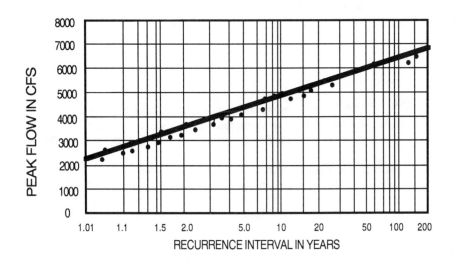

Figure 1 Example Frequency Curve of Annual Floods

Though certainly the magnitude and frequency of occurrence of floods are important factors affecting the severity of a flood (and implicitly a measure of the potential degree of conflict that may result) there are many other factors that impact the perceived severity of a flood. Some of these factors include:

- Season - the time of year of a flood, especially in agrarian societies, can contribute to vastly different perceptions of the severity of a flood event. Additionally, the season can affect the impacts of the flood through natural occurrences such as the presence of ice.

- Length of event - the duration of the flood event affects the degree of severity of the flood. Flood waters that linger for a long period certainly are more costly in terms of inconvenience and damages.

- Time since previous flood - though probabilistically a flood of a certain magnitude is expected to occur only once every n years, nature may inflict such a flood in succeeding years or at other intervals. A short interval between floods can be either more or less detrimental than such a flood occurring at an interval closer to its probabilistic expectation. Similarly, a long interval between floods can result in severe damage due to greater development in the flood plain and lack of understanding of the potential serious impacts of a flood.

- Preparedness and warning time - much of the detrimental impacts of a flood can be alleviated if a community is prepared to cope with a flood. Similarly, sufficient warning time can lessen the negative impacts of the flood.

- Development in the flood plain - the degree of development that has taken place in the flood plain has a significant affect on the impacts of a flood. Two communities on the opposite side of a river, but with differing development patterns, can be affected in a totally different manner by a flood of a given magnitude, duration, warning time, etc.

- Presence of flood control structures - In many cases, structural solutions such as dams and reservoirs, levees and channel improvements prove to be effective methods of mitigating the impacts of flood of a given magnitude or of changing the magnitude of the event.

As is evident, many factors influence the negative impacts of a flood and thus must be considered in characterizing its severity.

Droughts are generally characterized by the magnitude of the drought and the duration. Under most circumstances, a drought of short duration with extreme low flow is less severe in terms of its negative impacts than a longer duration drought with greater flow. However, the tradeoff between duration and magnitude depends upon the uses impacted by the drought. Graphically, droughts are represented by a probabilistic plot showing average flow as a function of recurrence interval for different durations. An example of such a plot is presented in Figure 2.

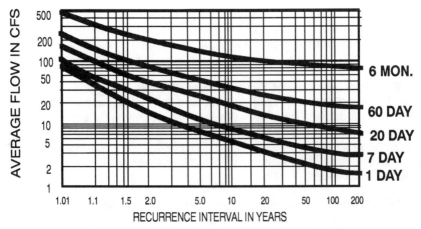

Figure 2 Example Frequency Curve of Minimum Flows

In addition to magnitude and duration of a drought, there are other factors which influence the severity of such an event. Many of these factors are similar to the factors affecting the impacts of a flood.

• Season - Drought conditions during the growing season or other times of high water need can accentuate the impacts of the drought.

• Time between droughts - A short period between droughts can lead to serious conditions because both the physical system and the economic system may not have sufficiently recovered from the previous drought.

• Relative water needs - Some uses are less tolerant to water shortages. Thus, at one extreme, for a flood plain area which depends on a yearly or periodic flood to replenish groundwater or provide nutrients, the absence of such a flood may be considered a drought. In other situations, such as in arid areas in which development has adjusted to limited water availability, only a severe absence of moisture could be considered a drought.

Temporal and Spatial Imbalances

Whereas extremal events are periodic occurrences of excessive or insufficient water, another hydrologic setting for conflicts is an imbalance in either the temporal or spatial availability of water. In a temporal imbalance, on average there is sufficient water available to support the uses but at times during the year there is either too little or too much water. In a spatial imbalance, there is sufficient water within a region but there may be too much in one part of the region and insufficient supply in another part of the region.

Published estimates of the availability of fresh water and the use of water by man (Overman, 1969), indicate that the overall supply far exceeds the worldwide demand for water. When the reuse of freshwater as it travels towards the ocean is considered along with the sub surface pool of water and, if needed, the huge supply of salt water in our oceans, it is evident that on a global scale that water conflicts may be attributed to spatial and temporal imbalances.

Spatial imbalances may range from small scale (a few hundred yards) to near global scale (thousands of miles) situaticns. At the small end, an imbalance may occur between two nearby plots of land where one has water and sewer service and the other does not or two adjacent areas which are subject to different levels of flooding due to elevation differences or difference in protective structures. At the other extreme, water transfers in the western U.S. of hundreds of miles are common and transfers of thousands of miles from Canada to California or from the Mississippi River to western regions have been postulated. The most ambitious spatial transfer of water that has and is still being considered is the transport of icebergs from polar regions to arid regions in the U.S. and the middle east. In each of these cases, potential conflicts can occur due to the spatial imbalance in the water resources and due to structural changes that alter these imbalances.

Temporal imbalances result from differences in the temporal availability of water and the temporal needs. Again, such imbalances may be small time scale imbalances of several hours to imbalances of many years. Natural diurnal variations in water quality and diurnal variations in water quantity due to hydro electric plant releases are examples of potential small time scale temporal imbalances. Natural cycles (seasonal and multi year) in hydrology can result in large time scale temporal imbalances.

Long Term Variations in Hydrology

Floods, droughts, and temporal and spatial imbalances in water availability are all phenomena which can generally be described in probabilistic terms. However, long term variations in climatology and hydrology or other long term trends which affect the availability of water are frequently caused by physical processes that we do not understand. Though we can postulate the existence of such trends, the uncertainty surrounding these trends is generally quite high. Global warming, contamination of groundwater supplies by toxic chemicals, and the deleterious impacts of acid rain on our inland lakes are examples of long term processes which are not fully understood, whose impacts cannot be predicted with much certainty and thus, are excellent examples of potential future settings for conflicts in water resources.

Catastrophic Events

Catastrophic events are similar to long term trends in that they are difficult to predict and can provide settings for future conflicts in water resources. However, unlike long term trends which are gradual processes, catastrophic events are generally triggered by a single (or set of) occurrences with resulting immediate negative impacts. Such triggering events could be natural events, man induced events or events caused by the interaction of natural events but exaggerated by the actions of man. Examples of catastrophic events that have been postulated with obvious negative impacts on water resources include: the sudden change in course of the lower Mississippi River, destruction of the main water supply tunnel feeding New York City, earthquake damage to water resources structures in California, contamination of a major surface water or groundwater supply, global impacts of a major volcanic eruption or collision of a meteorite with the earth. In each case, significant conflicts in water resources (and in other areas of life) would result with little chance for pre planning.

Competing Water Uses

Probably the most significant setting for conflicts in water resources are those resulting from competing uses of our water resources. Unlike other resources such as oil and minerals, where the primary conflict revolves around the relatively simple concept of who has the right to extract the resource, our water resources are much more complex. This complexity is due to many factors: water is a necessity of life for which there are no substitutes; water bodies are used as both a source of water and as a repository for wastes; the chemical, physical and biological reactions and transformations within a water body are complex and generally not fully understood; numerous regulations affect the quality and quantity of water at any given time and place; the availability of water changes with time; and water flows from point to point and moves through the natural hydrologic cycle so that the actions at one location can affect an area great distances away. Each of these phenomena surrounding our water resources contribute to the complexity of water as a natural resource and the competition surrounding its use.

Much work was done in the 1960's and 1970's by institutions such as Harvard University (Maass et al, 1966) and Resources for the Future (Kneese and Bower, 1968) to systematize the concepts surrounding competitive uses of our water resources. Concepts from welfare economics and terms such as "internalizing the externalities", "natural decision units", and "separable damage functions" all pertained to means of quantifying and systematizing competitive uses for water. This line of research and analysis has largely evaporated in recent years though the complexity of the situation and the impetus for conflicts remains as strong as ever.

Conclusions

Conflicts in water resources arise at the intersection of natural hydrologic events and man induced conditions and needs. Floods and droughts represent the classical situations associated with conflicts in water resources. However, other conditions that may foster conflicts include temporal and spatial imbalances in water availability, long term trends in hydrology and climatology, catastrophic events and competing uses for our water resources.

The commonalities among each of the possible settings for conflict are the existence of excessive quantities of water at any time or place relative to natural conditions or the developmental actions of man or insufficient quantity of water of sufficient quality at any given time or place to satisfy the needs of man. All of these situations can be placed under the flood and drought umbrella by broadly extending their definitions to reflect the intersection of the natural hydrologic conditions and the needs and actions of man.

Appendix

References:

Kneese, A.V. and Bower, B.T. (1968),"Managing Water Quality: Economic, Technology, Institutions", Johns Hopkins Press, Baltimore, MD

Maass, A. et al (1966),"Design of Water-Resource Systems", Harvard University Press, Cambridge, Mass.

Overman, M. (1969),"Water - Solutions to a Problem of Supply and Demand", Doubleday and Co., Garden City, NY

Analytical Aids to Conflict Management

Daniel P. Loucks, F.ASCE[1]

Abstract

Managing environmental-water resources conflicts typically involves complex phenomena, multiple issues, and institutions having differing objectives and responsibilities. The synthesis, understanding and communication of relevant data and the identification and evaluation of possible solutions with the aid of analytical and computer models is often proposed, and occasionally accomplished, to support one or more participants in a conflict management process. This paper reviews some proposed modeling approaches, their developers' and potential users' expectations, and some experiences and lessons learned in the use or implementation of modeling aids to integrative conflict management exercises involving environmental and water resources issues and systems.

Introduction

Anyone asked to address a topic as broad as the assigned title of this paper must decide what part of it to discuss. Even a brief review of the current literature on analytical aids to conflict management would require much more time and space than permitted here. Hence I will assume my task to be that of presenting a non-mathematical overview of some different analytical modeling approaches that have been applied to conflict management. Based on the experiences of the analysts involved, I will try to draw some conclusions as to the utility of applying analytical models as aids in a conflict management situation, and suggest some guidelines for increasing the likelihood of successful model use.

This paper will be further constrained by focusing on conflict management problems involving environmental and water resources issues. Environmental-water resources conflicts have some characteristics that distinguish them from many other types of conflicts. Frequently the disputes are less of the distribu-

---

[1] Professor, School of Civil and Environmental Engineering, Cornell University, Ithaca, New York 14853, USA.

tive kind (where what one party gets another party loses and hence offers and counter-offers are made, often in the absence of complete or truthful information), but rather are more often of the integrative kind. Integrative bargaining involves discovering how all parties in conflict can benefit from cooperating, and then determining how these added benefits can be apportioned equitably.

Conflicts over the management of a shared resource arise because of differing objectives and interests among different interest groups or institutions. Frequently each party in conflict fails to comprehend fully the interdependence of the complex issues and institutional objectives and constraints in conflict. So it becomes a learning process -- an integrative bargaining process. Such conflicts particularly arise when the resource -- say the river basin -- and its management institutions are under stress due to some rare event, such as a drought, a flood, or a severe toxic waste spill. This stress is often exacerbated by:

a) the involvement of multiple public and private interest groups and institutions each having multiple goals and aspirations as well as limited responsibilities and authority,

b) uncertainty with respect to the availability of the shared resource, or the duration and impact of some event reducing its quality or suitability for certain uses,

c) various legal and institutional constraints on the use or transfer of the resource,

d) the lack of an adequate or common data base or set of mutually agreeable assumptions regarding the characteristics of the shared resource, and

e) a lack of experience with unusual or extreme events that may be the cause of the conflict among interest groups or institutions.

Of all the analytical modeling aids available to conflict managers, this paper will focus on those designed to bring about a more complete understanding and consensus among all parties in conflict. This ignores, then, a large number of analytical aids developed for use in a more advisarial conflict management situation, such as when engaged in distributive bargaining. In any conflict management process, both distributive and integrative bargaining will be taking place to some extent. Not including models specifically designed to aid distributive bargaining processes does not imply they are any less important than models designed to aid integrative bargaining processes. It implies that integrative bargaining activities are, in my view, more likely to benefit from information resulting from the use of analytical models.

All of us are conflict managers to some degree. Life involves living with and managing conflicts. Most of us manage our conflicts without the aid of analytical models. But even if we had them, they would not replace the need for us to manage our conflicts. If true at a relatively simple level of conflict management, clearly analytical aids are not going to replace managers of complex environmental-water resources conflicts involving many institutions in conflict and each under their own political pressures. At best, such models can serve only as aids. If successfully integrated into the institutions involved in the conflict management process, these aids can serve to support this process. However this support is only a part of all that is needed to manage conflicts successfully.

Perhaps models can bring to the conflict management process a scientific or technical perspective, but not, very well, other important and relevant perspectives. These other perspectives can be represented by individuals trained in such subjects as political science, sociology, law, history and psychology, to mention a few. Modelers must recognize this need for a multi-perspective, multi-disciplinary approach to conflict management. Models can occasionally aid such processes, but not replace any of the other perspectives needed and involved in these processes.

Having stressed the limitation of analytical aids, it is also important to realize that any conflict involving shared resource distribution, value differences, disputed facts and differing opinions, complex interdependent impacts over space and time, and complicated multi-institutional jurisdictions and decision-making processes, can be substantially assisted by better information and improved means of communication. The more complex a problem is, the more likely some modeling will provide insights into that complexity. A number of analytical aids, commonly termed support systems of one kind or another, seem to be suited for such roles. Some have been and are being used, and used successfully, as will be discussed shortly. But it takes time to evaluate just how effective a given analytical approach can be in different conflict management situations. Newness does not always imply effectiveness.

The remainder of this discussion is divided into three parts: alternative analytical approaches for aiding conflict managers, modeler's and user's expectations versus reality, and some experiences and lessons learned from which guidelines can be suggested for model use. The paper ends with a few conclusions and challenges to those who strive to develop and apply analytical models to aid those responsible for environmental-water resources conflict management.

Alternative Analytical Approaches

Analytical aids to integrative conflict management may serve different purposes. Some are aimed at providing useful information and increasing communication and understanding concerning various issues in conflict. Other analytical aids are oriented towards aiding the conflict management process itself by identifying and evaluating alternative strategies and stable solutions. Each of these two groups of analytical aids requires their users to accept some assumptions concerning the issues, the shared physical resource being managed and used, and the institutional framework in which the conflict management process is taking place. All participating in the conflict management process bring to it their perspectives and assumptions. If the selected analytical aids can adapt to varying perspectives and assumptions, the information they provide will more likely be of value in the conflict management process.

To apply any analytical aid to complex ill-structured conflict management problems, some simplifying assumptions are necessary. Different analytical aids fit different sets of assumptions and often serve different purposes. Isard and Smith (1982) describe over 100 different types of analytical aids for conflict management. There are undoubtedly many more. Among the numerous approaches available for integrative conflict management, those that seem to predominate include multi-objective (and sometimes multi-level) decision making, decision analyses, and cooperative game theoretic methods. More recent methods include applications of artificial intelligence or expert systems and interactive gaming and simulation models. These are often labeled as some type of computer-aided support system.

Multi-objective and multi-level optimization

Multi-objective optimization is a technique for identifying those particular combinations of values for each of multiple, often conflicting objectives that are not dominated. Such efficient solutions have the characteristic that, if one objective value is to be improved in the bargaining process, at least one other objective has to be made worse. What one interest group must give up of one or more of their objective values to improve some objective value considered important by another interest group is called a tradeoff. In some cases, it is useful for various parties in conflict to know the tradeoffs among their different objective values.

Numerous texts, articles and other documents describe various multi-objective optimization models available for use to generate these efficient, non-dominated solution sets. Since most readers of this paper will be familiar with many of these approaches, and their limitations, I will not discuss them further. Their use is well documented in the environmental-water resources planning and management literature.

Multi-level optimization can be used to identify possible solutions to problems involving a hierarchy of decision makers, each having their individual objectives and decision variables, i.e. variables whose values they can control, but which influence the actions and values of the objectives of others. In a conflict management situation, the leader (e.g. a third party such as the UN or World Bank, or the stronger country or institution) decides what they want to do knowing that whatever they do the followers, in satisfying their own objectives, will affect the value of the leader's objectives. The leader, of course, has influenced the value each follower can get from his or her own objective.

Consider, for example, a government agency able to set wastewater effluent charge rates in a river basin and the users of water in the river able to control how much wastewater is discharged back into a river. Both the government's and each user's objective contain variables each can control, and those that others can control. The government's objective of improving stream quality by setting the amount of money charged per unit of wastewater discharge will be based on its perception of the user's reaction to those charges.

The high-level objective is being satisfied (or optimized) subject to the satisfaction (or optimization) of the lower level objective, which for a water user may be, in part, to minimize the total cost of wastewater treatment and disposal.

Anandalingam (1988) views many water resources conflict management problems as bi-level linear programming problems. He and his colleagues show how bi-level linear optimization can identify the advantages each of three parties can have by taking either a leadership role or a follower's position in a conflict. Of course where one is in the hierarchy of decision making may not be an option.

Decision analyses

Decision tree analysis involves the construction of a tree-like network that identifies all possible events, decisions, and their possible outcomes, together with their probabilities. By backtracking from each branch down to the trunk's base -- the current state -- one can identify the most desirable set of decisions and their expected impacts based on some selected criteria. Decision trees have generally been applied to distributive rather than cooperative or integrative conflict management, but this doesn't preclude its use for both types of conflict management (Raiffa, 1982). Their use in aiding actual environmental-water resources conflict management processes seems to be limited.

Game theoretic approaches

Applications of game theory are perhaps among the most prevalent types of analytical aids to conflict management found in the literature. It would appear that game theory was designed for just such situations, hence it is somewhat surprising that its actual application or use has not been very widely observed. Rogers (1969), Sheehan and Kogika (1981) and Fraser and Hipel (1984, 1988) are among many authors who show how various versions of cooperative game theory can be applied to integrative conflict management. Fraser and Hipel and their colleagues have developed a meta-game extension, called Conflict Analysis, that has been applied successfully to a variety of environmental-water resources conflicts.

Cooperative game theory addresses what can be done to increase the benefits or reduce the costs, however measured with however many different objectives, and how to apportion fairly the increased net benefits that result when interest groups and institutions in conflict work together to achieve the potential gains of collective action.

Using the jargon of game theory, parties in conflict are called players. The actions they can take, or not take, are called options. Some options may be independent of other options; some may be dependent on whether or not other options are taken. A combinations of options is called a strategy. Each player's feasible strategy and its potential outcome or consequence can be ranked in order of preference. Game theoretic models such as Conflict Analysis (Fraser and Hipel, 1984) require a knowledge of each player's options and preferences. It then identifies possible stable solutions or strategies for managing conflicts. A variety of recent applications of Conflict Analysis are reported in Volumes 26 and 27 of the Journal of Environmental Management (1988).

Sheehan and Kogiku (1981) present a number of simplified examples of the use of cooperative game theory to identify better cooperative strategies and to help determine how to allocate among themselves the additional gains obtained, say by individuals in conflict who decide to pool their resources to purchase a shared item for much less than the total would be if each purchased their own. There is no ideal procedure for determining how additional benefits should be shared. Concepts of what is fair can range from "equal sharing" to "might makes right" and on to more esoteric approaches such as Shapley values (where those whose cooperation results in the largest net gain get the largest share of that net gain). Finally there is the suggestion made by someone a long time ago: "Do unto others..."

Rule-based decision support

Kersten and colleagues (1988) have explored the use of expert systems as aids to conflict managers. They describe the management process in terms of rules similar to a decision tree analysis. Rules are specified for the system (e.g. a river basin) whose use is in conflict. These, in the jargon of this discipline, are called domain rules. The domain rules contain elementary entities, or facts (which are either true or false), subgoals and goals. Goals are groups of subgoals and facts. Quantitative measures, required in most prescriptive decision (optimization) models, are not required. Expert system shells (programs that operate on the rules) make it possible to manipulate the domain rules. Meta rules (rules operating on other rules) can simulate reasoning and modify domain rules.

This rule-based modeling technique provides a representation of the problem in a decision-analysis hierarchical manner, permits consistency checking, and can give explanations about the reasoning leading to a particular recommended strategy or decision. The so-called inference engine (a computer program) provides a means of simulating and supporting the conflict management process.

Conflict management involves learning. As the management process takes place, each interest group involved in the conflict may be learning more about their opponent's interests, requirements and options, as well as more about the physical system (the shared resource) and its capabilities. As a result, changes in problem representation, the domain rules, may be needed. Kersten et al. (1988) argue that their rule-based approach can indeed adapt to these changing attitudes and knowledge.

Interactive simulation

Since the advent of the relatively powerful and inexpensive microcomputer and workstation and their interactive graphics capabilities, there has been a growing interest in the development and application of interactive graphics-based simulation models. These have been applied, over the past decade, to a variety of environmental-water resources conflict management problems (e.g. Straus and Clark, 1980; Sheer et al., 1989).

Simulation modeling itself has been an important tool of water resources and environmental managers since the early days of using the computer to study such problems (Maass et al., 1962; Hufschmidt and Fiering, 1965). For resource systems whose development or management are in dispute, it seems obvious that having a simulation model of the resource system that is user-friendly, i.e. interactive, flexible and readily modifiable and adaptable to various assumptions regarding input data and operation, could be an aid to better understanding and communication. Such a tool, addressing "what-if" questions, can be used to estimate the impacts of alternative assumptions regarding hydrology, water quality prediction parameters, operating policies, and so on.

The widespread availability of interactive computer graphics as a means of displaying information and managing the simulation process itself permits the involvement of the human and his/her subjective judgments in a computer-aided analysis of issues. This so-called man-machine-model interaction enhances considerably the ability to test and communicate alternative ideas, and their possible consequences, for conflict resolution. This in turn can promote a greater understanding of the system under conflict as well as a greater understanding of the important conflicting issues that the conflict management process should address.

There is little doubt that interactive simulation can serve as a useful aid in a conflict management process. But like other analytical aids that are potentially useful, whether or not they will be useful will depend on many factors. One that the model developer can control is the degree the model can be understood and accepted by all its potential users. This will depend in part on how easily it can include alternative sets of data and assumptions; in fact, how well it can support the positions of its users, and how well it can identify which issues in conflict need further attention and which do not. For example, it may turn out that a simulation indicates that differing assumptions regarding hydrologic flows and advection-dispersion parameters will not make much difference with respect to the resulting quality of water in a river at a particular site. Yet alternative upstream reservoir operating policies do make a difference. Attention should therefore focus on reaching an agreement on reservoir operation and need not get bogged down on finding a common hydrological or water quality parameter data base.

Simulations can serve to shift the debate from issues that may not be very important in the conflict to those issues that are. They can serve to present "facts" based on alternative sets of assumptions, and allow the political process to debate the validity or acceptability of the assumptions. But for simulation models to do this, the assumptions incorporated into them must be readily apparent and changeable.

Sheer and colleagues (1989) have applied interactive simulation to the management of a number of conflicts over the use of shared water in several river basins in the U.S. They have extended this methodology from an inter-active simulation of the physical system to a simulation of the conflict management process to increase the communication and understanding among participants in that process. Their gaming-simulation involves decision makers who are in conflict in a dialogue with the interactive simulation model in a simulated conflict management exercise. Participants can request information from the model regarding the condition of the system containing the shared resource. Responses to these data are in turn simulated. This in turn alters the state of the resource system. This interactive man-machine-model exchange provides a way to learn more about the system, how it can perform, and what each participant can gain or lose by cooperating with each other.

Expectations vs. Reality

There is, and perhaps always will be, a gap between any structured view of a conflict management process and the real world in which conflict manage-ment takes place. All analytical aids to conflict management must assume some structure. Analysts are trained to deal with structured systems. They create artifacts of these systems, not the complex social-physical systems them-selves. The creation of multi-objective, multi-level, multi-variable decision or simulation models is not the same as making decisions under actual time con-straints and numerous conflicting political pressures. Solving models is not the same as solving problems. In the real world, solving one problem usually creates other problems. Improvements in public health and water supplies can lead to population stress. Controlling annual floods in the Nile, for example, has increased the need for fertilizers and irrigation systems, and so on.

By developing models to find a "best" or an "optimal" compromise solution to a conflict, we tend to miss the fact that organizations and societies strive to increase their options, rather than reduce them to a single best. They seek to minimize the adverse consequences or impacts associated with the possibility of failure rather than maximize the probability or likelihood of success. Ecolo-gical systems evolve in ways that make them resilient to failure, rather than fail-safe or failure-free.

Paraphrasing Linstone (1986), any discipline, including those involved in the development of one or more types of analytical aids for conflict manage-ment and decision support, tends to feed on itself, grow, and generate a self-reinforcing "group think." Systems dynamics leads to industrial dynamics leads to world dynamics. The number of disciples multiplies as do the number of workshops, conferences, papers, journals, books, professional societies, and awards. Shared interest and reinforcement lead to model refinements and extensions, often without regard to what is really relevant in reality. Quantita-tive analyses tend to drive out qualitative analyses just because the latter are "less rigorous." Analysts tend to think they are being objective, neutral or producing rational, or even optimal, tools and solutions. We modelers are an optimistic bunch, but we must take stock occasionally and become involved in the processes we are trying to assist. It is those who have done this who have developed the more useful analytical aids to various conflict management situations.

The perspectives provided by analysts and their analytical aids cannot by themselves include all the wisdom and experience needed for successful management of complex conflicts. Multiple perspectives, only one of which comes from the technical analyst or modeler, are critical to the successful management of most complex environmental-water resources conflicts. Taken together, the organizational-societal-institutional-legal (i.e. political), the personal-sociological-psychological, and the technical-scientific-engineering perspectives together provide the wisdom and information and experience needed for successful conflict management. Analytical aids, even if successfully implemented, can be only a part of the conflict management process.

Lessons Learned -- Some Guidelines for Model Use

The experiences of those involved in the use of analytical aids provides a basis for defining some guidelines for further research, development and model use. Undoubtedly no two conflict management situations are the same, and hence the experiences and conclusions steming from one situation may differ from those stemming from another. Even though some conclusions may differ, and in fact conflict, it seems appropriate to conclude this brief discussion on analytical aids by drawing from various experiences some guidelines for those involved in developing and using models for aiding conflict management processes.

From a review of the literature cited in the references at the end of this paper, and from discussions with colleagues involved in several research projects related to model use in solving transboundary conflicts recently carried out at the American Academy of Arts and Sciences, Harvard University, Massachusetts Institute of Technology, and the International Institute for Applied Systems Analysis, the following guidelines are suggested for consideration, when appropriate:

1. Confidence in any model is critical for its successful use. All potential users should have an opportunity to participate in the development of the model, or at least to change assumptions in the model and evaluate its effect, and to run the model under different assumptions to compare the results with conventional wisdom. Even if a model is never used for supporting actual conflict management, the process of various parties getting involved in model development and testing increases understanding and the chances of inventing new solutions.

2. One of the greatest problems in environmental conflicts is the development of quantitative measures and indices. Participants in conflict management must be given sufficient time to gain an understanding of various quantitative measures and what they mean or, even better, to define these measures and indices themselves.

3. Every analytical aid has its internal logic and limitations. The dynamics of conflict management processes also have their logics and limita-

tions, which are changing as the processes evolve towards some agreement. Analytical aids that can adapt to changing styles, logic and procedures in the conflict management process will be of greater value in that process than those that cannot.

4. During the development of any analytical aid to the management of conflicts, it is important to incorporate, if possible, the capability for a) subjective judgments, b) interaction between models and individuals, c) identifying relevant information needs and displaying that information in ways that maximize understanding and communication, d) considering important intangible factors as well as tangible quantitative ones, and e) producing the information needed in a timely manner, i.e. when and as needed.

5. Very often the modeling activities associated with supporting conflict management processes should be done away from the room where the debate among those in conflict is taking place. There is a chance the average participant in the process may be distracted by the technology and place undue importance on the technical rather than on the other aspects of the conflict management process. Human interaction should not be constrained by computer technology.

6. Participants in a conflict management process should use shared analytical aids to help them understand each other's objectives and constraints.

7. In a gaming simulation, use the fact that it is a simulation of a hypothetical conflict situation to encourage all participants to experiment with innovative alternative solutions. Representatives from each party in conflict should become involved in generating and analyzing alternative solutions.

8. Data input to analytical models should be easy to modify as should the logic and parameters of the models themselves in order to test the impacts of alternative views of the real world situation. The output of these models should be in a form that permits its rapid interpretation, evaluation and comparison. Watching the reactions of each interest group to new information resulting from models can lead to a better mutual understanding of the issues of greatest importance to each party.

9. Sometimes focusing individuals involved in conflict management on how to beat the previous computer results, rather than how to beat the other individuals, tends to focus attention on items of mutual rather than individual benefit. Joint ownership of solutions makes reaching an agreement easier, just as joint ownership of an analytical aid makes it much easier to accept and benefit from the information derived from it.

10. Models that support conflict management need to be scientifically credible, but also fit into the institutional and political environment in which conflict management is taking place. Model builders, and especially model users, must be well acquainted with, and involved in, the process. Use of models should not be postponed until the end of model development and documentation. There is a close connection between model building and model

use and acceptance by all parties involved.

11. Since analytical models run on computers, access to the needed hardware, access to individuals that can run and change the models when and as desired, and having a user-friendly interface between model users and the models themselves, is crucial to the successful use of models as aids in conflict management.

12. Models as aids to conflict management processes can be used as sources of information for defending a politically established position and to work out its scientific or technical details. They can also be used to foster better articulation of positions and as a means of estimating some of the impacts of alternative possible solutions or agreements.

Some Conclusions and Challenges

It is clear that some applications of analytical methods have provided useful information in support of conflict management processes involving water resources-environmental systems. But it is also clear that effective model use is not accomplished without substantial attention to fitting that activity into the broader political-social context in which conflict management takes place. It is not sufficient to develop an interesting analytical approach for some assumed conflict management scenario or structure. It is often necessary to become part of the conflict management process itself, and to get all potential users of the model involved in model development and evaluation prior to its actual use. On occasion, this has taken place, and models have successfully served to support the management of very complex and political conflicts over environmental-water resources issues.

One forum where conflict management was discussed occurred in the Fall of 1986 at the International Institute for Applied Systems Analysis (IIASA) in Laxenburg, Austria. The Workshop on the Management of International River Basin Conflicts (Vlachos, Webb and Murphy, 1987) brought together negotiators, ambassadors and diplomats, social and natural scientists, and a few model builders -- the systems analysts. The workshop participants identified the following needs (relevant to analytical aids) that they have experienced in conflict management situations:

1. Expanding the factual basis for decision making.

2. Identifying, acquiring and packaging or presenting information in a consistent and comparable manner.

3. Developing comprehensive models for generating a richer menu of alternative options for resolving conflicts.

4. Establishing coherent decision-support systems for improved data management, communication and generation, and understanding of innovative alternatives.

5. Using theoretical and computational advances without overwhelming or ignoring the non-quantitative intangible needs of all parties and individuals involved and the importance of the historical and socio-cultural context of each problem and issue in conflict.

6. Reducing the uncertainties caused by limited technical or analytical support and data regarding proposals about which leaders are asked to risk considerable political and financial capital.

It seems clear, from the needs and opinions expressed in this workshop and in the current literature on conflict management, that analytical models can serve to help bring about improved understanding and agreements among various parties in conflict. But in our efforts to develop improved modeling approaches that will serve the needs expressed above, we should not forget that models will, at best, be only aids to conflict management. Their use can, and has on occasion, provided information that has made a substantial difference in the outcome of some conflict.

Acknowledgment

I am indebted to Lance Antrim, Alan McDonald and many others associated with the research related to conflict management carried out over the past several years, mainly in Cambridge, Massachusetts, and at IIASA in Austria. The part carried out at Cornell University has been supported by the Ford Foundation. I also thank Ernest Thiessen for his help in collecting and reviewing much of the literature used as a basis for this discussion.

References

Anandalingam G. and V. Apprey (1988). "Multi-Level Programming and Conflict Resolution in International River Management." Mimeo, Center for Research in Conflict and Negotiation, College of Business Admin., Penn State Univ., and Dept. of Systems, Univ. of Pennsylvania, Philadelphia.

Anon. (1987-1988). Conservation Exchange, Vol. 5, No. 2, National Wildlife Federation (several articles on computer simulation).

Anson, R., M.T. Jelassi and R.P. Bostrom (1987). "Negotiation Support Systems: Computer Support of Mediated Conflict Resolution." Working Paper Series #W712, Inst. for Research on the Management of Information Systems, Indiana University, Bloomington, IN.

Antrim, L.N. (1985). "Computer Models as an Aid to Negotiation: The Experience in the Law of the Sea Conference." In: Coastal Zone and Continental Shelf Conflict Resolution: Improving Ocean Use and Resource Dispute Management, Sea Grant Information Center, MIT, Cambridge, MA.

Balakrishnan, P.V. (1988). "A New Analytical Process Model of Two-Party Negotiation in Channels of Distribution." Ph.D. Thesis, Univ. of Pennsylvania (Vol. 50/03-A of Dissertation Abstracts Intnl., p. 737).

Bard, J.F. (1987). "Developing Competitive Strategies for Buyer-Supplier Negotiations. Management Science, Vol. 33, No. 9, pp. 181-1191.

Bendahmane, D.B. and J.W. McDonald, Jr. (eds.) (1984). International Negotiation: Art and Science. Foreign Service Institute, U.S. Dept. of State, Washington, DC.

Bendahmane, D.B. and J.W. McDonald, Jr. (eds.) (1986). Perspectives on Negotiations: Four Case Studies and Interpretations. Foreign Service Institute, U.S. Dept. of State, Washington, DC.

Binmore, K. and P. Dasgupta (eds.) (1987). The Economics of Bargaining. B. Blackwell Publ., Oxford, New York.

Delli Priscoli, J. (1988). "Conflict Resolution in Water Resources: Two 404 General Permits. Institute of Water Resources (Army), Fort Belvois, VA." J. Water Resources Planning and Management, ASCE, Vol. 114, No. 1, pp. 66-77.

Eliashberg, J. (1984). "Arbitrating a Dispute: A Decision Analytic Approach." Management Science, Vol. 12, No. 8.

Fisher, R. and S. Brown (1988). Getting Together: Building a Relationship That Gets to Yes. Houghton Mifflin, Boston, MA.

Fisher, R. and W. Ury (1983). Getting to Yes: Negotiating Agreement Without Giving In. Penguin Books, New York, NY.

Fogelman-Soulie, F.D. et al. (1983). "Bivariate Negotiations as a Problem of Stochastic Terminal Control." Management Science, Vol. 29.

Fraser, N.M. and K.W. Hipel (1984). Conflict Analysis: Models and Resolutions. North-Holland, New York, NY.

Fraser, N.M. and K.W. Hipel (1988). "Using the DecisionMaker Computer Program for Analyzing Environmental Conflicts." J. Environmental Management, Vol. 27, pp. 213-228.

Grace, W., Jr. (1979). "The Effects of an Interactive Computer Simulator (KSIM) Upon the Resolution of Mixed Conflict in a Negotiation Situation." Ph.D. Thesis, Bowling Green State Univ. (Vol. 40/10-A of Dissertation Abstracts Intnl., p. 5247).

Hatami, R. (1984). "A Management Decision Support System for Labor Contract Evaluation." Ph.D. Thesis, The Univ. of Texas at Austin.

Holznagel, B. (1986). "Negotiation and Mediation: The Newest Approach to Hazardous Waste Facility Siting." Boston College Environmental Affairs Law Review BCERDX, Vol. 13, No. 3, pp. 329-378.

Hufschmidt, M.M. and M.B Fiering (1965). Simulation Techniques for Design of Water-Resource Systems. Harvard Univ. Press, Cambridge, MA.

Isard, W. and C. Smith (1982). Conflict Analyses and Practical Conflict Management Procedures: An Introduction to Peace Science. Ballinger Publ., Cambridge, MA.

Jarke, M., M.T. Jelassi and M.F. Shakun (1987). "MEDIATOR: Towards a Negotiation Support System." European J. of Operational Research, Vol. 31, No. 3, pp. 314-334.

Jeffers, J.N.R. (ed.) (1988). "Conflict Analysis." J. Environmental Management, Vol. 27, pp. 130-228.

Jones, E.H. (1988). "Analytical Mediation: An Empirical Examination of the Effects of Computer Support for Different Levels of Conflict in Two-Party Negotiation." Ph.D. Thesis, Indiana Univ. (Vol. 49/10-A of Dissertation Abstracts Intnl., p. 2849).

Kersten, G.E. (1985). "NEGO - Group Decision Support System." Information and Management, Vol. 8, No. 5, pp. 237-246.

Kersten, G.E. et al. (1988). "Representing the Negotiation Process With a Rule-Based Formalism. Theory and Decision." Intnl. J. for Philosophy and Methodology of the Social Sciences, Vol. 25, No. 3, pp. 225-257.

Kersten, G.E. (1988). "Generalized Approach to Modeling Negotiations." European J. of Operational Research, Vol. 25, No. 1, pp. 142-149.

Lakos, A. (1989). International Negotiations: A Bibliography. Westview Press, Boulder, CO.

Linstone, H.A. (1986). "Multiple Perspectives: Bringing the Technologist and the Negotiator Together." In: Contributions of Technology to International Conflict Resolution (Chestnut and Haimes, eds.), Case Western Reserve Univ., Cleveland, OH.

Maass, A. et al. (1962). Design of Water Resource Systems. Harvard Univ. Press, Cambridge, MA.

Mermet, L. and L. Hordijk (1987). "On Getting Simulation Models Used in International Negotiations." Mimeo, IIASA, Laxenburg, Austria.

Mumpower, J., R.G. Milter and J.W. Rohrbaugh (1985). "An Experimental Study of the Use of Computer-Assisted Conflict Resolution Techniques in Mediation." Proceedings, Assoc. of Labor Relations Agencies.

Myerson, R.B. (1986). "Negotiation in Games: A Theoretical Overview." In: Uncertainty, Information, and Communication (Heller et al., eds.), Cambridge Univ. Press, Cambridge, MA.

Nierenbery, G.I. (1986). The Art of Negotiating. 1st Fireside Edition, Simon & Schuster, New York, NY.

Raiffa, H. (1982). The Art and Science of Negotiation. Belknap Press of Harvard Univ. Press, Cambridge, MA.

Richardson, J.M., Jr. (1986). "Explaining Political Violence: A Dynamic Modeling Approach." In: Contributions of Technology to International Conflict Resolution (Chestnut and Haimes, eds.), Case Western Reserve Univ., Cleveland, OH.

Rogers, P. (1969). "A Game Theory Approach to the Problems of International River Basins." Water Resources Research, Vol. 5, No. 4, pp. 749-760.

Roth, A.E. (1979). Axiomatic Models of Bargaining. Springer-Verlag, New York, NY.

Roth, A.E. (ed.) (1985). Game-Theoretic Models of Bargaining. Cambridge Univ. Press, New York, NY.

Salewicz, K.A. and D.P. Loucks (1989). "Interactive Simulation for Planning, Managing and Negotiating: Closing the Gap Between Theory and Practice." IAHS Publ. No. 180, pp. 263-268.

Sheehan, M. and K.C. Kogiku (1981). "Game Theory Analysis Applied to Water Resource Problems." Socio-Economic Planning Sciences, Vol. 15, No. 3, pp. 109-118.

Sheer, D.P., M.L. Baeck and J.R. Wright (1989). "The Computer as Negotiator." J. of the American Water Works Association, Vol. 81, No. 2, pp. 68-73.

Srikanth, R. and M. Jarke (1987). "Individual Negotiation Support in Group DSS." In: Office Systems: Methods and Tools (G. Bracchi and D. Tsichritzis, eds.), North-Holland, Amsterdam, The Netherlands.

Straus, D.B. and P.B. Clark (1980). "Computer-Assisted Negotiations: Bigger Problems Need Better Tools." The Environmental Professional, Vol. 2, pp. 75-87.

Susskind, L. and L. Van Dam (1986). "Squaring Off at the Table, Not in the Courts." Technology Review.

Thomson, W. and T. Lensberg (1989). Aximatic Theory of Bargaining With a Variable Number of Agents. Cambridge Univ. Press, Cambridge, MA.

Vlachos, E., A.C. Webb and I.L. Murphy (1987). The Management of International River Basin Conflicts. Proceedings of Workshop, Graduate Program in Science, Technology and Public Policy, George Washington Univ., Washington, DC.

THE ROLE OF NEGOTIATION IN MANAGING WATER CONFLICTS

Gail Bingham[1]
Suzanne Goulet Orenstein[1]

Introduction

It is virtually certain that those involved in solving water resource problems will encounter conflict at some point in the process of achieving their goals. Conflicts over water resources are familiar to anyone concerned about wise use of those resources, and dealing with such conflict effectively is becoming an increasingly important skill for any water resource manager or individual concerned about the use of these precious resources.

As a nation, a consensus is emerging that water supplies are limited, valuable, and vulnerable, and that future challenges lie in managing those supplies more effectively and efficiently. This realization is demonstrated in recent public policy decisions, including efforts to address soil conservation and contaminant run-off concerns, wetlands preservation, and water quality issues in large bodies of water like the Great Lakes and the Chesapeake Bay.

Cost-sharing for water projects has become a reality, as have requirements for controlling non-point source pollution. Programs for groundwater protection and reallocation of federally-stored water are under consideration in many states. Increasingly, water users are being asked to pay for more efficient water projects, and for programs to end groundwater contamination and depletion.

In addition, states are revising water laws to stimulate conservation and permit easier water transfers, and recognizing the value of instream water uses as a matter of standard operating policy. Innovative solutions are being sought for improving waste water treatment and for reconciling differing strategies for water supply and demand decision making.

[1]The Conservation Foundation, Washington, D.C.

These developments do not imply any reduction in the number and intensity of water conflicts, however, perhaps because this focus on cost-effective, environmentally-sensitive water management in turn places a new emphasis on broad participation of all affected interests. While water development decisions has traditionally rested in the hands of politicians, developers, and engineers, the debates over water management now involve much wider constituencies. The power of paralyzing litigation and the visibility of battles over budgetary priorities have given a variety of other groups -- from Native Americans and farmers to environmentalists and taxpayers associations -- a share in the decision making process.

If sound, comprehensive water management is to work, it requires that all significant interests and their concerns be recognized, and that the full range of management options be available to meet their varying needs. Political and technical feasibility require that policy stalemates be broken by improving the procedures through which water conflicts are resolved, and that substantive innovations (like water marketing or conservation measures) be used appropriately to address the interests that produce those stalemates. This combination of innovative decision-making processes and innovative technical solutions can be critically important to creating workable solutions to controversial water resource problems.

Defining Negotiation and Mediation

Negotiation and mediation are processes which increasingly have been used to resolve conflicts over water resources. The term negotiation refers to a voluntary process in which parties meet face-to-face to reach a mutually acceptable resolution to the issues at hand. Negotiation is probably the most common dispute resolution strategy used for all kinds of conflicts. For example, ninety-five percent of all lawsuits filed are settled before trial through some form of negotiation.

Mediation involves the assistance of a neutral third party to a negotiation. The mediator should have no direct interest in the outcome of the dispute (neutrality), and does not make a decision about who is right or wrong or what the best settlement for a conflict should be. Instead, a mediator helps the negotiating parties to hold constructive discussions by calling meetings, establishing a framework for the negotiation within which all parties agree to

participate, and facilitating communication in meetings
and between meetings. Mediators often assist the
parties in identifying where they may be able to agree
or ways in which they can address their disagreements,
for example, through joint fact-finding. They also
assist by drafting, facilitating discussion of, and
refining agreement language that is then reviewed for
implementability by all parties.

Both mediation and negotiation involve processes in
which the parties have significant control over the end
result of the negotiation. Decision-making power stays
in the parties hands, and is not passed on to a judge or
arbitrator. Since the settlement rate for mediation of
environmental disputes averages nearly 80 percent,[2]
strategies for how parties can achieve the best possible
settlement for each specific situation -- solutions
that achieve the greatest satisfaction of interests for
all parties -- are necessary and worth understanding
well.

Negotiations are often difficult processes,
especially when they involve such public issues as water
policy questions, which are both politically and
technically complex. The large number of parties,
disagreements about the facts, and other complicating
factors often create circumstances in which the
negotiators give up or reach impasse. Mediators have
increasingly been called upon to prevent impasse in
conflicts, including those over water resources, or to
assist parties to continue negotiating when their
discussions have broken down.

History of Mediation in Environmental Conflicts

The first environmental dispute in which a mediator
was used to assist in a negotiation involved a water
resource conflict. The case occurred in 1973 when
Daniel J. Evans, then governor of the state of
Washington, invited mediators Gerald Cormick and Jane
McCarthy to help settle a longstanding controversy over
the siting of a flood control dam at the entrance to the
Alpine Lakes wilderness area in the Snoqualmie River
Valley east of Seattle. An agreement was reached, but
the dam was never built in part because the geology at
an alternative site did not prove suitable, although
studies done within the time constraints of the
negotiation gave a preliminary indication that the site
met technical criteria.

The second mediated environmental dispute involved
a transportation issue, also in the Seattle area -- the
expansion of Interstate 90 from Seattle's suburbs,

across Lake Washington, and into the city of Seattle.
The agreement in this case was more successfully
implemented, and has paved the way for perhaps as many
as four hundred environmental mediations in the
succeeding fifteen years.

Other water resource cases mediated have included
such varied issues as state and national groundwater
strategies, state-wide water supply plans, water rights
disputes, thermal pollution issues, nutrient control
strategies, sewer hook-up issues, in-stream flow for
endangered species habitat and many more.

Mediators have convened groups to discuss new
policy options and directions (in processes often called
policy dialogues) over controversial state and national
issues. They have also provided mediation for site-
specific controversies, concerning pollution standards,
hydroelectric facility permits, and recreational
boating controversies. Enforcement actions for water
quality and permit violations are increasingly being
submitted to mediation processes, and mediators have
assisted agencies convene negotiating groups to draft
regulations that are tailored to be implementable on
groundwater protection and other multi-jurisdictional
matters.

Among the water projects that have been the
subject of mediated negotiations was the controversial
(then and now) Two Forks Dam dispute, considered as part
of the agenda of the Denver Metropolitan Water
Roundtable.

In the early 1980's when construction of the Two
Forks dam became a high priority for the Denver Water
Board, then Governor Richard Lamm asked that opponents
and proponents of the dam consider negotiating a
settlement. The initial obstacle was getting agreement
on the question to be negotiated. Proponents wanted to
negotiate ways to build the dam in the most
environmentally sensitive manner. Opponents wanted the
question of whether the dam was needed to be the focus
of the discussion.

Mediators from ACCORD Associates succeeded in
obtaining agreement from all parties to meet to discuss
the question of how Denver would meet its water demands
in the year 2010, and many months of negotiations among
31 parties ensued. The result of this process was a
series of agreements on water storage projects, water
use efficiency, groundwater use, and integration of
Roundtable issues into a subsequent EIS process
conducted by the Army Corps of Engineers.

This case illustrates several important themes discussed in this paper. Agreement on the question for negotiation was essential to getting the parties to work together at all. The case also provides an example of how non-structural solutions may assist in meeting multiple interests.

Conflicts over the need for the dam were not resolved once and for all by this mediation, and the Two Forks situation is once again a hot political topic. However, as with other decision-making processes, negotiations are often only one part of a much more complicated series of public decisions and strategies used by participating parties to achieve their goals.

One participant in the Denver Metropolitan Water Roundtable recently assessed the pluses and minuses of the negotiation by saying that the Roundtable provided a forum for anticipating problems that would arise in the subsequent EIS process, and provided a valuable learning experience for members of the various constituencies. While the negotiation did not resolve the entire problem, it did allow the parties to more clearly focus issues and plan for subsequent decision-making steps.

Judging success for negotiated and mediated processes should be based on a variety of factors. Implementation of the agreed upon settlements is probably the most important measure of success, but factors like improved relationships among the parties, balancing of gains and losses, and some (if not complete) progress toward settlement as a result of the negotiation may also be productive outcomes of negotiations.

In Bingham's study, success at reaching agreement was documented in 78 percent of the cases, with little significant difference between site specific disputes and policy discussions. There were differences, however, in the implementation that resulted from these agreements. Site-specific negotiation agreements were implemented more often than agreements on policy. Eighty percent of the agreements reached in site-specific cases were fully implemented. However, only 41 percent of the agreements reached on policy questions were fully implemented, which may reflect the exclusion of government agencies from early policy dialogues between industry and environmental groups.

Creating Efficient and Effective Problem-solving Processes for Water Conflicts

Water conflicts seem especially amenable to negotiated solutions. Water by nature flows across jurisdictional boundaries, and thus effective water resource management requires obtaining agreement among multiple agencies as well as private interests. In addition, the impacts of certain water related activities are often borne by downstream or off-stream users, so diverse needs and interests must be considered as water resource management decisions are made.

Negotiations are constant in decision-making about water. They may be integrated into permitting decisions, part of determining what technical studies are needed, integral to lobbying and public involvement activities, and often are essential for interaction among multiple government agencies.

Thus, more efficient and effective negotiations in water conflicts are essential. Efficient negotiations involve "doing it right the first time," i.e. anticipating problems that will arise, be they technical or political, and planning to address those problems in the course of the negotiation. For example, this advance planning can help avoid problems that arise when implementation of negotiated agreements is blocked by a party not included in the negotiations and re-negotiation or litigation of the same dispute is required.

Effective negotiations are those that begin with an understanding of the various interests that need to be represented and satisfied, and end with workable plans for meeting those multiple interests. Agreement for agreement's sake will not necessarily constitute the best policy for a given situation. Getting agreement on criteria for determining what is good policy can be a first step to increasing the effectiveness of negotiations. Making sure that the information used in decision making is as accurate and complete as possible and that the broadest range of options has been considered also can help to create good quality agreements.

On-going efforts to resolve disputes concerning Mono Lake, which provides 17% of Los Angeles' water supply, are a helpful illustration of the search for an efficient and effective settlement. A group of California environmentalists, the Mono Lake Committee, sued the Los Angeles Department of Water and Power over increasing environmental damage to the Mono Lake

ecosystem. The goal of the suit was to address
diminishing lake levels and the impact of those declines
on salinity of the lake and fragile wildlife habitats.
As the litigation progressed, a second, multi-interest
committee, the Mono Lake Group, was formed to provide a
negotiation forum for reaching agreement on future
directions for policies affecting the lake.

Recent reports of a settlement among the members of
the Mono Lake Group have been encouraging. The group
includes representatives of the Los Angeles Department
of Water and Power, the Mono Lake Committee plaintiffs,
the Los Angeles City Council, the Los Angeles Mayor, The
U. S. Forest Service, the Mono County Supervisors, and
the California Department of Water Resources, with the
Environmental Defense Fund acting as a consultant on
innovative solutions. The members of the negotiating
group have agreed on an overriding principle for any
settlement they develop. They are seeking a settlement
that will not transfer the environmental problems at
Mono Lake to some other area or ecosystem, and thus have
rejected more traditional settlements based on political
competition for water supply that might have the result
of transferring the ecosystem damage elsewhere.

As a result of this principle, the negotiating
group has searched for solutions that will produce gains
with minimum losses for all concerned. They have used
their Environmental Defense Fund consultants to identify
alternative sources of water for Los Angeles that do not
require structural solutions or environmental
impairment. EDF has sought to purchase water rights for
both Los Angeles and for Mono Lake restoration from
agricultural interests. The agricultural interests will
be free to use the funds they obtain from the sale to
enhance and improve their current water conservation
strategies, which should result in no net loss of water
to them.

A similar example of a joint gains (or win/win)
settlement is an agreement between Imperial Valley water
users and the city of Los Angeles in which Los Angeles
agreed to pay for irrigation improvements that would
enhance water conservation in exchange for rights to the
water that was conserved. In this example, a non-
traditional technical solution -- lining irrigation
ditches to promote conservation -- was coupled with
negotiated trading to promote an efficient and effective
settlement.

In both of these situations, a combination of
creativity regarding technical solutions and realistic
problem solving made possible by negotiations (which

would probably have been impossible as outcomes of
judicial processes) have increased the options available
for truly resolving these conflicts. Negotiated
processes, when conducted well, can create benefits by
focusing on interests (avoiding environmental harm,
ensuring water supply for a metropolitan area) and by
allowing participants opportunities to generate
solutions.

Requirements for Successful Use of Conflict Resolution Processes

Creating successful negotiations and joint gains
requires excellent negotiation skills and an
understanding of the complex dynamics of environmental
conflicts. Addressing these two factors can improve the
frequency with which efficient and effective outcomes
result from these processes.

Excellent Negotiation Skills

Negotiators need to know when to negotiate; when
and how to share information about interests and goals;
how to use good communication, good preparation, and
strategic planning for negotiations; how to manage
negotiation teams and large problem solving discussions;
and how to handle complex technical information.
Negotiators also need to know when to settle, and how to
establish criteria and principles on which to base
agreements.

A very helpful analysis of some operational
principles for improving negotiations and developing the
skills needed can be found in the book Getting To Yes by
Roger Fisher and William Ury. According to these
authors, the essence of successful negotiations is to
avoid bargaining over positions. They outline some
very helpful principles for how to do this effectively:

Discuss and address interests. It is more
important to ask **why** one side is asserting a particular
position on the issues, and to understand their
underlying interests or what outcomes they really need
to achieve. Mediators assist negotiators to identify
and discuss interests, and that is an important element
in their success. Interests can be met in many ways;
positions are much more rigid.

**Understand the role of interpersonal dynamics in
negotiations.** Fisher and Ury call this "separating the
people from the problem," which really means understand
the role that emotions play in a dispute and try to get
the parties to address the presenting problem on its

merits and not in terms of personal preferences,
prejudices or prior history.

**Generate a wide range of options, minimizing
judgments at first.** An example of this principle is the
common technique of brainstorming, in which creative
ideas are encouraged by having participants list all
possible ideas for resolving something, regardless of
practical feasibility. The seeds of some feasible and
creative options may lie in those infeasible ideas.

Agree on criteria by which to judge options for
resolution. It may be easier to list the requirements
for a particular outcome than to develop every specific
settlement component simultaneously. An example of an
agreed upon criteria might be that of "no net loss" for
wetland permits, a standard by which settlements
regarding wetlands development can be judged.

**Understand the outcomes that you can achieve
without negotiating and use this information to decide
when to settle.** Fisher and Ury call this alternative
outcome a BATNA -- Best Alternative to No Agreement. If
you know that you can get a better outcome in another
forum, you should not settle for less in negotiation.
Of course, the certainty with which you "know" what you
can achieve elsewhere varies, so probability and risk
analysis need to play a role in this determination.

Choose options that allow all to gain something.
Opposing interests are not always mutually exclusive,
and trading-off what is of lesser priority to me but of
higher priority to you for something of higher priority
to me allows an integration of our gains and minimizing
of the costs or losses. An example of an integrated
solution is the Imperial Valley agreement referred to
above.

There are many criticisms that can be (and have
been) made of the Fisher and Ury approach. The fact is
that not every negotiation can be entirely interest
based -- eventually the pie can't be made any larger and
a certain amount of competition is inevitable in
dividing up the pie -- nor can the effect that
political power plays in negotiation dynamics be
ignored. But their principles do allow negotiating
parties to minimize competition and maximize creativity
to create more "joint gains" -- an essential ingredient
in sound policy solutions to complicated water problems.

Understanding the Dynamics of Complex Disputes

In addition to improving their basic negotiation
skills, negotiators in water conflicts need to
understand the special dynamics complicating water
policy negotiations and the needs that organizations
bring to the negotiating table.

In particular, analysis of the political, economic,
and technical circumstances of water resource disputes
is crucial. Negotiators must plan for implementation
of a potential settlement from the very beginning.
Agreements that won't work, whether politically,
institutionally, economically, or technically, are not
very valuable. Thus, identifying and including in the
negotiation those who can affect or block the
implementation of an agreement is essential, as is
gathering information and assessing the feasibility of
options before the parties as they negotiate with one
another.

Several factors complicate efforts to negotiate
environmental conflicts, like water resource disputes.
It is often these factors that induce negotiators to
seek the assistance of mediators.

Establish an agreed-upon framework for negotiation.
In most environmental disputes, negotiation processes
are convened on an ad hoc basis. Thus, clear agreement
may not yet exist on fundamental assumptions that shape
the negotiating relationship -- such as who will be at
the table, what issues will be on the agenda, what
authority the parties have to implement agreements
reached, deadlines, and other groundrules. Therefore,
one cannot simple convene a meeting. All of these
assumptions must be negotiated prior to the first
meeting. In order to establish a framework for
negotiations, it is important to involve all the
affected interests, get agreement on the objective of
the negotiation, build an agenda acceptable to all
(remember the Denver Metropolitan Water Roundtable
example of the question for negotiation), agree on a
time table and deadlines, and agree on the choice of a
third party mediator if one is involved.

**Recognize interorganizational and institutional
complexities.** Water resources conflicts are between
institutions and organizations, not individuals. The
individuals at the table, although negotiating with one
another, must also get proposals ratified before an
agreement can really exist. And, each negotiating
organization has its own internal decision-making
process which will affect the negotiation. It is

important to know the degree to which negotiators can
speak for their constituency or organization and the
freedom each has to make proposals and settle.
Negotiators must work hard to keep their organizations
informed about progress and problems, and must keep good
communication going within their team of interest group
members. The role that settlement approval and
ratification will play is an important element to
understand from the beginning of the negotiation.

Develop procedures to deal with technical uncertainty and complexity.

A third complicating factor
is the technical component of these kinds of conflicts.
Often, "battles of the experts" occur, and negotiators
need to devise a strategy for obtaining and analyzing
useful data. Often joint factfinding can provide a
common basis of information for negotiated decisions.
Steps useful for this task are to define the problem(s)
before seeking solutions, identify what is and is not
known, identify what is in dispute, articulate and
discuss the underlying assumptions in the technical
information, devise methods for sharing and reviewing
information, and develop a strategy for how to handle
decisions that must be made in spite of technical
uncertainty. Integrating technical information into
policy discussions and vice versa, poses significant
communication and problem solving problems, because
often scientific and policy negotiators speak different
languages. Recognizing where the parties need to seek
common terminology is important to dealing with
technical questions in negotiations.

An interesting illustration of strategies for
handling technical information is the mediation of
dispute between upstream and downstream governments over
nitrogen and phosphorous levels in the Patuxent River in
eastern Maryland. The State of Maryland had issued a
draft "nutrient control strategy" in an attempt to
comply with guidelines for obtaining EPA construction
grant funds. However, the strategy was challenged by
downstream users of the Patuxent River, who were
concerned about nutrient impacts from upstream urban
sewage facilities on fishing and recreation activities.
Downstream interests felt that the draft strategy did
not reduce phosphorous levels enough and did not
address nitrogen levels at all.

In October 1981, with a funding deadline
approaching at the end of the year, mediator John
McGlennon was asked to help the parties resolve their
dispute. The mediator constructed a steering committee
representing key interests to help guide the consensus-
building effort, and with its help devised a two-stage

process. In the first stage, technical representatives
of the various parties met to discuss what was clearly
known, not known, and in dispute about the water quality
of the Patuxent. This narrowed the issues requiring
discussion. The results of the technical meeting were
then presented to a group of forty representatives of
various governmental, industrial and environmental
interests from both the upstream and downstream
communities. After three days of meetings, during which
the technical experts were available for consultation, a
new nutrient control strategy was drafted and agreed
upon.

The agreement called for nutrient loading
reductions by upstream treatment facilities through an
experimental land disposal method for treated waste.
The downstream communities agreed to develop a non-point
source pollution control plan to further reduce
nutrients placed in the river. The State of Maryland
issued this plan, and funding for its sewage treatment
facility was assured.

As with the Snoqualmie Dam case, even the best
efforts don't always produce the intended outcome,
whether the policy is set through negotiated agreement,
legal action, administrative decision, or legislation.
Nutrient loadings in the Patuxent were reviewed five
years after the agreement and were found to be only
somewhat reduced.

**Plan for the large number of issues and parties
that are involved**. The number of parties involved in
water resource negotiations, coupled with the fact that
each party is concerned about several issues, creates a
need to structure the negotiation carefully. Sometimes
coalitions can be formed, as in the Mono Lake case, in
which several parties can be represented by one
negotiator. Also, sub-committees can be formed so that
sub-sets of issues can be addressed by smaller groups.
However, linkage of the work of sub-committees to the
larger, decision-making group must be assured and
opportunities to link solutions on one set of issues
with solutions on other issues preserved so that trade
offs can occur. All of these processes can require
significant time commitments to the negotiation process;
to be effective, negotiators need to plan to devote the
time necessary to allow full discussion and reach
resolution. (The time required for negotiation is often
cited as a disincentive for negotiations to go forward,
but comparisons with alternative forums may not be that
unfavorable.)

Address imbalances in power and resources.
Differences among negotiators in the power and resources
they have available for the negotiation can create
negotiation problems. More and more often,
traditionally powerful parties are realizing that they
need the cooperation of others who may have fewer
resources but the capacity to block action and will not
only agree to negotiations but will underwrite
participation expenses for those unable to come to the
table otherwise. Obviously, all parties want to
maximize their power, but it may not be quite so obvious
that the stability of settlements is increased if all
parties obtain and use as many kinds of power as
possible. Sources of power can be alliances, information
or technical facility, precedents and models, good
alternatives, and more subjective sources like the power
of persuasion or the power of a good idea. The Mono
Lake settlement may illustrate the power of a good idea
in its use of water market transfers to discourage other
less benign methods of water acquisition.

**Public decisions require public, not private,
decision-making forums.** A final characteristic
complicating water resource conflicts is the fact that
the issues in dispute are public issues that need to be
resolved in public forums. Often, an important part of
the negotiation is finding ways to involve the public
and to meet the public's need to know and approve of a
specific outcome. Dealing with the press and open
meeting laws must be done with sensitivity, and outcomes
must be able to withstand public scrutiny and comment.
Public institutions are often unable to be flexible for
fear of setting precedents, and maximizing the
flexibility within these agencies while holding
negotiated solutions to the same legal and regulatory
standards to which any decision would be subject is a
challenge for negotiators.

Mediators can often be helpful in assisting parties
to address institutional constraints. An example
occurred in a recent mediation over water quality in
Sheridan, Wyoming. Several residential water users in
Sheridan had access to and used untreated water from a
water conduit leading to the municipal water treatment
system. The U.S. EPA sued these individuals because the
water they used did not meet EPA health and safety
standards. But bringing treated water to these homes
was expensive, and the homeowners could not pay the
costs involved. The issue remained a stalemate.

A mediator was called in because the lawyers on the
case saw an opportunity to explore some creative
solutions that would not be available if the case

proceeded to trial. The mediator, Ben Moya of Western
Network in Santa Fe, New Mexico, met with the parties
and learned that in a nearby town there was a need for a
new water treatment facility. He obtained the agreement
of the parties to broaden the negotiations to include
regional and local government representatives for both
towns, and the negotiation concluded with a plan for a
new water treatment plant that could meet the needs of
the larger region and could include the Sheridan
residences. Costs for the new facility were
apportioned among a much larger group of water users,
making it more affordable, and EPA did not have to
proceed with an unproductive suit required by its
institutional standards.

Conclusion

The increasing need for and availability of new
technical solutions and open decision-making processes
for resolving water conflicts has emerged as an area of
challenge for water resource managers over the past
decade. Computer models, water rights transfers, user
fees, environmental trusts, conservation strategies and
other non-structural water management programs, all have
changed the capacity of states, regions and localities
to make tough decisions about water supply and water
quality.

The decision-making contexts for these discussions
have also changed a great deal. As Native Americans and
others assert their water rights claims and as
environmentalists conduct their own studies of economic
feasibility of water projects, attorneys, courts and
administrative agencies are forced to seek solutions
for water conflicts that meet the interests and needs of
multiple and opposing groups.

The institutional inflexibility already mentioned
is a major source of discouragement to those trying to
produce efficient and effective settlements for water
conflicts. Water disputes can have very long time
horizons, and very long and negative histories. Water
managers find themselves working with the constraints of
past decisions, in highly charged political contexts,
with conflicting mandates from those responsible for
solving the problems. The interplay of federal policies
and state and local policies alone can create decade-
long impasses on water projects.

Water managers tell us that the potential for water
conflict resolution also can be affected by myths and an
atmosphere of pessimism. Common views about the
inviolability of water compacts, the assumption that

tradeoffs on quality of life must be made to accommodate growth, and the perception that ever-changing power politics make negotiations impossible on major water projects can create obstacles to resolving conflicts. The examples we have presented in this article may begin to address some of the pessimism about the potential for resolving water conflicts, but we are not naive enough to discount their effect entirely.

As we have shown, meeting the needs of varying political interests in a constructive manner can require new decision-making processes that use some form of negotiation to focus the discussions. It is important to remember, however, that effective negotiation requires facing the differences that divide groups and developing strategies that allow constructive solutions in spite of those differences; it does not necessarily require eliminating those differences. Furthermore, lawsuits, political action, public education and other strategies for resolving disputes will still be needed -- mediation and negotiation are not appropriate strategies for resolving every water conflict. The decision to negotiate is a strategic one that should be made with full information about the availability of alternative strategies and their potential for success.

When the need to agree is paramount -- because data must be jointly gathered and analyzed, many good minds are needed to resolve a problem, or implementation must be coordinated -- negotiated processes, with or without a mediator's assistance, can bring considerable benefits. Efficient and effective settlements can be precedent setting, and more and more, persistent negotiators and forward thinking technical experts are showing the way by negotiating more truly useful solutions for tough water conflicts.

Bibliography

Bingham, Gail. Resolving Environmental Disputes. Washington, DC: The Conservation Foundation, 1984.

Fisher, Roger, and William Ury. Getting To Yes: Negotiating Agreement Without Giving In. New York: Houghton Mifflin, 1981.

Fisher, Roger. "Negotiating Power: Getting and Using Influence" American Behavioral Scientist 27, No. 2 (1983): 149-66.

Folk-Williams, John A. Water in the West. Santa Fe, NM: Western Network, 1982.

Gusman, Sam, and Verne Huser. "Mediation in the Estuary." Coastal Zone Management Journal 11, no.4 (1984): 536-52.

Talbot, Allan R. Settling Things: Six Case Studies in Environmental Mediation. Washington, DC: The Conservation Foundation, 1983.

Footnotes

1. Gail Bingham is Vice President of The Conservation Foundation, directing its Program on Environmental Dispute Resolution, and is the author of Resolving Environmental Disputes: A Decade of Experience. Suzanne Goulet Orenstein is a Senior Associate in the Program on Environmental Dispute Resolution. Both authors gratefully acknowledge the contribution and inspiration of Dr. Edwin Clark, II.

   The Conservation Foundation conducts research on a variety of environmental issues, including water policy and conflict resolution, and convenes negotiations among representatives of various interests on new approaches for resolving longstanding problems. In recent years, the Foundation's water policy work has focused on groundwater protection, through a National Forum on Groundwater Protection chaired by Bruce Babbitt, former governor of Arizona, and through the development of a handbook for local groups on implementing groundwater protection strategies. The Foundation also convened the National Wetlands Policy Forum, chaired by New Jersey's Governor Thomas H. Kean, whose goal of "no net loss" for wetlands is being adopted by both federal and state authorities. The Foundation's mediators also have facilitated a state groundwater forum in the state of Tennessee, as well as negotiations on wetlands delineation, underground injection rules for hazardous waste, pesticide effects assessments, water front development, and superfund cleanups.

2. G. Bingham, Resolving Environmental Disputes: A Decade of Experience (Washington DC: The Conservation Foundation, 1986).

Expanding the Role of the Engineer in Conflict Management

Ernest T. Smerdon, P.E., M. ASCE[1]

The law is a tool, not an end in itself. Like any tool, our judicial mechanisms, procedures, or rules can become obsolete. Just as the carpenter's handsaw was replaced by the power saw, and his hammer was replaced by the stapler, we should be alert to the need for better tools to serve the ends of justice.

-- Warren E. Burger

Abstract

The cost of litigation is shown to be a major drain on the economic strength of this nation. Conflicts and lawsuits deter us from becoming a highly productive society. Ways in which engineers might help reduce water-related conflicts are analyzed and examples given to illustrate. Finally, some actions that engineers might initiate are presented.

Introduction and Background

In this introduction of the topic of the engineer in conflict management, I first look at the costs of conflicts. I rely heavily on the several papers published in the Fall, 1983, issue of _National Forum_ -- a special issue devoted to Conflict Resolution and Peacemaking. Abraham Lincoln more than 125 years ago said: "Discourage litigation. Persuade your neighbors to compromise whenever you can. Point out to them how the nominal winner is often a real loser -- in fees, expenses and waste of time."

---

[1] Dean, College of Engineering and Mines, The University of Arizona, Tucson, Arizona 85721

What is the real cost to the U.S. of our litigious society? What is that cost in terms of the diverted energy of very bright lawyers toward tasks that produce no wealth? Nothing is added to the nation's productivity by conflict and the costly court actions associated with these conflicts. What is the effect of excessive litigation on our nation's competitiveness at this time when the Japanese are dominating us in technological progress in consumer goods, including many high-tech consumer goods? What is the cost in terms of our nation's economic health and international balance of payments?

Let's look at some figures on the U.S. and the Japanese legal systems. Japan has about one-half the population of the United States, but only one-fortieth as many practicing lawyers (Cannon 1983). Japan has about one-fiftieth as many civil lawsuits as in this country. The number of degrees in engineering granted in Japan, however, is much greater relative to its population (DEC 1988). The following table summarizes these figures:

	Japan	U.S.
Number of Lawyers	15,000	600,000
Civil Suits	281,500	13,000,000
Number passing the Bar Exam/year	525	15,750
Lawyers per 1,000 population	0.13	2.5
% Baccalaureate grads in Engineering	19	7

Lester Thurow, Dean of the Sloan School of Management at MIT, reported that a Japanese steel official once said that the difference in the number of lawyers and our propensity for civil suits is why his country will eventually beat ours (Thurow 1983). Thurow acknowledges that the steel official was correct in a sense because a litigious society is not a highly productive society. Derek Bok, Harvard President and former law school dean, seems to agree (Bok 1982). In relation to legal regulations Bok has noted: "Legal regulations seem burdensome to the point that they conflict in dealing with progress, productivity and initiative." He continues: "The total cost of our system of enforcing rules and settling disputes appears more and more excessive." University of Virginia law professor A. E. Dick Howard estimates that the total cost of legal services in the U.S. amounts to 2% of the nation's GNP. That is more than the entire steel industry (Howard 1982). Is it no wonder that the Japanese steel official dared predict that the Japanese will eventually beat us in economic competition?

No doubt the Japanese nation spends more of its national productive energy on the development of its economy, focusing on new products that it can export. The Japanese probably have a better engineered society than we do in terms of consumer goods. That fact troubles engineering deans, such as myself. In Japan, 19% of the total baccalaureate degrees granted are in engineering, compared to 7% here. Derek Bok sounded the alarm that law in the U.S. "...attracts an unusually large proportion of the exceptionally gifted. Far too many of those rare individuals are becoming lawyers at a time when the country cries out for more talented business executives, more enlightened public servants, more inventive engineers, more able high school principals and teachers." Bok is on target in my view.

We have drifted away from what our founding fathers envisioned more than 200 years ago. They wanted laws to protect individual freedom through common rules with the judicial system functioning in an important but limited sphere. The Founders would likely be surprised at the current attitude of, "meet you in court." They wanted to avoid the condition that Yale College President Timothy Dwight mentioned to the 1776 Yale graduating class when he referred to "costly and needless litigations which retard the operations of justice" (Cannon 1983). It appears that, as Chief Justice Warren Burger once suggested, "we are well on our way to a society overrun by hordes of lawyers, hungry as locusts, and brigades of judges never before contemplated" (Burger 1983). Consider the cost of litigation by looking at some figures on the case load increase in our judicial system.

Increase in Litigation in the U.S.

Activity	Time Period	Increased Load
Federal District Court --		
civil case filings	1940 to 1981	35,000 → 180,000
case load per judgeship	1940 to 1981	190 → 350
Federal Court of Appeals --		
civil case filings	1950 to 1981	2,800 → 26,000
case load per circuit judgeship	1950 to 1981	44 → 200
State Courts --		
appellate court filings	1967 to 1976	8x population growth
trial court filings	1967 to 1976	2x population growth

In this introductory section I have looked at the relative number of engineering graduates in the U.S. as compared to Japan and also the relative number of lawyers in each country. Although many factors determine progress in improving the standard of living, productivity is a key one. Comparisons in recent progress of Japan and the U.S. are of interest. In 1960, Japanese citizens had a per capita personal income one-sixth as large as in the U.S. Today, the average Japanese enjoy a personal income equivalent to what we have in this country (Cannon 1983). That progress was made with few lawyers and few civil law suits. Instead, emphasis has been placed on the aspects of society that enhance productivity, particularly engineering.

By comparison, the U.S. standard of living has dropped in recent years. According to the Council on Competitiveness, the U.S. standard of living index in 1987 was only 78.9 percent of its 1972 value (Council on Competitiveness 1988). The Council also noted that the U.S. Productivity Index in 1986 was only 68.7 percent of its 1972 value. The Council stated, "Our worst performance has been in the area of productivity. Since 1972, Japan's Manufacturing Productivity Index has increased eight times faster than America's." These comparisons provide a sobering assessment.

How Might Engineers Reduce Conflicts?

Conflicts in water resources may result from several types of misunderstanding. I mention some of the reasons for conflicts. First, attitudes toward water resources change. To illustrate, during the first half of this century or more, water was judged to be a key factor in economic development. Our national goal was economic development and few citizens then questioned the water development projects that were proposed by agencies such as the Bureau of Reclamation or the Corps of Engineers. The economic importance of the projects was the overriding justification. Now, there are many other considerations that various groups insist be part of the decision matrix. This expands the potential for conflict.

A second reason for conflict is because the scientific data may be misunderstood or interpreted differently by different groups. One example relates to the question of environmental quality versus risk. A good question might be termed, "How safe is safe?", which was the title of a recent paper on this subject (Waterstone and Lord 1989). Waterstone and Lord discuss the risk of five parts per billion of trichloroethylene (TCE) in water. Epidemiological data suggests that drinking two liters of such water per day over a 70-year lifetime would lead up to two additional cancers per million people. The issue of balancing risk emerges when attempting to assess the additional threat due to this drinking water when one remembers that 200,000 to 250,000 people among those typical one million will develop cancer from other causes. How do you compare risks due to drinking this water with those from other sources and avoid potential conflict when there is no universally accepted way to measure risk? Clearly, we see the potential for conflict.

Another possible source of conflict may occur because engineers tend to think in discreet, analytical terms. To us, things tend to be -- yes or no. The grey areas of human judgment are difficult for engineers to cope with. We may fall into the trap of rejecting the notion of compromise, and instead see any compromise as a sign of weakness. In a recent conference someone said: "In America, real men don't mediate." In our complex society, this is a frightening thought. We may subconsciously be too quick to adopt that narrow view, even if we would not state it openly. The academic disciplines usually viewed as important in streamlining dispute resolution procedures are sociologists, social psychologists, political scientists, anthropologists, economists and lawyers. Unfortunately, few think of engineers in that role.

For three years I held a joint appointment in Civil Engineering and the LBJ School of Public Affairs at The University of Texas at Austin. There, in my teaching, I became painfully aware that engineers have to convince the typical person that we can be open-minded and consider human factors as well as the "physical and chemical facts" when making judgments. Those bright graduate students in the LBJ School, working on Master of Public Affairs degrees, had widely divergent undergraduate study backgrounds. However, seldom was it engineering. The initial view of the LBJ School graduate students was a general skepticism that engineers could adequately consider human preferences in the engineering decision matrix. Most of these students initially would have doubted that engineers could play a useful role in helping resolve disputes.

I had the good fortune to work with these students for a full academic year on each of three policy research projects -- a required year-long course for all students in the LBJ School of Public Affairs. It was a good experience for me as an engineer. I believe it was a good experience for those LBJ School students as well. I believe all involved quickly came to recognize that engineers should play a much larger role in public affairs work, including conflict resolution. However, to be totally effective in doing so, we engineers must broaden our views. We must learn to look beyond the hard facts of scientific data and recognize the human dimension. This means that engineering educators must begin to include some public policy courses in their course of study. I should hasten to add that it is also very important for those in the social sciences to include more courses in science and technology in their course of study. That way, the bridge of understanding can be better approached from both directions.

Reducing Conflicts By Early Involvement of Engineers

Twenty-one years of my professional life have been spent in Texas. I am most familiar with water resources issues in that state. I cite three examples from Texas issues where conflicts have existed or may occur in the future. I briefly discuss how some of these conflicts might be reduced if engineers were more involved at an early stage.

In Texas, there are currently 1,225 water districts and authorities (Smerdon and Gronouski 1986). Some of these are no longer active, but nonetheless exist on the books. At one point each achieved legal status through an appropriate approval process. There are perhaps twenty major river authorities and major municipal water supply districts among this group. In several cases, there is more than one river authority with jurisdiction in a given river basin. In other cases, a separate ground water management district may be responsible for a ground water aquifer that underlies a river basin that is managed by a totally separate river authority. Since the ground water laws in Texas are essentially independent of surface water laws, the potential for conflict is quite evident.

The Stacy Reservoir Conflict on the Colorado River in Texas. There are two principle institutions which share the management of the surface water on the Colorado River in Texas. The Colorado River Municipal Water District (CRMWD) is responsible for the upper reaches of the river. Its boundaries include the cities of Odessa, Big Spring and Snyder, as well as the Colorado River drainage area above the east county line of Coleman County (Smerdon and Gronouski 1986). The CRMWD is governed by a 12 member board of directors

representing the three cities. The purpose of this District is to supply water for the municipalities it serves and it does so through surface reservoirs and ground water wells.

The Lower Colorado River Authority (LCRA) has a service area of 31,000 square miles, encompassing ten counties in the lower reaches of the Colorado River. The LCRA is governed by a board of fifteen directors appointed by the Governor with the advice and consent of the Texas Senate. The LCRA is heavily involved in power generation with the lion's share of its revenue coming from that source. Therefore, the LCRA is involved in hydroelectric power, as well as water supply. The CRMWD has jurisdiction on the upper reaches of the Colorado River, and the LCRA is responsible for the lower reaches. Both institutions own reservoirs and both are responsible for providing water to customers in their respective regions.

On May 25, 1979, the Texas Water Commission granted a permit to the CRMWD to construct the Stacy Dam and Reservoir Project at the confluence of the Colorado and Concho Rivers (Booth 1985). The location was in the upper reaches of the Colorado. It provided 113,000 acre-feet of water per annum to meet future municipal and industrial needs of CRMWD customers.

The LCRA objected to this project. An issue of concern was the meaning of "unappropriated water" and how return flow was considered in the unappropriated water determination. This resulted in the Texas Supreme Court reversing the decision of the Texas Water Commission, and remanding the matter back to the Commission with instructions to reconsider the Stacy Dam application in view of the Supreme Court's ruling on unappropriated water. This in effect killed Stacy.

Here was a conflict that seemed to be resolved because the Supreme Court had acted. However, there was a larger issue at stake. The political leaders in the state of Texas had been working on a financing package involving state-

supported bonds for several water activities including water
supply, water quality, flood control, regional systems (sewer,
water, and reservoirs), water conservation in irrigation and
others. The referendums had been prepared for submission to
the voters and broad-based political support was needed for
acceptance.

Although the Stacy Dam conflict appeared to have been
resolved in the courts, it was not a good solution for the state
because it polarized the voters -- West Texas versus East
Texas. All of the regional problems which political leaders had
worked hard to resolve with a broadly based bond package to
finance water projects, which would benefit all citizens of
Texas, had been rekindled. The effort of the political leaders
appeared to be for naught unless a satisfactory compromise to
the Stacy conflict was reached.

Texas politicians do not give up easily on issues such as
the Stacy Dam conflict. They decided to play hardball politics
with the governing boards of the two water institutions
involved. A law was passed placing all river authorities and
water districts in the state under a sunset review. Since many
districts operated facilities, the districts themselves could not
be abolished. However, the law provided that the sunset
review could result in the current governing board members
being removed and a substitute board be appointed by the
Governor. The Governor, Lieutenant Governor (who heads the
Texas Senate), and the Speaker of the House of
Representatives met individually with the boards of directors
of the CRMWD and LCRA regarding the Stacy case.
Remarkably, within a very short period of time the two
contending governing boards reached a mutually acceptable
agreement. That ended the fight. The Stacy conflict had come
to an end, but only after the Legislature had passed a sunset
law providing the potential to reorganize water agencies. The
statewide water development and environmental programs
provided in the bonding program could proceed.

In the required referendum, bond proposals amounting
to over $1 billion were supported by more than seventy

percent of the Texas voters. Of 256 counties, ranging from desert western counties to humid southeastern counties, only 24 opposed the proposition. No vote on a water financing referendum since 1897 had received such widespread support, save the water bond issue of 1957 which followed the most severe drought on record in Texas.

How could this costly conflict in Texas, which was only resolved as a result of astute political leadership by the Lieutenant Governor and others, have been avoided? I believe that when two quasi-public water agencies operate on the same river basin and do so essentially independently, conflict is unavoidable as the water resource of the basin is stretched to its limit. If engineers and hydrologists had been more directly involved in framing the water institutions on this river basin, I believe the potential conflicts could have been minimized. The upstream versus downstream development issue involves complex hydrology that should be treated before the issues come to court, as opposed to having hydrologists as expert witnesses supporting the arguments on each side. Laws creating water districts which adhere to political boundaries and ignore hydrologic reality are an open door to conflict.

Edwards Underground Water District/The Guadalupe-Blanco River Authority/San Antonio River Authority Case. Here is a case where the Guadalupe-Blanco River Authority (GBRA) and the San Antonio River Authority (SARA) have responsibility for management of surface waters in two adjacent river basins covering a region in the vicinity of San Antonio, Texas, and to the east and southeast of that area. The GBRA serves ten counties, but not the entire basins of the Guadalupe and Blanco Rivers. Its nine member board of directors is appointed by the Governor. The SARA covers four counties including Bexar, where the city of San Antonio is located. SARA is governed by a twelve member board elected with half from Bexar County, and two each from the other three counties. The Edwards Underground Water District (EUWD) is responsible for managing the ground water in a portion of the   Edwards Limestone Formation, and it overlaps

GBRA and SARA in several counties. The two river authorities have responsibility for managing the surface water, including water conservation, water supply and environmental quality. The EUWD is responsible for the conservation, protection, and enhancement of recharge of the Edwards Aquifer. Since the Edwards Aquifer exists in a karst topography subject to rapid recharge of the limestone aquifer in certain areas. Where the formation intersects the surface, there is a direct interplay between the surface water hydrology and the ground water hydrology. This fact was not recognized in the approval of the three various entities and each governing board manages its operations essentially independent of the other. The potential for conflict is large.

While the conflicts that have existed so far have been relatively minor, it makes little scientific sense to have water management organizations structured as these are. The EUWD would like to build detention structures in the recharge area to detain surface flow for recharge into the aquifer. This purpose could agree with the flood control mission of SARA, but it certainly conflicts with the objective of GBRA, which is more involved in water supply and hydroelectric power production. Therefore, GBRA wishes to maximize flow to its surface water reservoirs for subsequent sale and power production, as well as other uses. San Antonio is currently 100% dependent on ground water and the city has a close tie with EUWD as regards water management.

Again, like the Stacy case, this example is presented to show that water institutions that are organized without adequate attention to hydrologic realities pave the way to conflict. Again, engineers and hydrologists should involve themselves to a greater extent in the political process of formulating such institutions so that potential conflicts are minimized.

Water Supply for the City of Houston. This case comes from a study by Dan Sheer which illustrates the importance of operating procedures in maximizing the water yield from various combined supply sources. The city of Houston is located in the San Jacinto River Basin. Its water supply comes from Lake Houston and Lake Livingston, which are owned by the city, and potentially from Lake Conroe, which is owned by the San Jacinto River Authority. The city also uses ground water which is now managed by the Harris-Galveston Coastal Subsidence District, a district created to control subsidence which has amounted to nearly ten feet since the turn of the century in the most critical areas. Maximum safe ground water yields have been determined based on the requirement of controlling subsidence. The Brazos River, managed by the Brazos River Authority, is a short distance west of Houston and it flows directly into the Gulf of Mexico. There is no bay or estuary system at the mouth of the Brazos River so the environmental benefits to fish spawning and nursery areas of periodic flood flows does not exist there.

Here we have a case of four institutions having the potential for helping provide water supply to the city of Houston. Sheer has shown that the independent safe yield of the three lakes is 1,533,000 acre-feet per year. Safe annual ground water yield is 337,000 acre-feet per year, giving a sum of independent yields from the three lakes and ground water of 1,870,000 acre-feet per year. This assumes uncoordinated, independent operation of the three reservoirs. If the three reservoirs were operated jointly, the dependable safe yield would increase from 1,533,000 to 1,660,000 acre-feet per year, an increase of 8.3%. If the three reservoirs were operated jointly with ground water supply, recognizing that temporary overdrafts of ground water would not create severe subsidence problems, the joint yield increases from 1,870,000 acre-feet to 2,220,000 acre-feet per year, an increase of 18.7%. This clearly indicates the scope of water supply increases which are possible by jointly operating water supply systems. If the surplus flows of the Brazos River, which serve no significant beneficial use in the Gulf of Mexico, were captured, an additional 200,000 acre-feet of water could be provided.

This study, one of many of this nature by Sheer, clearly indicates the potential for increased dependable water supply through integrated management of water resource systems. However, such joint management is not easy when so many independent water institutions are involved. Potential conflicts may exist in the future which could have been avoided if the hydrologic facts of the water systems were better understood when the water agencies were established. This, again, illustrates the increasingly important role that engineers can play in avoiding water conflicts by being more pro-active in the political decisions regarding water institutions.

Action We Might Take

Certainly, the engineers need to look at the factors which are key to the feasibility of water projects. Sometimes the key reason for our work is improvement of a needed service to people and our job is to find a way to solve the problem. We may come up with physical solutions to the problem and in so doing lose sight of the real problem. We need to better explain our assumptions and the precise meaning of the terms we use. An example is the expression, "dependable water supply." I could ask you to define "dependable water supply" and I venture to say that many of you would give me a different answer. So, we have communications problems which may lead to misunderstanding and conflict.

I suggest that on every project we should do an "analysis of potential conflict" (APC). I am not interested in building bureaucracy, but when a project involving the public is built, I think we should do an APC. It should be part of the project documentation. The engineers and hydrologists should look at the potential conflicts and how these could be resolved. We should think of the potential conflicts which might result from the various uncertainties, the lack of knowledge, the assumptions, etc. Then we might come up with expert systems (artificial intelligence) approaches to resolving conflicts. We could even use simulations to help with the process. Ideally, we might develop with a procedure whereby we can look at various types of conflict and establish a framework for solving them before they actually exist. It is difficult to be totally rational in the heat of a contentious battle. The APC process would allow us to play "what if" games beforehand and, thereby, avoid conflicts or quickly resolve them if they occur.

Engineers need to relook at some of our programs with an eye toward conflict resolution. We have many cooperative programs in our engineering colleges. These coop programs are involved with industry. It would be fantastic for engineers who work with water resources problems to engage in an experimental coop program involving the agencies concerned with conflict resolution. This would give the engineers experience in interacting with the public. It would illustrate how we can play an important role in helping to solve these problems. It could involve an internship type of experience.

I say to students that I don't care how good the engineering solution is, if the public doesn't want it then it's not a solution. Moreover, if it is likely to result in conflict, it is not a good solution. So, I think that having some of our colleagues who have actually experienced internships involving public policy and conflict resolution issues would be extremely important.

At one time, water development was driven by physical potential for development. And now the overriding question is whether the activity satisfies the desires of the public. Many have blamed the engineers for projects developed in the past. But that's what the political leaders wanted and it's best we not forget that fact. Nonetheless, we need to adjust the way we do things. Perhaps we need to look at some modifications in our curricula. Engineers will always play a role in natural resources and, therefore, should prepare ourselves to better interact with the decision makers on water projects. We must be up front with our input on resolving conflicts. If not, too often the courts will have the last word.

References

Bok, Derek (1982). A Flawed System. Harvard Magazine.

Booth, Frank R. (1985). Implications of the Stacy Dam Case. Water Law Conference, The University of Texas (at Austin) School of Law. October 3 and 4, 1985.

Burger, Warren E. (1983). Conflict Resolution -- Isn't There a Better Way? National Forum. The Phi Kappa Phi Journal. Fall Issue.

Cannon, Mark W. (1983). Contentious and Burdensome Litigation -- A Need for Alternatives. National Forum. The Phi Kappa Phi Journal. Fall Issue.

Council on Competitiveness (1988). New Economic Index Reveals United States Outperformed by Major Competitiveness, Washington, D.C.

DEC 1988. The 1988 Technology Institute for Engineering Deans. Digital Equipment Corporation. p. 13.

Howard, A. E. Dick (1982). A Litigation Society? The Wilson Quarterly. Summer.

Sheer, Daniel P. (1985). The Importance of Operating Procedures in Determining Yield of Water Sources Available to the San Jacinto Basin, Texas. Annex 1, Chapter V, Texas Water Management Issues, Technical Report 221, Center for Research in Water Resources, The University of Texas at Austin.

Smerdon, Ernest T. and John A. Gronouski (1986). Texas Water Management Issues. Technical Report No. 221. Center for Research in Water Resources. The University of Texas at Austin.

Smerdon, Ernest T., John A. Gronouski and Judith M. Clarkson (1988). Approaches to Water Resource Policy and Planning in Texas. Water Resource Bulletin. AWRA. 24(6):1257-1262.

Thurow, Lester (1983). Death by a Thousand Cuts. J. C. Penny Forum. May.

Waterstone, Marvin and William B. Lord (1989). How Safe is Safe? National Forum. The Phi Kappa Phi Journal. Winter Issue.

FROM HOT-TUB TO WAR:
ALTERNATIVE DISPUTE RESOLUTION (ADR) IN THE
U.S. CORPS OF ENGINEERS

by
Jerome Delli Priscoli, Ph.D.*

Abstract

This paper reviews the U.S. Corps of Engineer
Alternative Dispute Resolution (ADR) program. It begins
by defining ADR. Then the paper outlines selected social
and organizational trends which are encouraging the
adoption of ADR techniques, and the guiding principles
of the program. A brief description of a continuum of
ADR techniques which is central to the program is
described. This description is followed by summaries of
selected Corps experiences using ADR in contract claims,
Water Resources and other areas. The Corps three-tier
approach to institutionalizing ADR is summarized. The
paper concludes with five summary goals for the ADR
program.

Introduction

A new age of resolving disputes has come upon us.
Unless we find better ways to resolve disputes, we will
be buried by them. Chief Justice Burger (1984) has
stated, "Our system is too costly, too painful, too
destructive, too inefficient for truly civilized people.
To rely on the adversarial process as the principle means

---

* Dr. Jerome Delli Priscoli is Senior Policy
Analyst at the U.S. Army Corps of Engineers Institute
for Water Resources, Casey Building, Fort Belvoir,
Virginia, 22060. He manages the Corps ADR program. The
views and opinions expressed in this paper are those of
Mr. Delli Priscoli and do not necessarily reflect the
policy of the Corps of Engineers.

70

of resolving conflicting claims is a mistake that must be corrected." The Corps of Engineers has responded to this challenge by instituting a major alternative dispute resolution (ADR) program. This program is sponsored by the Chief Counsel and Senior Corps executives. It stresses internal development of ADR skills along with the use of external advisors and consultants.

The ADR program is important to other Federal agencies for a number of reasons. First, the Corps is using ADR in a variety of administrative functions such as regulating waterways and wetlands; planning water development projects; designing engineering solutions; constructing and implementing projects; and operating and managing completed projects. Second, ADR has been used in a variety of traditional engineering fields such as hazardous and toxic waste cleanup; traditional water resources development; and infrastructure development. Third, the Corps' applications of ADR in contracting offer new alternatives for improving government contracting, reducing contracting claims and increasing contracting efficiency.

I.   What is Alternative Dispute Resolution (ADR)?

The term "Alternative Dispute Resolution" is imperfect because it defines the field in terms of what it is not, rather than what it is. ADR is not a replacement for our legal system. ADR is a means to "off-load" the pressure on that system so it may act more equitably and efficiently. This acronym, ADR, contrasts with normal litigation which is distinguished by: 1) an adversarial process; 2) a decision reached by a third party such as a judge; and, 3) an imposed decision whether or not it is acceptable to the parties.

In contrast, ADR strives for mutually acceptable decisions, although this sometimes occurs when the only remaining alternative is litigation. ADR rarely uses third parties who make binding decisions as a judge. ADR third parties are usually called "facilitators," "mediators," or neutral advisors and are used to facilitate and encourage resolution and to counsel on possible bases for resolution. But in ADR it is finally up to the parties to reach agreement.

Because the emphasis is on voluntary agreement, ADR processes emphasize mutuality and interdependence. Many of the adversarial practices associated with litigation such as formalized procedures, limited communication between actual parties, and efforts to withhold information, are not appropriate with ADR. ADR uses processes which are designed to increase communication, encourage informal discussion, reinforce relationships and build trust. The reason is simple; communication, trust and improved relationships create a climate in which it is easier to reach a voluntary agreement. Also, if and when such agreement is achieved, it is more likely that the agreement will stick. And it is likely that the parties in the future will be better able to deal with one another.

II.   Why is the Corps Interested in ADR?

Numerous broad social and more immediate organizational trends are converging to generate an interest in ADR. The following paragraphs describe a few:

a.   Some broad social trends

o Our institutional means for achieving environmental quality are increasingly inappropriate to meet the needs of environmental and economic health. Public awareness and concern for the environment across all the industrial world continues to grow (Milbraith; 1980). While solutions to many of our immediate environmental threats require engineering skill, much of our public engineering resources are housed in traditional development agencies outside the mainstream of our public environmental organizations. The gap between growing public concern for environmental health and quality and our capacity to apply the Nation's public engineering resources to such concerns must be narrowed.

For example, look at the water resources field as described in Figure 1. The figure shows that water resources spending accounted for 61% of total Federal spending for natural resources and the environment in 1965. In 1988 it accounted for 27%. At the same time, pollution control and abatement has grown from less than 10% to approximately 33% of the total Federal spending for natural resources and the environment. In other words, the Federal concern for natural resources, a traditional concern for the civil engineer, is rapidly being defined in environmental terms. Yet, public engineering institutions seem not to fully reflect this shift.

The point can be stated more simply. To achieve environmental quality ends will require engineering means, and applying engineering means will increasingly be rationalized in terms of environmental ends. We are in a period of adjusting to a new public understanding of this environmental ends-engineering means continuum. ADR can be seen as a tool to adjust the institutional public engineering inertia to a changing sense of public values.

Figure 1

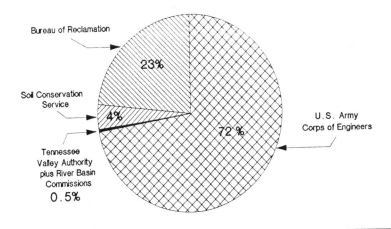

Federal Spending for Water Resources in 1988
(Estimated 1988 Outlays of $4.15 Billion)

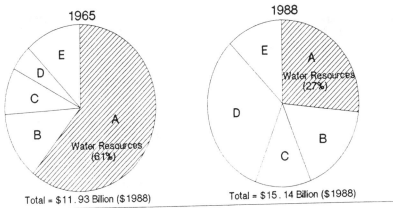

Total Federal Spending for Natural Resources
and the Environment

A - Water Resources   C - Recreational Resources   E - Other Natural Resources
B - Conservation & Land Management D - Pollution Control & Abatement

Source: Office of Management and Budget, 1988. Historical Tables. Budget of the United States Government FY 1989.
         U.S. Government Printing Office, Washington, D.C.

Beyond public engineering, the National Science Foundation (1979) and the National Research Council (1986) show that the science of environmental impact analysis is deficient and should be upgraded. Environmental impact statements (EISs) have become a major instrument in raising the environmental consciousness and leveraging environmental concerns in the decision processes. However, the EIS debate focuses primarily on procedure and, to some degree, inhibits the substance of scientific concerns from being considered. Posturing and positioning dominate the discovery of substantive interests (Stakhiv, 1988).

The EPA has begun to revitalize and change the contract management methods to better achieve environmental goals of the Superfund law. Similarly, the Department of Energy (DOE) is reconsidering its environmental management structure partly in response to recent criticism of environmental compliance. These are only a few examples beyond the Corps of how other agencies and instruments designed to deal with environmental health concerns are themselves becoming dated.

o <u>We are increasingly mired in a psychology of constraints and limits</u>. While reacting to and stopping projects has been useful in raising our environmental consciousness, or even as a precondition, it is not sufficient to achieve environmental and economic health. A "When in doubt do nothing," rule cannot be sustained forever. As long as we continue to make policy in the spirit of constraint and limits, we will be increasingly dominated by a fear of the future. Therefore, we must overcome that fear and act to create rather than simply react to trends.

Public policy must move beyond the "impact fixation" institutionalized in the alphabet soup requirements of impact assessment such as RIA, SIA, EIA, etc. Often, it appears that we have institutionalized negativism. That is, the way to be heard is to object. Many have the power to stop, but few seem to exercise the power to create. In a world of such fractionalized power, or to put it scientifically, reductionism, the power to stop seems to be "over" rewarded. Impact assessments are crucial for both informed technical and good moral decisions. We must know to the best of our ability the consequences of our actions. However, we must move beyond being paralyzed by our understanding of such consequences. The demand for ADR exists, in part, because of such paralysis. ADR offers a route out of paralysis toward action.

o <u>There is a changing understanding of professionalism throughout society and the Corps of Engineers</u>. This term, professionalism, is so often used that we assume its meaning to be self evident and shared throughout the engineering community. But, it is not. There are many images of professionalism.

In the Corps many see themselves first as professional engineers; most see themselves as professional civil servants; some see themselves as military servants. As the Corps has evolved, lawyers, economists, new types of scientists, engineers and even social scientists have sought to blend their own professional images into that of the public engineering service the Corps provides. The reality of having to deliver goods, services and products has forced accommodation, if not synthesis, among these different professional images. It has also forced the organization to seek definitions of professionalism that transcend individual images. The psychiatrist R.J. Lifton (1987) notes that:

"The history of the idea of a profession reveals that the pre-modern image of profession as advocacy based on faith gave way to the modern image of technique devoid of advocacy. What we need is a post-modern model of professions that would include both knowledge and skill on the one hand and specific advocacies and ethical commitments on the other."

Throughout society, the very meaning of professionalism is changing. Patients no longer say, "Cure me": they participate with doctors in their own diagnosis and treatment. Clergy may no longer maintain strict distinctions between the "lay" and "religious" and may no longer consider themselves the sole salvation mediators between heaven and earth. Lawyers can no longer neglect avenues of ADR or avoid linking their individual actions to the overall state of social justice. Should engineers be surprised when citizens who use a power plant exercise a right in influencing its design and location?

Professionalism includes not only the final goods and services provided, but also the means employed to deliver those goods and services. The means by which the goods and services are delivered establish a relationship with the public clients and our customers. ADR is once again a means to help professional engineers cope with these changing demands emanating from a new understanding of professionalism throughout society.

o **The changing nature of administrative processes in the democratic state.** Since the late 19th century, the United States has blended the separation of powers doctrine with a distinction between administration and legislation. Technical agencies such as

the Corps have come to recognize the blending as a
distinction between technical versus political.
Although this is theoretically plausible, the distinction rarely fits reality. Nevertheless, the Corps often
holds an image of technically pure and competent
professionalism with high integrity. Obviously, that is
a good image and must be held. However, it cannot be
held by retreating into narrow technicalism. Leaders
have to publicly recognize that our "technical" agencies
operate, more and more, in the area between technical
and political. The integrity and professionalism of
engineers in such agencies will be found in the way they
explicitly blend, rather than separate, the issues as
technical versus political.

The administering of laws has come to look
increasingly political. Legislatures seem to write
legislation that is more general than specific. Judges
shy away from substantive judicial review and review
procedure. Thus, technical agencies such as the Corps
are placed in the position of distributing benefits and
costs of the programs to the people. This is especially
true in the environmental area. It is in the
implementation of the programs that the distribution of
the benefits and costs become clear. ADR offers tools
to the administrators and managers for managing this
gray area between technical and political. In fact, ADR
may become some of the most important tools in the
managers toolkit.

    b.   Some immediate organizational trends.

Beyond these external trends, the Corps, like
many large organizations, is involved in numerous
immediate disputes. As managers of construction for
some of the largest public works projects in the world,
the Corps is often involved in claims and disputes among
the Corps, contractors and sub-contractors. These
involve interpretations of the contract, differing site
conditions, change orders, and the relationship between
design and construction.

Beyond construction, the Corps' operations and
maintenance program has steadily been growing. Today it
is estimated to be over 60% of the total civil works
budget of the Corps of Engineers. In managing many of
the Nation's largest dams and locks, the Corps makes
decisions which are potential sources of disputes, such
as the level of flood protection provided, the available
water supply for communities and industry, navigation
rules along the river and the water level of reservoirs
which are used for recreation as well as for flood
protection. Indeed, projects which have existed for a
number of years find themselves in new demographic
situations and therefore confronted with new sets of

demands for the allocation of the resources they represent.

Because of its legislatively mandated role as regulator of the Nation's wetlands and the free flow of navigation, the Corps must often address disputes over how much development should be allowed in wetlands or in navigable waterways. Since the Corps receives over 14,000 permit requests a year, the opportunity for disputes and the need for efficient and equitable means of resolving those disputes is clear.

Even in its military construction role, disputes often arise between the Corps and its "clients" both within the Army and other service organizations. For example, there may be different expectations about what is required about the differing schedules and about different ways of operating projects. In the environment of changing military requirements and commanders, and satisfying clients, even if that client is another Federal agency, negotiations can become fraught with disputes.

Under the Defense Environmental Restoration Program (DERP), the Corps of Engineers represents the Department of Defense (DOD) in negotiating cleanup of hazardous waste contamination at current and former DOD installations. Representing DOD, the Corps will have to negotiate an allocation of responsibilities for cleanup with a variety of parties such as: previous site owners, current owners of parallel sites, various affected publics and others. Scientific studies and engineering analyses, alone, are unlikely to demonstrate responsibility. Supplemental negotiations will undoubtedly be needed.

Currently, many of the disputes arising in these areas are resolved through litigation or other highly adversarial processes. In the case of the Corps' relationship with its military "clients," disputes aren't resolved by litigation but may result in impasses which can pollute the relationship among the organizations. This can result in increased cost to the U.S. taxpayer.

Whether the result is litigation or impasse, there are costs to the organization and to the public. For example, contract claims against the Corps have more than doubled in the past eight years. This has created new costs for additional staff, attorneys, and courts. The contract appeals boards, which themselves were developed as an ADR mechanism, are overloaded. "Fast track" claims can take over one year and still be appealed. The average time for a claims settlement, including accelerated processes, is over 400 days. The average time for claims not on the accelerated process can be two to four years. There may also be consider-able delays in the completion of projects or cost overruns due to the failure to resolve issues in a timely manner. When disputes remain unresolved for prolonged periods, there is damage to important relationships.

There are also internal costs when disputes remain unsolved. For example, studies have shown that 30% of first line supervisors' time and 25% of all management time is spent in resolving disputes. More than 85% of those leaving jobs do so because of some perceived conflict. Almost 75% of job stress is created by dis-putes (Delli Priscoli, Moore, 1989).

III. Guiding Principles of the Corps ADR Program

The Corps ADR program has utilitarian, strategic and normative components. In the utilitarian sense, the program seeks to add "tools" to the "toolkit" of the manager. In the strategic sense, the program encourages executives to evaluate expected values generated by various dispute management approaches and to actively manage dispute, rather than routinely turning such management over to others. In the normative sense, the program actively encourages and assists Corps' managers and executives to embrace ADR. The Corps' ADR program is built on the belief that there are numerous advantages to using ADR techniques such as: (Delli Priscoli, Moore, 1989)

o Getting better decisions: because agreements reached between the parties meet the parties' interests, they are likely to do a better job of resolving disputes than the all-or-nothing court decisions.

o Creating a better climate for resolution: people use ADR techniques because they think they'll do a better job of resolving the dispute. No one is coerced and this in itself creates a better climate for dispute resolution. It may also create a better climate for the sharing of infor-mation.

o Expediting procedures: because ADR techniques are less formal and can be scheduled at the discretion of parties, they often result in considerable time savings. However, savings can be counterintuitive: "up-front" costs can be heavy, while the costs of implementing and main-taining a settlement once achieved should be reduced.

o Reducing Costs: normally, ADR techniques can also save money particularly when they are compared to litigation.

o Enhancing flexibility: because ADR procedures are under the control of the parties themselves, they can adapt to specific needs and circumstances.

o Providing more control over the outcome: because the decisionmaking is retained by the parties rather than delegated to a judge or third party, the parties have more control and there is more predictability to the outcomes.

o Encouraging control by managers who know the organization's needs best: ADR seeks to put control in the hands of the line managers who are best able to assess the impacts of any proposed decision in the organization and have the greatest flexibility in developing creative solutions.

o Increasing the probability that decisions will hold up: because all parties have an interest in making an agreement work, mutual agreements are more likely to hold up over time and prevent future problems.

IV. From Hot-tub to War: A Continuum of ADR Techniques

Figures 2 and 3 describe a continuum of ADR techniques. This continuum is the central metaphor throughout the Corps ADR program. Figure 2 outlines a general continuum of ADR procedures while Figure 3 describes ADR procedures found in the middle third of the continuum, roughly from point 2 to point 17 on Figure 2. Turning to Figure 2, point A represents what is colloquially called the "Hot-tub Approach." That is, we all jump into the Hot Tub and somehow come to agreement. Point B represents the opposite extreme. That is, we go to war or use a highly adversarial approach. ADR addresses the numerous possibilities between these points. Some are well known, others are emerging and most make common sense.

Four points should be made about the continuum in Figure 2. First, as we move from move from point A to point B, we gradually give over the power and authority to settle to outside parties. A dividing line, roughly two-thirds of the way from A to B symbolizes that point at which the power to resolve disputes moves out of the hands of the disputants and into the hands of an outside party. The thrust of the Corps' ADR program is to encourage managers and executives to explore techniques

Figure 2
A Continuum of ADR Techniques*

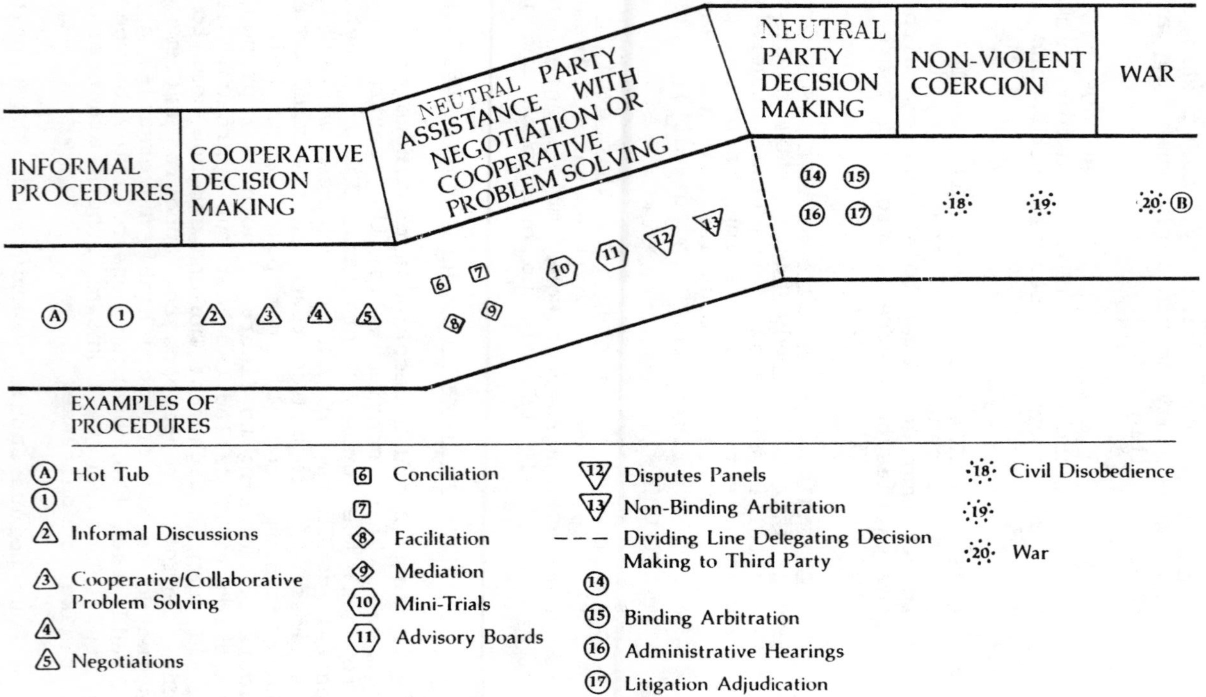
INFORMAL PROCEDURES
COOPERATIVE DECISION MAKING
NEUTRAL PARTY ASSISTANCE WITH NEGOTIATION OR COOPERATIVE PROBLEM SOLVING
NEUTRAL PARTY DECISION MAKING
NON-VIOLENT COERCION
WAR
EXAMPLES OF PROCEDURES
A Hot Tub
1
2 Informal Discussions
3 Cooperative/Collaborative Problem Solving
4
5 Negotiations
6 Conciliation
7
8 Facilitation
9 Mediation
10 Mini-Trials
11 Advisory Boards
12 Disputes Panels
13 Non-Binding Arbitration
--- Dividing Line Delegating Decision Making to Third Party
14
15 Binding Arbitration
16 Administrative Hearings
17 Litigation Adjudication
18 Civil Disobedience
19
20 War

* Delli Priscoli and Moore, 1989

to the left of this dividing line which will enable them to retain decisionmaking authority and resolve disputes efficiently and effectively.

Second, the basic principles of interest-based negotiations and bargaining as explained in Fisher (1981), can be applied with any technique along this continuum. Interest-based bargaining, in contrast to positional bargaining, can be appropriate for facilitation, problem solving meetings, mediations, mini-trial deliberations, and fact finding.

Third, the unnamed points in the continuum are meant to indicate that there is much to learn. Possibilities exist to create new procedures across the continuum. The last word on ADR is not in. In fact, the Corps' program invites managers to innovate and to create new ADR procedures.

Fourth, since communications contain, at least, content and process, the way we talk, or our process of dialogue, often can determine how and if people listen to the content of that dialogue. A premise of ADR techniques is that by separating the process and the content roles in a dispute we can better manage the discussions and promote agreement. The separation of process and content roles often leads to using neutral parties, sometimes called "interveners." Such neutral parties, in a variety of ways, become caretakers to the process of dialogue in the dispute. Figure 3 describes techniques from cooperative to third party decision-making. It groups these techniques into the following categories: unassisted procedures; relationship building assistance; procedural assistance; substantive assistance; advisory and non-binding assistance; and binding assistance (Delli Priscoli, Moore, 1989).

To some, this continuum and categorization may seem either too discrete or overly defined. However, the point of the continuum is to show managers that numerous techniques are available. It also attempts to show managers that many possibilities for innovation also exist. In other words, the continuum tries to place techniques in a context which helps us to catalog and share our growing ADR experiences.

V.   Selected Summary of Corps Experiences

In varying degrees the Corps has used techniques across this whole continuum. The following examples are meant to provide a flavor of the Corps' ADR activities. Under neutral party advisory and non-binding assistance (Figure 3), the Corps' primary experience has been with non-binding arbitration. While Federal agencies may not

Figure 3
A Continuum of ADR Techniques (In-Depth)*

COOPERATIVE DECISION MAKING	NEUTRAL PARTY ASSISTANCE WITH NEGOTIATIONS OR COOPERATIVE PROBLEM SOLVING				NEUTRAL PARTY DECISION MAKING	
Parties are Unassisted	Relationship Building Assistance	Procedural Assistance	Substantive Assistance	Advisory Non-Binding Assistance	Binding Assistance	
• Conciliation • Information Exchange Meetings • Cooperative/ Collaborative Problem-Solving • Negotiations	• Counseling/ Therapy • Conciliation • Team Building • Informal Social Activities	• Coaching/ Process Consultation • Training • Facilitation • Mediation	• Mini-Trial • Technical Advisory Boards/ Disputes Panels • Advisory Mediation • Fact Finding • Settlement Conference	• Non-Binding Arbitration • Summary Jury Trial	• Binding Arbitration • Med-Arb • Mediation-then- Arbitration • Disputes Panels (binding) • Private Courts/ Judging • Admin Hearing	

* Delli Priscoli and Moore, 1989

use binding arbitration, they can participate in non-binding arbitration.

In arbitration, disputes are submitted to a neutral individual or panel for either an advisory non-binding or binding decision. The neutral parties are often technical experts, lawyers or judges, although this is not a prerequisite. At either a binding or non-binding arbitration hearing, each side's arguments are presented in a quasi-judicial manner. Time is allowed for cross examination and closing statements. After the case presentations, the arbiter issues an opinion which may be non-binding or binding depending on the prior agreement reached by the parties, or the conditions which have been set up by some other contract mechanism (Edelman; 1989). Non-binding arbitration has been used in a number of construction contract cases.

Of the substantive assistance procedures, the Corps has used the mini-trial, disputes panels, and fact finding. The mini-trial has become the best known of all Corps' ADR procedures. It is the first ADR method developed to resolve disputes in government contracting (Edelman, et. al,; 1989). The term mini-trial is somewhat of a misnomer. It is not a trial. Essentially it is a structured negotiations technique. The mini-trial is a process which is designed to expose the senior decisionmakers to the strengths and weaknesses of one another's case and to help bring them to the point of directly negotiating an agreement.

The mini-trial is a voluntary, expedited and non-judicial procedure. While the mini-trial is a flexible procedure, it usually involves the commitment of top management, a willingness to give authority to senior management to make a deal, and often a neutral advisor. A mini-trial process also usually includes development of a mini-trial agreement, discovery of information as defined in the mini-trial agreement, an exchange of position papers, a preliminary meeting between the neutral advisor and the management representatives, the mini-trial conference itself and, finally, negotiations following the conference and the documentation of any agreements reached (Edelman, et. al; 1989).

Neutral advisors in the mini-trial have been judges who are acting as neutral facilitators rather than judges, mediators and others. The role of the neutral party is flexible. For example, that party may or may not be present when the senior executives negotiate after hearing the positions.

Most mini-trials should be completed within three months. This includes time for the discovery and for the conference. Parties agree to limit deposition,

interrogatories and other discovery devices. The actual
mini-trial conference is informal. Time allowed for
case presentation and rebuttals is scheduled in advance
and adhered to during the conference. No transcript of
the hearing is produced and rules of evidence and
procedure are not used. The mini-trial is not
adversarial. It seeks to quickly establish the principles and facts underlying the dispute. The sides
present their best case, but there is no attempt to
limit the other attorney's presentations. The contents
of the conference are kept confidential and neither
party may use the hearing in subsequent litigation. At
the end of the informal conference, the principals meet
privately to discuss the dispute (Edelman, et. al;
1989).

The Corps has successfully used mini-trials in
cases ranging from several hundred thousand dollars to
several million dollar claims. Perhaps the best known
case is a construction claim for 55.6 million dollars
involving aspects of the Tennessee-Tom Bigbee Waterway
construction. This dispute arose over differing site
conditions. A three day mini-trial, followed by a one
day mini-trial, was completed and a settlement of 17.25
million dollars was reached. The Defense Department
Inspector General (IG) investigated this settlement.
The IG found that the settlement was in the best
interest of the government, and concluded that the mini-
trial in certain cases is an efficient and cost effective means for settling contract disputes. After the
Ten-Tom, the Corps has employed the mini-trial on
several other contract claim cases. The Administrative
Conference of the United States (ACUS) and others have
reviewed these mini-trials (Crowell and Pou, 1987;
Endispute, 1989).

Recently, the Corps used the mini-trial to reach
agreement on responsibility for a toxic waste site
cleanup under its new DERP responsibilities. The dispute was over the cost allocation for cleanup of
groundwater contamination at the Phoenix/Goodyear
Airport. The total cleanup estimate was to exceed 12
million dollars. The dispute include the Department of
Justice, Environmental Protection Agency, Department of
Defense and Goodyear (Endispute; 1989).

The mini-trial process began in January 1988 and
was completed by the end of May 1988. This process
started after a previous year of notices and discussions
and failed attempts at negotiations. It used a neutral
advisor who was a well known environmental mediator and
resulted in an agreed assignment responsibility for
cleanup costs. In this case, both Goodyear and the
Corps, representing the Department of Defense, felt they
had strong arguments for why the other should bear the

majority of the costs. This application demonstrates
that the mini-trial is flexible and can be used beyond
contract claims. This mini-trial demonstrates a model
which could be used in other Superfund cases to perhaps
break a deadlock and enhance the efficiency of cleanup.

Dispute panels, although new to the Federal
government, have been used by several state governments
on large construction projects. In this technique, a
panel is chosen before construction begins and parties
agree to let contract disputes be voluntarily submitted
to the panel for an opinion as they occur during construction. Thus, the disputes panel acts to prevent
unnecessary conflict and the aftermath of protracted
conflict.

Under the Corps' ADR program, disputes panels will
consist of three private technical experts. The
government and the contractor each select one member of
the panel and the third is selected by the agreement of
these two members. The procedure provides for the
disputes to be submitted quickly to the panel in time to
make a non-binding, written recommendation to the
contract officer and contractor.(Edelman, 1989) Unlike
a mini-trial or other techniques, the disputes panel is
composed of technical, not legal, personnel. Disputes
panels, like non-binding arbitration, will probably be
used on claims and cases involving lower dollar claim
figures (Endispute, 1989).

Fact finding is the third of the substantive
assistance procedures used by the Corps. Fact finding
originated in the attempt to resolve labor disputes, and
has been used in a number of other areas. Basically, an
impartial and acceptable neutral party is selected by
the disputant parties or by an agency or individual.
This person is authorized to investigate the issues in
the dispute and issue a report. This report could
either be a situation assessment which organizes and
describes issues, interests, potential settlement
options and possible procedures to resolve the conflict,
or a specific non-binding procedural or substantive
recommendation about how the dispute may be settled
(Delli Priscoli, Moore; 1989).

Ideally, the fact finding report would be seen as
unbiased, fair and equitable and help parties move
towards the acceptance of the facts and a negotiated
settlement. In a recent case, the Corps participated in
a fact finding surrounding the environmental cleanup of
a chemical company's operations. More than four hundred
potentially responsible parties (PRP) were identified
and a neutral fact finder was appointed. The potential
cleanup costs at this abandoned dump site were estimated
at around 35.5 million dollars. The process presented

PRPs with the facts regarding involvement in the contamination and offered options for participating in the cost of the cleanup.

The Corps of Engineers has substantial experience in facilitation and mediation techniques which use neutrals to assist in the procedure or process of dialogue. Both are essentially "caretakers" to the process of dialogue. The mediator, however, may become more involved in the substantive settlements. For example, the mediator may call caucuses or help parties to formulate possible alternatives and to be a vehicle by which alternatives can be placed on the table. Mediation is most known in cases where there have been limited parties and limited clearly identified issues. Facilitation usually is used where there are multiple parties and multiple issues.

The facilitator is typically and primarily involved in the conducting of meetings among the parties. A facilitator will be sure that all parties feel listened to, will make sure that the meetings stay relevant, and may suggest procedures which are helpful in arriving at a solution. (Creighton, et.al, 1983) Actually, the distinction between facilitation and mediation is not always clear. An individual some people call a facilitator may actually engage in many of the behaviors of a mediator, depending on what the situation requires, and also what the disputant parties desire.

Facilitation and mediation have traditionally been used in civil works planning. The first known case of environmental mediation was used in the mid-1970s in the Corps' water resource development planning process. One of the most exciting uses of facilitation has been in the Corps' 404 permit program. Under its permit authorities, stemming from Section 404 of the Clean Water Act, the Corps must review permits submitted to it for projects involving the use of wetlands and navigable waters. (Lefkoff in Creighton, et. al, 1983)

For the Sannibel Island of Florida and for exploratory drilling for petroleum in the Gulf Coast region, the Corps used its authority to write general permits. Facilitation and mediation were used to bring potential disputants together, and reduce the amount of litigation and time required to issue these permits. Essentially, the Corps identified potential disputants and suggested that they come together and talk about their different interests and positions (Delli Priscoli, 1988). If the parties could come to some agreement on the acceptable conditions for individual permits in their various areas and activities, those conditions would then become the special conditions for a general permit.

Thus, individual permits would be facilitated without loss of environmental and other considerations.

Each case involved neutral facilitators, who acted as both facilitators and mediators. In both cases, agreement was reached among Federal, state, local, private, and public sector representatives. The neutral parties helped the representatives of the potential disputants to understand shared interests. For example, the private sector expressed an interest in a more certain future even if that would mean less development. Environmental groups also expressed their interests in a stable future, so that their limited resources could be spent in fighting battles in other areas. Both cases produced general permits which were in place for five years.

A general permit reduces the amount of time for individual permits. It can also reduce the number of conflicts that will arise surrounding an individual permit. In the case of exploratory oil drilling, officials could expect several hundred permit requests a year. In the case of the Sannibel Island, there were 11 to 12 requests a year. In both cases, the use of the neutral party helped potential disputants anticipate and thereby prevent unnecessary conflict by assuring that major interests would be met and served before they were solidified into public positions.

The Corps also has substantial experience with techniques further to the left on the continuum. One of the more interesting, and perhaps precedent setting uses of ADR, is occurring at this end of the continuum. At one 80 million dollar lock and dam replacement project, the Corps has, from the beginning of the project, fostered a new team building or partnering relationship between the contractor and itself. Typically, a project this size will have a large dollar value of outstanding claims at its completion. The Corps sought to finish the project on time without outstanding claims and at projected budget. To do this, the Corps, with the initial help of a facilitator, sat down with the contractor before the contract began. The purpose of this meeting was to discuss common interests, communication channels, the potential areas of disputes and how the Corps and the contractor would settle these disputes.

Several areas of shared interest were identified. Among them were the profit margin of the contractor. Clearly, it was in the interest of both the Corps and the contractor to make a profit. However, that profit could be made without outstanding claims at the end of the contract and undue delays. The Corps and the contractor developed a multi-step procedure by which disputes, once identified, would be handled. Also, the

Corps and representatives of the contractor would meet
periodically to discuss their progress on the resolution
of disputes and disagreements.   In this way, a team
building relationship--rather than an adversarial
relationship--was set up from the beginning.   Both the
Corps and the contractor see themselves as "in it"
together.   To date, the contract is ahead of schedule
with no outstanding claims.   This is a case of anticipating potential conflicts and acting to prevent
unnecessary conflicts, with the goal of achieving basic
management objectives.

A number of other cases can be seen in our review
of various Corps' publications.   Overall ADR experience
is growing.   Also, ADR does not wholly mean dealing with
conflict that has solidified almost to the point of
litigation.   It also means anticipating conflict based
on experience of what may happen, and acting to prevent
unnecessary conflict by identifying and addressing
interests before disputes explode into extreme positions.

VI.   ADR and the New Era of Water Resources Development

With the 1985 Supplemental Appropriations Act (P.L.
99-88), and the Water Resources Development Act of 1986
(P.L. 99-66), the Corps of Engineers entered into a new
era of water resources development and planning.   Local
cooperation agreements (LCAs) now require a new mandatory
cost sharing arrangement and consequently sharing of
risks and responsibilities.   Non-Federal sponsors are
required to put more money up front for the project and
to participate in the project planning.   The costs to
project sponsors can include items such as providing real
estate interests needed for the projects, other non-
Federal obligations including operating and maintaining
the project after completion (except for navigation
projects), and agreeing to indemnify the Corps for damage
claims not resulting from negligence of the Corps and its
contractor (Edelman; 1989).

This new era of local cooperation agreements has
been called an era of partnership and planning.   However,
regardless of legal mandates, this partnership does not
assure freedom from dispute, especially disputes among
sovereign entities.   With more sharing of cost and
participation by sponsors, it is not difficult to see how
traditional project management issues such as "project
modifications, construction schedules, evaluation of real
estate, accounting methods, and application of Federal
social legislation in the local arena could generate
disputes (Edelman; 1989).

To avoid unnecessary litigation and negative public
reaction that could result from disputes among sovereign
entities over project responsibilities, the Corps added

an ADR clause to all of the LCA project structuring agreements. This clause is general and simply commits the parties to trying an ADR mechanism before resorting to court. To date, this clause has not been activated since the LCA process is new. However, we can speculate that both procedural and substantive assistance techniques could be applicable here.

V. The Corps Program: A Three-tier Approach

The Corps has adopted a three-tier program to encourage the use of alternative dispute resolution techniques. The three-tier approach is based on the successful model to institutionalize public involvement that the Corps of Engineers used in the late 1970s and early 1980s. The three tiers are training; research and development and evaluation; and field assistance and, networking.

a. Training

If ADR is to be adopted, mindsets must change. The Corps has found that mindsets can be changed and that skillfully developed training is crucial to this change. The key is to reach a broad cross section of the organization. This cannot be done on a "one shot" approach. Therefore, the Corps developed an ADR training program which would become part of the mainstream training options for managers and executives.

Annually, over the last five years, the Corps has presented two to four sessions of a five-day conflict management and negotiations training course for mid-level to senior level employees. More than 350 Corps' employees have attended this course, which covers ADR philosophy, techniques, applications, negotiations and bargaining. The course is built on a "learn by doing" model.

The Corps has developed and begun a special two-day executive training course for all senior Corps' executives and commanders which will complement the five-day training. Over the years, many of the mid-level managers have responded positively to the training course, but also said that their senior supervisors would not let them implement the techniques and philosophies they had learned. Now since the Chief of Engineers has suggested that all senior commanders and senior executives attend the executive training course, this course exposes senior executives to the range of ADR techniques and asks them to encourage their subordinates to use ADR.

This executive course also uses case studies and hands on training. However, it is geared to the strategic management of conflict. The course is designed to acquaint managers with the strategic options available to them for resolving disputes. It also provides experience by which managers can choose various options in simulated case studies. The overall objective is to establish executive and mid-level management training that will be available on a routine basis and included in the core curriculum of managers as they progress up the supervisory ladder within the organization.

   b.   Field Assistance and Networking

      Technical assistance is vital to adopting new ideas in any organization. Throughout the 1970s, the Corps instituted an effective technical assistance program to support the use of new public involvement technologies. A similar program for ADR is now being developed. This program supports Corps' field activities by:

   o Designing special "on-site training", based on specific real time problems;

   o Helping commanders prepare for negotiations by: scoping optional approaches to negotiations/ bargaining; identifying issues, interests and positions of major interested parties;

   o Assisting in the development of single text negotiation techniques including drafting and revising text;

   o Applying principles of interest based bargaining conciliation, mediation, and third party intervention to specific Corps functions;

   o Mediating disputes both where the Corps is a party and where the Corps is a facilitator;

   o Employing ADR techniques to internal Corps conflict situations where appropriate and requested by field offices and others;

   o Assisting field offices in locating and employing credible third parties where needed.

   c.   Research and Evaluation

      Like all programs, ADR evaluation and feedback is important, but rarely done. The ADR program is setting up a monitoring program to determine what works and what does not work, and how the costs and benefits should be assessed. A number of case study assessments have been completed and more are planned (Endispute; 1989). Success stories need to be documented and disseminated throughout the agency and the government to show others the possibilities of ADR. Likewise, failures need to be documented to understand the risks associated with applying ADR within an organization. The focus of this evaluation program is case studies and retrospective assessments.

Institutionalizing ADR in the Corps is in many ways similar to institutionalizing public involvement in the 1970s (Delli Priscoli; 1978). Beyond writing guidance and regulations, there is considerable debate on a number of similar issues. For example, what is the best way for the agency to respond, through regulation, legislation, executive orders? Should there be some special organization instituted for ADR, such as special assistance for ADR or special offices? Is the best way to implement ADR from the top down or from the bottom up? How do we deal with the real needs expressed due to professional resistance to compromise or negotiation over "truth."

Like public involvement attempts in the 1970s, institutionalizing ADR constantly can appear to disrupt agency routine. The question underlying this perception is how to get ADR accepted as a mainstream and not an add-on to management's thinking. Finally, what is the appropriate balance between using outside or inside facilitators or mediators? These and several such questions once again have surfaced just as they did in the late 70s and 80s. This is because ADR cannot be reduced to just a set of techniques. ADR comprises a philosophy and an approach, and in this sense requires mindset and attitude change.

VI. Conclusions - Goals

The goals and expectations implied and expressed throughout this paper can be summarized in the five following points:

1. ADR seeks to change management culture. Managers must actively and strategically manage conflicts and not, routinely, hand them off to others for decisions.

2. ADR seeks to reduce the cost of litigation, appeals and other expensive adversarial rela- tionships, while helping to build better relations with contractors and other potential disputants.

3. ADR seeks to improve public contract admini- stration. The Corps' ADR experience may show how ADR is a way to regain control of contracts

and claims, and, thus, be a model for DOD and the Federal government.

4. ADR is a means to help one of the world's largest public engineering organizations cope with changing public values and with redefining public engineering services.

5. ADR is a way to forge a new synthesis between environmental quality ends and public engineering means.

BIBLIOGRAPHY

Bureau of National Affairs. ADR Report, "Practice and Perspectives," Volume II, October 13, 1988, pages 365-367.

Chief Justice Warren Burger. Annual Report on the State of the Judiciary, American Bar Association, February 12, 1984.

Creighton, James, Jerry Delli Priscoli, C. Mark Dunning. Public Involvement Techniques: A Reader of Ten Years Experience at the Institute for Water Resources, IWR Research Report 82-R1, May 1983.

Delli Priscoli, Jerome and Christopher Moore. The Executive Seminar on Alternative Dispute Resolution (ADR) Procedures: The U.S. Corps of Engineers, CDR Associates, Boulder, CO and Institute for Water Resources, U.S. Corps of Engineers, Fort Belvoir, VA, 1989.

Delli Priscoli, Jerome. "Conflict Resolution in Water Resources: Two 404 General Permits," Journal of Water Resources Planning and Management, Volume 114, No. 1, January 1988, pages 66-77.

Delli Priscoli, Jerome.   "Enduring Myths of Public Involvement," in Citizen Participation, Spring, Lincoln Filene Center, Tuffs FTS, University, Medford, MA

Delli Priscoli, Jerome. "Implementing Public Involvement Programs in Federal Agencies," in Citizen Participation in America, Essays on the State of the Art, edited by Stuart Langton, Lexington Books, DC Heath & Co., Lexington, MA, 1978.

Delli Priscoli, Jerome. "Public Involvement, Conflict Management: Means to EQ and Social Objectives," Journal of Water Resources Planning and Management, Volume 115, No. 1, January 1989, pages 31-42.

Delli Priscoli, Jerome. "To Be Environmental Engineers for the Nation," Strategic Working Paper #89-3, Office of Strategic Initiatives, U.S. Corps of Engineers, Office of the Chief of Engineers, Washington, D.C., April 24, 1989.

Edelman, Lester. "ADR in Government: An Agency's Experience," address at the ABA Annual Meeting, Administrative Law and Public Contract Law Sections, Honolulu, 1989.

Edelman, Lester, Frank Carr, James L. Creighton. The Mini-Trial, Pamphlet One, Alternative Dispute Resolution Series, U.S. Corps of Engineers Institute for Water Resources, Fort Belvoir, VA, 1989.

Edelman, Lester. "Statement before the Committee on the Judiciary Subcommittee on the Courts and Administrative Practice," United State Senate, May 25, 1988.

Endispute, Inc. Using ADR and the U.S. Army Corps of Engineers, a Framework for Decisionmaking, Alternative Dispute Resolution Series, IWR Research Report 89-8-ADR-R-1, August 1989.

Fisher, Roger and William Ury, 1981. Getting to Yes: Negotiating Agreement Without Giving In, Huton Mithlin Co., Boston, MA.

Lifton, Robert J., 1987. The Future of Immortality and Other Essays for the Nuclear Age, Basic Books, Inc., N.Y., NY.

Milbraith, L. (1984). Environmentalists: Vanguard for a New Society. SUNY Press, New York.

Stakhiv, Eugene V. 1987. "Environmental Analysis in Water Resources Planning" in Water for the Future: Proceedings of the International Symposium on Water for the Future. A.A. Balkema: Rotterdam, Boston, 1987.

Innovative Compensation Arrangements for Resolving Water Transfer Conflicts

William E. Cox[1] and Leonard A Shabman[2]

Abstract

Transfer of resources on the basis of compensation arrangements among the affected parties is a common transaction in market economies, but water is not a typical resource. Water use and development are subject to significant influence from political decision making. Removal of water allocation decisions from political processes is not a reasonable goal, but greater reliance on negotiation of compensation agreements as a conflict resolution mechanism has potential to mitigate some of the deficiencies of political decision making. Such agreements continue to be approved in certain cases, usually as a result of special institutional arrangements that remove traditional obstacles. These agreements generally provide for innovative compensation arrangements that increase payments to the area of origin for a proposed transfer in exchange for removal of opposition to the transfer. Greater reliance on mechanisms that encourage negotiation prior to final regulatory or judicial decision has significant potential to improve management of water transfer.

Introduction

Transfer of water from areas of abundance to areas of scarcity has been a common aspect of water management during much of history, but major transfers have become increasingly difficult to implement. Transfer proposals

---

[1]Professor, Department of Civil Engineering, Virginia Tech, Blacksburg, VA 24061

[2]Professor, Department of Agricultural Economics, Virginia Tech, Blacksburg, VA 24061.

generate substantial opposition within the intended area of origin and from environmental interests. This opposition is expressed through administrative and judicial proceedings, often resulting in protracted conflict.

Water-transfer conflict in the United States occurs within the framework of a market economy where transfer of resource ownership generally occurs on the basis of compensation from the recipient to the previous owner. For many resources, such transactions occur continuously and facilitate the coordination of supply with demand. Compensation agreements usually answer all significant questions of ownership and legal rights of use.

But water has not been considered a typical resource to be managed through compensation agreements. While negotiated compensation agreements play a role in water use and development, they occur less frequently than in the case of many resources. Due to water's characteristics (and perhaps to philosophical views regarding water), water use and development are subject to significant governmental direction. These influences are manifested through a variety of means such as limitations inherent in the definition of water rights, governmental regulation of water use, and direct governmental participation in water use and development.

The extent of governmental involvement in water-use decision making is generally explained by the fact that water possesses values normally not captured by market prices. Such values tend to receive inadequate attention in market processes because they are not priced and exchanged by conventional means. In these cases, political decision making offers the theoretical advantage of being able to consider these values along with those that are recognized in markets.

But in spite of these theoretical advantages, political processes exhibit major deficiencies as resource allocation mechanisms. Decision makers in the public sector lack the insights and incentives that drive individual decisions concerning resource use, and they tend to become subject to behavioral influences adverse to general concepts of best resource use. A major weakness is the difficulty of assessing the legitimacy of claims and hypothetical demands on the resource by the various participants. Since claims associated with particular values need not be supported by willingness to pay for the use in question, claims are likely to be exaggerated. Incentives to engage in political action are not tempered by the requirement that any gains achieved be accompanied by payment for the benefit received. Because of the potential for a winner-take-all decision, a spirit of compromise may be missing. As a result of these characteristics, political decision processes tend to be protracted and may produce outcomes not in the best interests of the immediately or indirectly affected parties.

While complete removal of water allocation decisions from political processes is not a reasonable aim, greater use of negotiation relying on market-like processes has potential to overcome some of the deficiencies associated with political decisions. A primary advantage of placing greater emphasis on negotiation is the potential for fashioning compensation arrangements among the affected parties that reflect acceptable compromises seen as mutually advantageous by the parties. Negotiated agreements tend to be more socially acceptable and produce less residual animosity than do adversarial legal proceedings.

In fact, the advantages of negotiated solutions are so substantial that compensation agreements have continued to be developed as a basis for solution of transfer - related conflict in selected cases in spite of formidable obstacles. These compensation arrangements generally have not developed independently of political decision processes but instead have occurred as the result of special institutional mechanisms that provide forums for negotiation or remove impediments to development of compensation arrangements.

This paper examines cases where innovative compensation arrangements have been developed and explores the potential for greater reliance on negotiated agreements as a means to manage transfer-related conflict. It begins by investigating the reasons why negotiation of compensation agreements is difficult within the framework of typical water management institutions. Attention then turns to three case studies involving innovative compensation. The paper concludes by advocating development of institutions to facilitate and encourage negotiation prior to final governmental decision making.

Water Transfer Negotiations under
Conventional Water Management Institutions

Conventional water management institutions restrict the potential for negotiated settlements to water-transfer conflict because they fail to satisfy the basic conditions essential to negotiation. Three of these deficiencies of special significance are inadequacies in property rights definition, high decision making costs, and information deficiencies.

Property Rights Uncertainty

A basic requirement for successful negotiation is a clear definition of property rights in the resource in question. Without clear definition, the party desiring to acquire the resource will not have incentive to enter negotiations with the apparent holder of rights in the resource. First, the party desiring acquisition is not likely to negotiate if an ambiguous definition leaves open the possibility that this party may already hold a valid claim, making the consent of the alleged holder unnecessary. Second, negotiations are not likely where property-rights uncertainties create potential for claims in the resource to be successfully asserted by third parties. In this case, a negotiated exchange with the alleged holder of property rights will not create secure rights for the purchaser.

These definitional uncertainties that obstruct negotiation are inherent in the nature of water rights. Water rights traditionally have been viewed as "limited" or "qualified" property interests subject to constraints not affecting ownership of land and land-based resources. These limitations take forms such as restrictions on place of water use, time limitations on the duration of the right, forfeiture provisions in the event of non-use, and publicly imposed curtailment in times of unusual shortage. These potential limitations can be evaluated by consideration of individual theories of water rights applied by state governments.

The prior appropriation theory of water rights is generally considered to offer the greatest certainty. Where water within the area-of-origin of a proposed transfer is fully appropriated, the system of established rights provides a relatively concrete framework for negotiation. Transfer of ownership of appropriative rights is a commonly practiced activity.

However, transfer is subject to state approval and is conditioned on lack of unacceptable impacts on third parties and the general public interest. The large number of such parties and the scope of the issues may make conventional negotiation processes inoperable in the case of a major transfer proposal.

Compensation agreements are less feasible where transfer of unappropriated water is proposed. Unappropriated water is the property of the state and not the locality or the individual residents within the area of origin. Transfers of unappropriated water will generally be opposed by these parties through political means since a basis for a market transaction is missing.

Uncertainty is even more prevalent within the riparian doctrine. The mechanism of enforcement of property claims under this doctrine is the private lawsuit brought by an injured riparian landowner. Where surplus water exists, injured riparians to serve as plaintiffs will be absent. Riparian landowners and other interests within the area-of-origin generally oppose transfer, but the absence of well-defined property interests undermines the potential for negotiation with those wishing to transfer water.

Negotiated compensation arrangements involving riparian rights are also difficult where water is not surplus but is being used. Riparian rights are not quantified. They fluctuate with natural conditions because available flow, including drought flows, must be shared among all those with rights. In addition, established water uses must accommodate new uses based on the exercise of previously dormant water rights. The purchaser of a riparian right therefore cannot be certain of the continuing scope of the right acquired. Thus, a substantial disincentive to water-rights transactions exists.

A basic feature of both the appropriative and riparian doctrines is that property rights in surplus water, which is the most likely candidate for transfer, are generally not held by specific parties. The concept that such water is the property of the state is a key factor in disposition of transfer proposals. The public status assigned to surplus water is viewed as essential to the protection of the broad public interests in water that extend beyond those aspects encompassed by private property rights. But as well-intentioned as the public-ownership concept may be, it serves as a major hindrance to efforts to negotiate a solution to conflict associated with transfer proposals.

Just as property interests in surplus water are not held by individuals, they also generally are not held by local governments where the water occurs. Local governments can acquire water rights for specific water uses, but they typically are not directly involved in the administration of state water-rights systems. Local governments, therefore, are not in a strong position to bargain with respect to water transfer.

Yet local government is the focal point of significant values associated with the water resource. A state's political subdivisions are a major organizational entity both in the advocacy for water transfer and in transfer opposition. Local governmental interest in the water resource is generally perceived to be substantially greater than the sum of the individual interests of its citizens. Although studies have questioned the significance of the relationship between abundant water supplies and economic growth (see, e.g., Howe, 1968), the relationship is often perceived locally as a major reason to develop abundant supplies or, in the case of potential areas of origin, to protect existing abundant supplies from transfer to other localities. Related to this desire of areas of origin to preserve perceived growth benefits associated with water is the attempt to protect the local tax base. Projects proposed by outside governmental units have potential to remove substantial amounts of land from taxation.

Local governments within proposed areas of origin have a limited range of responses because of their lack of defined property interest in the water resource. With a negotiated settlement substantially hindered by this lack, opposing the transfer through political means becomes the logical strategy. Areas of origin can suffer considerable loss where transfers occur under conventional water allocation procedures. Traditional compensation rules, since they may limit damages to legally provable injury, may significantly understate total long-range costs. No compensation is likely to be awarded for indirect economic impacts and for damages that, although they eventually occur, are speculative at the time of the legal proceedings. Political opposition

to transfer may be the only rational response to a
proposed transfer under these conditions.

High Decision-Making Costs

    Related to the property-rights uncertainty issue is
the   tendency   for   traditional   water   management
institutions to impose substantial decision costs on
parties attempting to negotiate solutions to water-use
conflicts. High negotiation costs can consume water-
transfer benefits that otherwise would be available for
compensation to opponents of transfer.

    High decision costs arise under conventional water
management institutions because of the large number of
parties   involved   and   fragmentation   in   decision
processes. Involvement of large numbers of parties is a
consequence   of   the   existence   of   many   water-rights
holders on most bodies of water. Consolidation of these
multiple interests in judicial proceedings through class
actions   may   have   potential,   but   potential   for
consolidation outside judicial processes is limited.

    The costs of negotiation are also increased by the
concurrent operation of several decision processes in
the case of an individual water transfer proposal. In
addition to resolving the water-rights issue, the water
developer must comply with a variety of regulatory
requirements. At the federal level, for example, a
permit from the U.S. Army Corps of Engineers is required
for related construction below high water mark or within
wetlands (under 33 U.S.C.A. sec. 1344).   State
government   also   typically   imposes   restrictions   on
related construction. Local authority may involve
direct control over water facilities in some cases and
generally will include land use controls that apply to
facilities development.

    If these various constraints were administered
through a single proceedings, the decision process would
provide a forum for consideration of a broad range of
issues   and   establish   a   basis   for   negotiation   of
compensation   arrangements   to   address   objectionable
impacts   of   the   proposed   project.   Since   these
constraints generally are administered independently,
however, no such forum is provided, and negotiated
resolution of conflict is obstructed.

Information Deficiencies

A third obstacle to negotiated agreements under traditional water management institutions is lack of adequate information. Successful negotiation with respect to water transfer depends upon agreement among the parties concerning the impact of the transfer so that adequate compensation can be determined. Necessary information includes realistic projections of future water supply demands within the area of origin and likely environmental consequences of a transfer. Institutional mechanisms such as environmental impact assessments assist in developing necessary information, but information deficiencies continue to be common. In the absence of a definitive information base, proponents of transfer tend to underestimate potential impacts while opponents develop exaggerated damage claims. This often major disagreement on basic characteristics of a proposal creates a disincentive to negotiation.

Case Studies of Water-Transfer
Compensation

Although the obstacles to development of compensation agreements as a basis for water transfer are substantial, innovative arrangements have been developed in certain cases. Consideration will be given here to compensation arrangements developed in three transfer cases: New York City's diversion from the Delaware River Basin, Transmountain diversions in Colorado, and Virginia Beach's proposed diversion from the Roanoke River Basin.

New York City's Delaware Diversion

New York City's efforts to provide its population with water have resulted in major transfers from the Delaware River Basin to its northwest. This transfer has involved a variety of complex institutional arrangements. Resolution of related interstate conflict has involved an equitable apportionment decision by the U.S. Supreme Court (New York v. New Jersey, 256 U.S. 296 (1921)) and the creation of an interstate river basin commission. While this case presents some interesting interstate trade-offs (e.g., increased water treatment within New York State in exchange for the transfer's diminution in available dilution water), the compensation arrangements developed to resolve

intrastate conflict within New York are of greatest
relevance here.

The special compensation in this case is a result
of special state legislative provisions that authorize
transfer in exchange for several types of payments to
the area of origin in addition to the conventional forms
of compensation for direct takings of lands and water
rights. One form of compensation is that the City must
continue to pay property tax on its reservoir and other
lands as would a private landowner. This requirement
generates substantial revenue for the jurisdictions that
host the City's projects and prevent a major impact that
such projects can impose. Another benefit is that local
governments within the area of origin are authorized to
tap the City's system for their own water supply. The
City may charge reasonable rates for this water that
cannot exceed the rates applicable within the City.

Special compensation arrangements also apply to
individuals within the affected area. In addition to
compensation for property rights directly taken for
project purposes, provision is made for payments that
cover "unforeseeable damages" to individuals not
physically affected by the City's projects. Claims
under this provision typically involve indirect economic
losses. For example, the claim of a feed store owner
that business had declined because of the displacement
of some of his customers was resolved by an award equal
to two years of lost business. Claims of unforeseeable
damages must be filed within three years of project
completion and are adjudicated by three commissioners of
appraisal. One of these court-appointed commissioners
is from the City, one from the affected area, and one
from an uninvolved region (information for this case
study is from Covington, 1986).

Transmountain Diversions in Colorado

The water allocation law of Colorado (the
appropriation doctrine) generally allows the transfer of
water without compensation to the area of origin, but
special compensation requirements have been applied to
certain transfers. This special provision applies to
certain diversions of water from the Colorado River
Basin to the East Slope of the Rocky Mountains where the
majority of the state's population lives.

The compensation requirement arises from a state legislative provision that diversions of water by conservancy districts from the Colorado Basin cannot impair nor increase the costs of present and prospective water-rights holders within the Basin. This provision was initially interpreted as requiring the water exporter to build reservoirs in the Colorado Basin to provide compensatory storage to replace the exported water. Monetary settlements with potentially affected parties have also been used to satisfy the requirement. One such settlement involved a payment in excess of $10 million to the Colorado River Water Conservation District for planning and constructing water storage projects that may be necessary in the future (information for this case study is from MacDonnell et al., 1985).

Virginia Beach Proposed Transfer

The resort city of Virginia Beach, Virginia has been involved in a long-term effort to expand its water supply in response to substantial growth. The City's efforts to end its dependency on neighboring jurisdictions for water supply involve transfer of water from the Roanoke River, an inland river to the west of the City. The proposed project involves construction of an intake on an existing hydroelectric impoundment and a pipeline to connect to the existing water supply system. The proposed transfer has been opposed by the State of North Carolina since the Roanoke River flows into that state from Virginia, and related legal proceedings continue. This case study focuses on recently completed agreements between Virginia Beach and the Virginia locality within whose jurisdiction the proposed water supply intake would be located.

The bargaining position of the host jurisdiction is enhanced by a Virginia legislative provision that such projects require the consent of the host jurisdiction. If consent is denied, however, an appeal to a specially created court is authorized (for discussion of this process, see Cox and Shabman, 1983).

The agreement provides several types of compensation to the host jurisdiction in the form of a lump-sum cash payment. The largest component of this approximately $3 million payment is intended to settle the issue of potential development losses to the County associated with construction and operation of the intake. A second component of the payment is compensation for loss of tax revenues resulting from removal of the intake site from county tax rolls. A third component is compensation for impacts associated with pipeline construction.

The agreement also addresses other issues beyond compensation for potential impacts. Virginia Beach agrees to reimburse costs associated with monitoring and inspection of project construction. In addition, the agreement contains various assurances that Virginia Beach will not use its powers to interfere with use of the reservoir or surrounding lands. For example, the City agrees not to seek special legislation, regulations, or stricter discharge standards than would apply to other similar waters within Virginia. With respect to possible future requests for increased withdrawal of water, Virginia Beach agrees to resubmit to the local consent provision and to pay $1.675 million the County. Finally, the host jurisdiction agrees not to unreasonably obstruct the project by denial of local permits or to contribute funds to organizations opposing the project through litigation or other means (information for this case study is from "Contract between Brunswick County, Virginia and the City of Virginia Beach, Virginia, Aug. 16, 1989).

General Observations Regarding the Case Studies

Although these case studies involve relatively unique situations, they share certain common features. One of the most obvious characteristics shared by these examples is that the agreements in question were not the result of voluntarily initiated negotiation.

In the New York City case, the "agreement" was actually negotiated within the New York State Legislature and presented as a legislative solution. This approach is a compromise solution that prevents local obstruction of water transfer but in exchange ensures compensation to the area of origin greater than that likely under traditional riparian water law.

The Colorado example does not involve a specific state-mandated approach to the transfer issue, but state action does provide a necessary foundation for negotiations. A variety of approaches to implement the no-impairment requirement of state law would have been possible, but the availability of federal funds through the Reclamation Program facilitated adoption of the compensation storage concept. This approach may be less feasible where local parties must pay all costs of transfer. It is interesting to note that diversions out of the Colorado Basin by municipalities, which would likely be responsible for all associated costs, are not subject to the requirements of the no-impairment legislation applicable to conservancy districts.

The agreement concerning the proposed Virginia Beach transfer was also facilitated by a special institutional mechanism not generally available under traditional water management institutions. This mechanism is a local consent requirement concerning interjurisdictional water supply development that is subject to review by a special court. The agreement in question was signed shortly before this court was to make a decision in its review proceedings. State law establishing this mechanism therefore created a forum to bring the parties together and, while not expressly addressing negotiation, provided incentive for the parties to negotiate a mutually acceptable solution in lieu of a legally binding court decision.

Although agreements to resolve transfer-related conflict were achieved in each of the three cases considered, none of the institutional arrangements involved appears ideal for managing the transfer issue. In the New York example, the case-specific solution, while offering a possible model for broader application, offers little flexibility to the parties involved in a transfer proposal. The Colorado case involves a solution closely tied to federal funding programs and therefore has limited transferability. The agreement reached in the Virginia case resolves conflict between two localities but is narrow in scope. A variety of water rights and other issues remain to be resolved through other procedures.

Conclusions

This analysis suggests several factors important to an increased role for compensation agreements in resolving transfer-related conflict. In general, such an institution must mitigate the impacts of traditional obstacles to transfer such as property rights uncertainty, high negotiation costs, and information deficiencies.

A first step in overcoming these obstacles is creation of a forum to bring parties with interests in a proposed transfer together, particularly local governments that are affected. Traditional water management institutions fail to recognize adequately the interests existing at this level and provide limited forums within which negotiation may take place. Negotiation may be initiated after the parties have entered into a judicial proceedings (out-of-court settlements are not uncommon after a lawsuit is filed), but the act of filing a lawsuit in a court of general jurisdiction is a major decision: substantial resources must be committed and outcomes are unpredictable. Protracted conflict may, therefore, occur prior to initiation of judicial proceedings.

Simple mechanisms that provide the opportunity for negotiation can significantly improve the traditional situation. For example, the Virginia approach involving local consent subject to a special appeals procedure is a more workable process for resolving transfer conflict than previously existed in the state.

But a forum limited to a narrow set of issues has less potential than one of broader scope. For instance, expansion of the existing Virginia procedure to include water-rights adjudication would bring a wider range of affected parties together and increase the potential for negotiation to resolve conflicts. Property rights uncertainty is a major obstacle to negotiation under traditional institutions; the availability of a process for defining affected rights together with resolution of local governmental issues would represent a significant advancement since fragmentation of decision making and the associated costs would be reduced.

Another useful expansion of the mechanism existing currently in Virginia would be addition of a fact-finding capability. Information deficiencies are often central to water development conflicts, indicating the potential contribution of a mechanism that addressed basic information needs. This mission could be implemented through existing public agencies or by other contractual means. Since necessary investigations would be conducted by a neutral party, results would be more readily accepted by the interested parties.

Establishment of a forum of proper scope increases the potential for water-transfer compensation agreements, but further incentive may be necessary to ensure timely action that avoids protracted conflict. One such incentive is the vesting of authority in a decision-making body to impose its own conflict-resolving decision whenever negotiations arrive at an impasse. The proposal of this approach may appear contradictory to the general philosophy of this paper that negotiated solutions should be encouraged; however, provision of a clearly defined opportunity for negotiation prior to regulatory action places the regulatory approach in a back-up position while encouraging good faith negotiation.

As stated at the outset, the basic theme of the paper is that decisions concerning water use and development can be improved by greater reliance on negotiation between affected parties within the framework of general public sector control -- not that public sector control should be replaced by market processes. The proposed approach differs from traditional water management institutions primarily by providing opportunity and encouraging negotiation prior to regulatory decisions. Negotiation opportunities would be institutionalized and therefore would occur on a systematic basis rather than being left to chance ad hoc arrangements. Subject to review for consistency with third party interests and the general public interest, negotiated solutions should be endorsed by relevant decision-making bodies and incorporated into final decisions.

The institutional mechanism envisioned here (for a more detailed discussion, see Cox and Shabman, 1984) would require careful design to ensure proper functioning, but it need not take any particular form. In the case of a riparian-doctrine state such as Virginia, the proposed institution could operate in a manner similar to the existing procedure requiring local consent subject to judicial review. Necessary decision rules could be formulated as guidelines for the special court that conducts reviews of local consent decisions. In the case of a state with an administrative water-use permitting program, the proposed procedure could be administered as part of or coordinated with the permitting process whenever water transfer is proposed.

Development of necessary institutions will be more difficult where transfers are interstate in nature or have interstate impacts. Institutions developed in an

individual state have some potential to address
interstate impacts through such means as allowing out-
of-state parties to participate in negotiations, but
creation of an interstate management entity may be
necessary. Interstate agreements are complex and
difficult to establish.

Institutional change is a slow process subject to
many obstacles and much uncertainty. But the potential
gains from better management of water transfer provide
the needed incentive. Even with greater efforts to
control water demand, water transfer proposals will
continue to arise because of nonuniformities in
distributions of water and population. Traditional
institutions contribute to protracted conflict and high
decision costs and are likely to result in excessive
water supply expenditures by unnecessarily blocking cost
effective options. The potential to avoid these losses
indicates the importance of working toward institutional
change.

Acknowledgement

The research on which this paper is based was
supported in part by the U. S. Geological Survey,
Department of the Interior under grant number 14-08-
0001-G1481. However, the contents do not necessarily
represent the policy of that agency, and the reader
should not assume endorsement by the Federal Government.

Appendix - References

Covington, M.B., III. (1986). "A Proposal for an
Improved Institutional Mechanism to Facilitate
Interjurisdictional Water Transfers in Virginia."
Masters thesis submitted to the faculty of Virginia
Polytechnic Institute and State University in partial
fulfillment of the requirements for the Master of
Science degree in Civil Engineering.

Cox, W.E. and Shabman, L.A. (1984). "Virginia's Water
Law: Resolving the Interjurisdictional Transfer Issue."
Virginia Journal of Natural Resources Law, 3(2), 181-
234.

Cox, W.E. and Shabman, L.A. (1983). "Institutional Issues Affecting Water Supply Development: Illustrations from Southeastern Virginia" (WRRC Bulletin 138). Virginia Water Resources Research Center, Blacksburg, VA.

Howe, C.W. (1968). "Water Resources and Regional Economic Growth in the United States." The Southern Economic Journal, 34, 447-489.

MacDonnell, L.J., Howe, C.W., Corbridge, J.N., Jr., and Ahrens, W.A. (1985). "Guidelines for Developing Area-of-Origin Compensation" (Research Report 22-36). University of Colorado Natural Resources Law Center, Boulder, CO.

INSTITUTIONAL ASPECTS OF WATER DISPUTE RESOLUTION

William B. Lord[1]

Abstract

Institutions can be described as socially determined rules which shape human action. Such rules arise as attempts to resolve perceived problems. New or altered rules may hold the key to resolving water related disputes, but the kinds of rule changes invoked must be chosen carefully in consideration of the kinds of conflict involved and the ways in which rules alter the behavior of actors and lead to new outcomes.

Institutions Defined

One of the greatest impediments to effective analysis and communication is failure to assign a common meaning to the words that we use. The word "institution" has been given many meanings. Common language frequently equates "institution" with "organization," as when we speak of the University of Arizona as an educational institution. Social scientists most often use the term to refer to the glue which holds society and its parts together; which gives cohesiveness and continuity to social action. For example, the institutional economist John R. Commons defined institutions as "collective action in control, liberation, and expansion of individual action" (Commons).

Commons' definition points but does not define. I prefer Elinor Ostrom's definition of an institution as a set of rules which shapes human action (Ostrom). Such rules may be formalized and codified, as in the case of constitutions, statutes, and administrative regulations.

---

[1]Director, Water Resources Research Center, The University of Arizona, Geology Bldg., Rm. 318, Tucson, AZ 85721.

Institutions as Problem Solvers

They may be implicit and widely understood, but not set down in writing, as is true of the social mores and conventions which govern scientific discourse. The rules which hold a society together (indeed, which give meaning to the concept of a society) were originally the product of non-self conscious social evolution. Most rules still are. But the need to formalize and codify led to the explicit examination of rules, and eventually to their self-conscious and purposive creation. My colleague, Helen Ingram, calls this explicit and self-conscious process of creating rules "policy design," particularly if the process itself follows the rules of rational decision making.

If institutions are defined as rules, then one may ask to what kinds of games these rules apply. I find it useful to think of institutions as rules which society has adopted to facilitate the solution of the human problems which arise from interpersonal interdependence and interaction. Without a problem, or perhaps more accurately, following John Dewey (Dewey), a "problematic situation," there would be no need, and thus no stimulus, to undertake the often painful process of establishing new rules.

On this view, government is a collection of rules created to solve the problems of a community of persons necessarily interrelated through propinquity, technology, economies of scale, and dependence upon common resources, with emphasis upon lodging of rule making and rule enforcement authorities in organizations explicitly created to receive and exercise them. It leads to consideration of the effective linking of rules with the problems which they are to address.

Environmental Problems

There are many sorts of problems which political institutions have been created to solve. One broad class of such problems is that which we term "environmental." As in the case of "institution," it is well to ask what we mean by this term before we employ it as a fundamental tool for discourse. On the most general level, it is clear that "environmental" refers to the interaction between human beings and the physical environment which sustains them. Beyond that, I submit, is the notion that environmental problems are not simply problems which arise as humans interact with nature, but also involve in an essential way their interaction with each other. Ciriacy-Wantrup (Ciriacy-Wantrup) has defined a natural resource as an appraisal, by a planning agent, of his (or her) environment for the purpose of satisfying human wants. It is when these appraisals overlap or conflict that environmental problems arise.

Is it useful to go further and distinguish different kinds of environmental problems? I think that it is. I shall distinguish first of all asymmetric problems from symmetric ones. Asymmetric problems are those which are unidirectional. My action creates a problem for you but you do not cause one for me. Symmetric problems are those in which causation is multidirectional and all actors who are causal agents also suffer the resultant impacts. Symmetric problems are, in principle, easier to resolve because all of the actors share a common interest in doing so. One can go further and observe that one of the most effective approaches to resolving an asymmetric problem is to convert it into a symmetric one by linking it with another assymetric problem in which the direction of influence is reversed.

Economists have divided asymmetric problems into spatial externalities and temporal externalities (they have also distinguished other types of externalities, their word for asymmetric problems, but these are unnecessary for our purposes). A spatial externality arises when the creator of the externality is spatially separated from the bearer. A temporal externality is one in which that separation is through time. The classic case of the fisherman whose fishing is ruined by the discharges from an upstream paper mill is an example of a spatial externality. The equally classic case of the fisherman whose fishing is ruined instead by the overfishing of his predecessors is an example of a temporal externality.

Symmetric problems often originate in what economists call open access situations. These can be further divided into common pool problems, in which each actor's use of the resource diminishes its availability to all, and public goods problems, in which that subtraction principle does not apply. Ocean fisheries constitute a classic example of the common pool problem, while scenic vistas constitute an example of the public good problem. The common pool problem involves reciprocal externalities, hence its symmetry. The public goods problem involves a less direct interpersonal problem, arising from the fact that, since no user can be excluded from using the resource, no price can be charged for its use, and thus it is likely to be undersupplied.

Environmental Conflict

Environmental problems themselves, and certainly attempts to resolve them, often lead to conflict. In an earlier paper (Lord) I have distinguished three kinds of environmental conflicts. I called them social value conflict, interest conflict, and cognitive conflict. Social value conflict occurs when actors hold and pursue differing, or differently weighted, social values. By social values I mean those shared notions of what is right or wrong, or good or bad, which are instilled in individuals through the complex processes which we call socialization. Such social values are often rationalized through reference to the common good of the collective. Examples of social values include those environmental values often referred to by such names as preservationist values or existence values. They also include those ethically, empathetically, and/or religiously based values which are referred to by such names as equity and fairness.

Interest conflict arises when the direct or utilitarian interests of actors clash. The actions of one actor reduce, or threaten to reduce, the flow of of goods and services enjoyed by another. Examples include the externalities cited earlier. Interest conflict involves the direct flows of valued goods and services to the contending parties, whereas social value conflict is concerned with shared values. Both, however, relate to the process of valuing.

Cognitive conflict arises through differences in factual understanding. A disagreement over whether pollution found in a groundwater basin originated at a particular source is an example of cognitive conflict. So is a disagreement over the probability of failure of an existing or proposed dam.

As I pointed out in my earlier paper, the distinction between these three types of conflict is important because the kinds of actions which are likely to be effective in resolving them are so different. Cognitive conflict is addressed through collecting, analyzing, and effectively presenting factual information. It may involve the resort to specialists or experts, such as scientists and engineers. Such methods are likely to be ineffective in resolving social value or interest conflicts. Social value conflicts are resolved through invoking shared values, through persuasion, and often ultimately through voting when consensus cannot be achieved. These methods are unlikely to resolve cognitive or interest conflicts. Interest conflicts are best resolved through redistributing the incidence of benefits and costs through bargaining, whether in the market or in the legislature. Bargaining is not an appropriate way of resolving cognitive conflicts or social value conflicts.

The methods of conflict resolution just mentioned can be viewed as rules for changing the rules governing how resources shall be allocated and managed. In cases of environmental conflict, the rules to be changed are the rules which govern access to, and use of, natural resources. With this in mind, it is now time to return to the concept of rules as institutions.

Types of Rules

Following Ostrom, we may distinguish seven different types of rules:

1) Position rules are those which establish the positions or roles which actors may assume in an action situation. Examples of positions are owner, lessee, judge, plaintiff, and state engineer.

2) Boundary rules are those which prescribe how actors may or must enter or leave positions. Examples are diversion and beneficial use, execution of a lease, election, filing suit, and appointment, as well as forfeiture or abandonment, failure to pay rent, loss of an election, out of court settlement or court verdict, and retirement, resignation, or dismissal.

3) Scope rules are those which describe and delimit the possible outcomes of an action situation. Examples include administrative or judicial determination of water rights, a range of ambient water quality conditions in a surface or groundwater body, available water supplies in a basin, and population levels of a rare or endangered species.

4) Authority rules are those which stipulate the actions which are required of, prohibited of, or permitted of the occupant of a position. Examples include provision of surface water rights to offset groundwater pumping, compliance with emission standards, and right to divert water up to the limits of a water right so long as senior appropriators are not shorted.

5) Aggregation rules are those which describe how the actions of occupants of positions, as specified in authority rules, determine outcomes, as described and delimited in scope rules. Examples are application of the seniority principle in the doctrine of prior appropriation, use of design standards in achieving ambient or performance standards for environmental quality protection, market mechanisms for transferring water to higher uses, and voting rules for determining water allocations within an irrigation district.

6) Information rules are those which specify what kinds of information may, may not, or must be generated by, and transferred between, occupants of positions. Examples are rules permitting public testimony on proposed water development projects, prohibitions on revealing extraneous and prejudicial information to juries, and NEPA requirements for presenting alternatives to the recommended plan.

7) Payoff rules are those which prescribe how the benefits and costs resulting from the outcome of an action situation shall be distributed among the occupants of positions. Examples include cost sharing requirements, pricing and other marketing rules for public power projects, and Superfund rules for sharing of cleanup

costs.

In this paper I have attempted to present a vocabulary or a set of taxonomies which should facilitate the analysis of the institutional aspects of environmental conflict resolution. The analysis which must follow should be devoted to matching environmental problems with rule sets. We must ask what specific types of rules are likely to work in settling conflicts and thus resolving particular kinds of environmental problems.

References

Ciriacy-Wantrup, S.V., Resource Conservation: Economics and Policies, University of California Press, Berkeley and Los Angeles, CA, 1952, 381 p.

Commons, J.R. 1950. Economics of Collective Action, Mcmillian, New York, NY, 1950.

Dewey, J., Logic The Theory of Inquiry, H. Holt & Co., New York, NY, 1938.

Lord, W.B., "Conflict in Federal Water Resource Planning." Water Resources Bulletin, American Water Resources Association, Minneapolis, MN, 1979, Vol. 15, pp. 1226-1235.

Ostrom, E., "An Agenda for the Study of Institutions," Public Choice, Martinus Nijhoff Publishers, Dordrecht, Netherlands, 1986, Vol. 48, pp. 3-25.

NEGOTIATING WATER SUPPLY MANAGEMENT AGREEMENTS
FOR THE NATIONAL CAPITAL REGION

Robert S. McGarry[1]

Abstract

        Efforts by the Federal government, through the
U.S. Army Corps of Engineers, to insure adequate water
supply for the National Capital Region lasted more than
20 years with no resolution or agreement. Local
engineer managers took charge, formed political task
forces, introduced risk management/drought management
concepts and innovative regional operating techniques
to resolve the stalemate.

Introduction

        In July 1982 in the District Building in
Washington, D.C., representatives of Fairfax County
Water Authority, the Washington Suburban Sanitary
Commission, the States of Virginia and Maryland, the
District of Columbia, the Corps of Engineers, and the
Potomac Water Authority signed eight separate contracts
that resolved more than twenty years of conflict over
water supply for the metropolitan region of Washington,
D.C. Water supply for the region was assured through
the year 2010, cost sharing for the needed regional
reservoirs was established, and the responsibilities
for financing future facilities beyond 2010 were also
agreed to.

        This paper describes how the conflicts that had
prevented this resolution for so long were resolved.

        This is also a personal paper because I was in a
leadership role throughout the process that eventually
resulted in a resolution. In 1973 I was chosen to be
the District Engineer, Baltimore District, U.S. Army
Corps of Engineers (the Corps). The District's

----
[1]Director, Department of Transportation, Montgomery
County, 101 Monroe Street, Rockville, MD 20850.

116

responsibility includes all Corps activities in the Potomac River Basin. The District also operates the Washington Aqueduct Division (WAD), the water treatment facility for the District of Columbia. In addition to being the regulator, the channel maintainer, and the flood control agency for the Potomac River Basin, the Corps, through the District, has a unique responsibility of providing wholesale treated water for distribution by the District of Columbia.

In 1976 I was promoted to Brigadier General and transferred to another assignment. In 1977, I retired to become the General Manager of the Washington Suburban Sanitary Commission (WSSC), the regional water supply (and sewage treatment) agency for Prince George's and Montgomery County, Maryland. These two Maryland counties, Fairfax County, Virginia, and the District of Columbia, form the Washington metropolitan region.

As District Engineer, my responsibilities included both adequate water supply for the District of Columbia and the Corps' interest in resolving the long-term regional supply. As General Manager of WSSC, I was, of course, most concerned about the water supply for the two Maryland counties, but I knew, from my previous work, that the Corps' efforts very much affected WSSC.

The water supply problem to be solved in the Washington metropolitan region is fairly simple. The three water supply agencies: WSSC for Prince George's and Montgomery County, Maryland; the Washington Aqueduct Division (WAD) for the District of Columbia; and the Fairfax County Water Supply for Fairfax County, Virginia all depend on the Potomac River for their water supply. There have been droughts when the average daily flow in the Potomac was as much as 30 million gallons per day (MGP) below the peak daily demand of the 1980's. A repeat of these droughts would cause serious water shortages for the three jurisdictions. Because Fairfax and the two Maryland counties were growing rapidly, this problem became more serious with each year.

The Corps of Engineers Potomac River Basin Studies

In the mid-1950's, the potential water shortage for the Washington region was also of to Congress and the Corps of Engineers. Because of this concern, Congress authorized the Corps to prepare comprehensive studies of the Potomac River Basin. At this time, local elected officials and managers of the three utilities assumed that these comprehensive studies would develop a solution that would eventually be implemented through federal programs. A summary of the Congressional/Corps activity follows:

1963 - The Baltimore District Engineer completes the comprehensive study and recommends 16 reservoirs be constructed in the Potomac Basin for flood control and water supply. Storage needed to augment low flows for the District, as well as many other jurisdictions in the Potomac Basin would be provided by these reservoirs.

1969 - After a review, the Chief of Engineers finds six of the 16 reservoirs are urgently needed and should be constructed by the Corps as soon as possible.

1970 - The Secretary of the Army concurs, but finds that two of the six reservoirs are most urgent: Sixes Bridge near Frederick, Maryland and Verona near Staunton, Virginia.

1974 - Congress partially accepts the Secretary's findings and authorizes Sixes Bridge and Verona for design. However, because of objections to the reservoirs, Congress also directed construction of a pilot water treatment plant to determine if the water in the Potomac estuary could be treated and used as an alternative source of supply. Congress went further and directed another Metropolitan Washington Water Supply Study--a study to end all studies.

After twelve years of studies and review, two reservoirs were finally authorized for design, but the fact that Congress also directed the estuary study for water supply and yet another study of the water needs indicated that confidence in the eventual building of the two reservoirs was low.

While these studies were underway, a large Potomac reservoir at Bloomington, Maryland for water supply and flood control was authorized in 1962. Bloomington was one of the 16 identified in the study, and the authorization was accelerated, not because of water supply urgency, but as part of the Appalachian Redevelopment Program to create jobs. There was no opposition to Bloomington and construction started in 1975. However, the studies concluded that Verona and Sixes Bridge were urgently needed in addition.

By 1976 it was becoming very doubtful that Sixes Bridge or Verona would ever be built. Both reservoirs would have taken large amounts of land in areas far removed from the District of Columbia, and local residents objected strenuously. Also the environmental

impacts were severe. As stated earlier, even the
authorization by Congress was less than firm because an
additional study and the pilot estuary treatment plant
were authorized as alternatives.

In hindsight, and considering the form that the
solution eventually took, I can now see why, despite a
very sincere federal interest in the issue, it was not
resolved during fifteen years of activity. The first
reason for lack of success is that the traditional long
Corps process for study, authorization, and eventual
construction, in this case, took place when there was a
dramatic change in the public attitude regarding
reservoirs, the environment, and citizen involvement in
their destiny. The Congressionally-mandated process
for such projects is deliberately slow, in order that
only the most worthwhile projects eventually move
through the process and are constructed. But
attitudes, policies and laws changed dramatically
between 1963 when the District Engineer recommended 16
reservoirs in the Potomac River Basin and 1976. Had
the process moved quickly to authorize even two of
those reservoirs by 1964, they probably would have been
constructed before the public began to question all of
the Corps' activities, especially reservoirs. As the
process dragged on, citizen involvement and serious
questioning of the environmental impact of massive
public works projects caused an entirely different set
of procedures. By 1976, it was fairly clear that the
process that had been followed had not considered the
environmental impacts and certainly had not had
sufficient citizen involvement.

Second, local jurisdictions were not seriously
involved in these studies. They had, in essence,
delegated the problem to others and, since there seemed
to be plenty of time, had not concerned themselves too
much. In 1960 it was hard to believe that the
population would grow over the next 20 years so that by
1980 a very serious shortage was eminent. Also, the
local officials, like the Corps, had not counted on the
"rules" being changed so drastically as to perhaps
invalidate all previous studies. In 1963, a large
reservoir miles from the District of Columbia to solve
the metropolitan problem probably appeared like a very
reasonable solution. By 1975 the citizens living near
the proposed site were pretty outspoken in their
resolve not to give up their land in order to solve the
District of Columbia's problem.

A third issue that eventually killed the big dam
solution was the question of how much water was needed. When people became aware of the impact of these

reservoirs, serious questions were raised regarding the tradeoff of providing a very generous water supply for a very rapidly growing population in the Washington metropolitan region. Many responsible people asked, "Why can't you get by with less water? If you can get by with less, perhaps all these reservoirs aren't needed! How serious is this alleged crisis?"

Congressional Reaction

        Congressional committee members involved in these activities became very frustrated that their sincere interest and willingness to build facilities was stymied. As stated earlier, they directed the Corps to construct and operate a pilot estuary plant to use the water in the fresh but heavily polluted estuary of the Potomac and they directed another "final" water supply study. In the same act, they also included a provision to help force resolution. In the 1974 Water Resources Act, they directed that the Corps would not issue any permits for future withdrawals from the Potomac River until the D.C. metropolitan users had agreed on how they would allocate the water in the Potomac during periods of low flow. Congress, in essence, said, "Okay, if the basin won't accept the federal proposals, you will have to agree how to protect D.C.'s needs during periods of drought or there will be no more intakes."

        Thus, by 1976, the three water managers in the metropolitan region were faced with the facts that (a) the previous Corps-proposed solutions were, for all purposes, dead; (b) that another study was underway, the outcome of which was, at best, uncertain, since previous Corps efforts had failed; and (c) that if any additional intake structures on the Potomac River were to be permitted, they had to agree how to protect D.C. (the federal interest) during low-flow. This last restriction was very serious because both WSSC and Fairfax County Water Authority needed new intakes on the Potomac River. As the General Manager of WSSC, I knew that if our new intake was not authorized, we would face very serious shortages within five years. Fairfax faced the same situation. Our populations were growing so that we needed more water during normal flow. It was readily available in the Potomac, but we could not get permits.

The Maryland Bi-County Water Supply Task Force

        In 1975, frustrated by the inability of the federal process to resolve the issue, the elected officials of Prince George's and Montgomery Counties,

Maryland, and the Washington Suburban Sanitary
Commission, formed the Bi-County Water Supply Task
Force to determine if they could implement a local
solution that would assure the two counties of adequate
water supply. The Bi-County Task Force was very
important regionally for three reasons:

A. Local leaders had finally decided to address the
    problem;
B. The organization of the Task Force would become
    a model for achieving citizen and political
    consensus; and
C. The technical solution to the problem involved
    accepting droughts and managing them, rather
    than planning to provide all the water that was
    necessary even during droughts. The concept of
    drought management was an extremely important
    technical and political part of the eventual
    regional solution.

     The organization of the Task Force is
important. The Task Force itself was co-chaired by the
Presidents of the two County Councils. Other members
of the Task Force were the very senior appointed
officials, representing the County Executives and
WSSC. Most important was the the fact that the
co-chairs were elected officials who would eventually
be responsible, with other Council members, for
approving whatever recommendations were made. They
would eventually have to resolve the issues of the
public interest vs. environmental impact vs. cost.

     An equally important element of the Task Force
was the Citizens Advisory Committee (CAC). The CAC was
selected from interested, environmentally-oriented
citizens who were concerned about the future of their
counties. The CAC was involved in every step of the
decision process, and when it was finished, they
supported the recommendations and were very
instrumental in enlisting general public support.

     The third element, the Technical Group, provided
the supporting engineering and environmental studies
necessary. However, their work was definitely directed
by the Task Force with strong input from the Citizens
Advisory Committee.

     The CAC had a powerful influence on the work of
the Task Force. The CAC insisted that solutions that
might not be "fail safe" be developed. The Technical
Group was, at first, reluctant to analyze supply and
demand in this fashion. However, the Task Force
leaders insisted and the technicians began an analysis

that involved new concepts of drought management and risk management. Studies were developed that showed that if the region would accept water restrictions during severe droughts, the demand could be reduced significantly. Further, study showed that reasonable restrictions such as alternate day watering, slight reductions by the major water users in the region, and pricing mechanisms to discourage excessive use would be effective. First, the CAC, and eventually I (the Manager of WSSC) and my staff, became convinced that a major failing of all previous studies was the large size of proposed reservoirs that resulted from the assumption that the citizens would not and should not accept restrictions during periods of drought. After analysis, the Technical Group, the CAC and the Task Force decided that the bi-county area would and should accept an 8% risk that there would be limited shortages in any year and that water would have to be restricted. Accepting this risk reduced the need for additional supply by 2/3, with significant reductions in cost and environmental impact. Urged on by the CAC and the administration of WSSC, the elected officials accepted this principle and this concept was adopted. The Task Force had successfully completed their work and recommended that a small reservoir on Little Seneca Creek in Montgomery County be constructed by WSSC. With this additional reservoir and drought management, Prince George's and Montgomery Counties were assured of an adequate water supply through the year 2010. The Maryland portion of the region had solved the problem that had eluded the other jurisdictions for so long.

Potomac Low Flow Agreement

While the Task Force work was underway, WSSC and Fairfax County's need for new water intakes on the Potomac became more and more urgent. Even though both managers knew that, during periods of drought these additional intakes would not provide adequate water, they were needed to meet the non-drought demands of our growing populations. Because of the Congressional restriction on issuing additional Potomac permits without a low-flow agreement, Fairfax County and WSSC were forced to negotiate with the District of Columbia and the Corps of Engineers. After several months of negotiation, an agreement was worked out that allowed the two intakes the proceed, but made the regional situation more serious for WSSC and Fairfax. The low-flow agreement provided that the District would not be harmed by growth in the suburbs of Virginia and Maryland. Reluctantly Fairfax and Maryland agreed that their share of water in a period of drought should be based on the winter demands of the three jurisdictions

in 1975. Since the District was not expected to
increase in population, and therefore in need, the
agreement provided enough for D.C.'s needs. However,
for the Maryland and Virginia jurisdictions, increases
in population would make their share during a period of
drought less and less adequate. I clearly recall
advising the Chief of Engineers during these
discussions that, while such a plan was very
undesirable, it was better than no permit. In fact, I
stated that I doubted he could write a version of the
low-flow agreement that I would not sign. Our need for
an intake was urgent. I had a 1980 problem to solve,
and even though it made the 1990 or 2000 situation much
worse, I felt that I would get this permit now and
address the subsequent problem later. The analysis on
which the Bi-County Task Force based their conclusions,
had considered such a restrictive low flow agreement.
For Fairfax, the situation was much more serious.

However, another serious impediment to a "Maryland" solution arose. The Bi-County Water Supply plan
depended upon a new reservoir on Little Seneca Creek.
The leadership of the Corps and the Environmental Protection Agency advised me that they would be reluctant
to issue permits for the construction of a reservoir on
Little Seneca Creek without a regional solution. My
first reaction was that I doubted that the courts would
sustain this position. My second reaction, however,
was that we could be delayed for years even if we,
eventually, won in court.

By 1979 the federal government, in the form of
the Corps, had dramatically changed its position on
water supply for the region. As stated earlier, from
the 1950's to the 1970's, the Corps conducted studies
that were expected to result in the construction of
reservoirs to resolve the issue. By 1979 their
approach was that they would use their regulatory
authority regarding intakes on the Potomac River or
construction of dams to significantly increase the
pressure on local jurisdictions to cooperate. At the
time, I was, of course, very angry and frustrated by
this position. I felt that they had been unable to
solve the problem and now were trying to prevent WSSC
from proceeding until a regional solution was
developed. In hindsight, I must agree this was a
proper position. Had they allowed WSSC to proceed, the
regional solution that was to evolve probably would not
have occurred. I know I would not have worked so hard
for a regional plan.

The Corps' Washington Metropolitan Water Supply Study

In 1980 the Baltimore District of the Corps of Engineers completed the first phase of the final study mentioned earlier. During the study process, the local governments had asked the Corps to develop plans that could be implemented in the region, as opposed to larger reservoirs distant from Washington, D.C. The results of the first phase of this study, published in 1980, showed that if the reservoir proposed by WSSC were built and shared, if a mechanism were found to skim water from the Potomac during periods of normal flow to ensure that the local reservoirs available to Fairfax and WSSC were kept full and if there were a degree of regional cooperation regarding withdrawals and the use of water in the now-complete Bloomington Reservoir, then there was adequate supply for the region. It was a remarkable set of conclusions because the federal government, in the form of the Corps, had shown that the solution to the problem could be implemented by the three local jurisdictions. There was no federal involvement proposed, but also no federal, or for that matter local, mechanism to implement such a concept.

A very historic, important meeting took place in early December 1980. The District Engineer invited the General Manager and staffs from Fairfax County Water Authority, WSSC, and Washington Aqueduct to a meeting to present the findings of the study just mentioned and to discuss them. I clearly recall the meeting where we discussed the technical pros and cons of the skimming concept, the analysis done on the population projections and water needs, the status of WSSC's reservoir, and then paused in frustration with the realization that, for the first time, there were no recommendations for federal action that could solve our problem. It was clearly up to the region to solve the problem, and there was really no role that the Congress or the Corps could play in solving it, if we accepted these recommendations. I believe we, at first, thought of asking the Corps to do a second phase and look at other solutions that didn't involve such an impossible task as getting the three jurisdictions to agree to share costs and, in essence, operate their independent utilities as one system during periods of drought. I was particularly upset at first by the recommendation that our reservoir on Little Seneca Creek should be shared with the others. We had worked so hard to solve our problem, and now others wanted to benefit from our work. But I also was very worried, as I stated earlier, that the EPA/Corps insistence on a regional solution before issuing permits would delay or stop our reservoir.

After the meeting ended in no conclusion and utter frustration, the General Managers of Fairfax and Washington Aqueduct asked me to join them for lunch. At the lunch, they pointed out the success of the Bi-County Water Supply Task Force and asked me to consider attempting the same sort of solution on a regional basis. I agreed to try.

The Washington Metropolitan Water Supply Task Force

In late December 1980, I wrote to the Presidents of the Councils of the District of Columbia, Fairfax County, Montgomery and Prince George's Counties, and asked them to form a Washington Metropolitan Water Supply Task Force similar to the Bi-County Water Supply Task Force. I explained that the Corps study had clearly shown that a solution to our water supply problem was within our own boundaries and that we needed to begin the process to solve the problem ourselves. Fortunately, I knew each of the Presidents personally and, in addition to writing, I personally asked them to agree. In January 1981, they all agreed to form the Task Force.

We followed the same organizational model as the Bi-County Task Force. The Task Force was the four Council Presidents. We formed a Citizens Advisory Committee, again with informed, environmentally-oriented members from the four jurisdictions. The Technical Group was composed of experts from each of the three agencies, WSSC, WAD and FCWA.

In the work of the Bi-County Task Force, it was primarily the citizens who insisted on innovative approaches to water supply planning. In the case of the Washington Metropolitan Water Supply Task Force, it was the Technical Group, chaired by the General Managers of the water supply agencies, took the leadership in developing what I believe is a very new approach to water supply management.

About the same time that the Task Force was formed, Dr. Daniel Sheer of the Interstate Commission on the Potomac River Basin completed work on a model he had developed for predicting the daily flows of the Potomac River. In addition to predicting the flows, the model contained past weather data and past recorded demand data from the three water supply agencies. The model also included data on all the regional reservoirs. Bloomington Dam was complete. In addition, Fairfax County had a medium-sized reservoir, the Occoquan, and WSSC also had medium-sized reservoirs on the Patuxent River. The model also included the im-

poundment on Little Seneca Creek that had been developed as part of the Bi-County Water Supply study. At
that time it was planned that under certain drought
conditions the flow in the Potomac would be augmented
by fairly substantial releases of water from the
Bloomington Reservoir about 30 miles upstream from the
intakes. It also planned that the three agencies,
acting independently, would make decisions regarding
the use of their own reservoirs and withdrawals from
the Potomac River. Washington Aqueduct had no on-line
storage, but the Low-Flow Agreement would ensure that
at least their share of the water was available during
a drought. All the planning was on analyzing droughts
on a monthly basis. The technical breakthrough by the
Technical Committee, led by Dr. Sheer's model, was the
analysis of the behavior of the river and the three
suppliers on a daily basis. The historical daily
demand of the three agencies during periods of drought
is erratic. Even a minor amount of rainfall can cause
wide fluctuations in use, as can temperature. Based on
the history of past performance response to drought by
the three agencies, the model demonstrated that large
releases from Bloomington based on monthly projections,
would waste a good deal of the water. It was wasted
because it flowed by the three intakes during periods
of low daily demand. Historically, the three agencies
had not operated with the interests of the region in
mind, but, rather, as they deemed best for their
customers. Continuing the modeling, it was learned
that if the three utilities were operated as a system
and if the releases from Bloomington were made on a
daily basis, giving due consideration to the seven-day
time of flow to reach the intakes, the storage in
Bloomington was conserved. The three local reservoirs
could be used to smooth out peak demands and also to
meet any unexpected daily demand that the model did not
predict. The results of this work were indeed
profound. The existing reservoirs, plus the proposed
impoundment on Little Seneca Creek in Montgomery
County, provided sufficient water for growth through
2050, even with a repeat of the record droughts of 1930
and 1966, provided that the three water supply systems
were operated as a single utility during periods of
drought. Even the skimming concept in the Corps study
was not needed.

    It is very important to understand the
significance of this finding. For 20 years, studies
had shown that the only solution to adequate water
supply for the Washington metropolitan region was at
least two more very large impoundments. When the
existing system of reservoirs and utilities was
analyzed on a daily basis, something that had never

been done before, no additional reservoirs were
needed. There was enough water in the region if a
mechanism could be found to operate the three
independent utilities in three separate states, one
controlled by the federal government, as a single
system during periods of drought -- a profound finding
with profound implications.

The role of the engineers involved in our effort
at this point was very important. This type of
analysis had never been performed before and seemed to
disprove every previous study. The senior staff of the
three utilities plus the three General Managers had to
personally examine the findings; understand the model;
be satisfied with the data stored, the assumptions
made, the simulations performed, because the future of
their utility in a drought was at stake. We probed, we
questioned, we asked for different simulations, we
searched for fatal flows, and eventually the collective
judgment of the three staffs and the three General
Managers was that it, indeed, was a breakthrough and
would work.

The Technical Group presented these findings to
the Citizens Advisory Committee and the Task Force (the
four elected Council Presidents), who approved the plan
in concept. Another point regarding the role of the
engineer is important to note at this juncture. It was
not reasonable to expect the Citizens Advisory
Committee or the elected officials to understand or do
sufficient study to satisfy themselves that this
radical approach was sound and technically correct.
They had to rely on the judgment of their experts from
the three utilities. Both the citizens and the Task
Force members (the Council Presidents) were aware that
it was a radical approach and that the conclusions
differed from all other studies. They were skeptical,
but they accepted the findings because they had
confidence, built up over many years of efficient,
effective operation of the utilities, that the
engineering judgment was sound.

Having approved the concept, the Task Force
directed the Technical Group to work out the necessary
contractual agreements regarding operations and cost
sharing to perform such a plan. While this may appear
to be a somewhat mundane task for staff and attorneys,
it was perhaps the most difficult part of the whole
process. Eventually, there would be eight contracts
that would have to be signed by three states, two
independent water supply agencies, and the Corps of
Engineers for the federal government. Negotiating
these agreements involved another role for the engineer

in managing conflicts -- leadership and political involvement.

I recognized that, if this concept were to be implemented, someone would have to take charge of the negotiations and ensure that they were completed promptly. If negotiations dragged on for years, a tenuous concept would fall apart. Further, I felt that compromises and political trade-offs would have to be made to translate this concept into action. I decided I must take charge, establish tight schedules, give orders, and personally negotiate the compromises that would be necessary. Some examples of the myriad problems that we encountered in the approximately six months that we negotiated these agreements follow.

The issue of cost-sharing was one of the most difficult. As stated earlier in the paper, WSSC had planned to build a reservoir on Little Seneca Creek that was now to be part of the regional system. In exchange for sharing the water for regional use, I expected the jurisdictions to share the cost. I believed that elected officials in Maryland would be willing to accept the loss of water storage in exchange for lowering the cost to their rate-payers. We used the model of the Potomac River Basin to determine how much water would be used from Seneca Reservoir by each jurisdiction during periods of drought to determine each jurisdiction's share. The modeling showed that it was WSSC and Washington Aqueduct that needed the storage in Little Seneca. Because of the configuration of the Fairfax County water system, their Occoquan Reservoir was large enough to meet their needs during a period of drought without Little Seneca. While technically a sound analysis, this was, I felt, politically unacceptable. I believed then and I am convinced today that the elected leadership of Washington, D.C. and Prince George's and Montgomery Counties in Maryland would never have entered into this agreement without Fairfax sharing some of the cost of Little Seneca Reservoir. But the Fairfax County Water Authority could demonstrate that Little Seneca was not needed for their purposes. I arranged a personal meeting with the Fairfax County Executive, with whom I had a close relationship through other regional issues. I carefully explained to him that, while technically they did not have to share in the cost of Little Seneca, it was my belief that politically they must. We negotiated and he agreed to urge the Fairfax Water Authority to share 10% of the cost of Little Seneca Reservoir. I accepted this and later convinced Maryland the D.C. officials to accept this compromise.

An important political regional issue was the
Maryland counties north of the metropolitan region who
also depended on the Potomac River for water supply.
When Bloomington Dam had been authorized, they had
participated in an agreement to eventually purchase a
portion of the water supply in Bloomington Reservoir.
Details of the purchase had never been worked out, but
they clearly had a right to this water. Our analysis
of the total water supply showed that they were not
consumptive users. Their demands were so small and
were returned via sewage discharge and runoff. They
would have virtually no impact on our regional
solution. However, I felt that politically they might
delay the agreements if we insisted they meet their
previous agreement to purchase Bloomington storage.
This was a political judgment. I proposed that the
three D.C. jurisdictions purchase all the Bloomington
water, but not restrict their use. The first reaction
of the D.C. utilities was unfavorable because they felt
everyone should bear some cost. However, after
producing various model simulations of the situation, I
was able to convince them that upstream withdrawals
would have no impact on our supply, but to negotiate
cost-sharing with these counties would seriously
jeopardize the whole process. It was finally accepted
that the three utilities in the Washington area would
purchase all of the water supply in Bloomington and
guarantee that the two Maryland counties north of the
region would get the water they needed during a drought.

Finally, the eight contracts were ready for signature by all the participating jurisdictions. Close,
but by no means finished. Each jurisdiction has a process to go through to authorize the signature of documents such as these, and this is complicated and uncertain. I assumed the responsibility for assuring that
these documents moved through each jurisdiction promptly. I personally followed the process through each,
using every political connection I had to assist. For
example, one of the members of the Citizens Advisory
Committee from Virginia had strong political connec-
tions in Richmond. Through this individual, I was able
to track the process and arrange for him to make key
calls to appropriate political leaders to keep the
contracts moving and assure approval.

July 22, 1982, in a ceremony at the District
Building appropriate representatives from all parties
signed eight contracts that ensured that the water
supply needs of the Washington metropolitan region had
been met through the year 2050.

The regional water supply system would be

completed for about $31 million, whereas the cost of the federal reservoirs that had been proposed would have been about $400 million. The high-flow skimming concept proposed by the Corps for an additional $70 million would not be needed. The cost savings are impressive, but nothing would have happened had a regional water system not been developed where none had existed before.

Engineer/managers were in leadership positions throughout the 20-year history of this effort.

A. The engineer/managers of the three water supply agencies had finally realized that the efforts of the Corps and of the Congress, though sincere, held out no hope of resolving the issues.

B. The engineer/managers were instrumental in creating two task forces that were chaired by elected officials. They recognized that the elected officials would make the decisions, not the utilities. This technique of a task force of elected officials was instrumental to the solution, and it was the engineer/managers who used the task forces to address the problems.

C. The three engineer/managers were seriously committed to citizen involvement, recognizing that without such involvement the controversy would continue. The Citizen Advisory Committees of informed, concerned, environmentally-oriented citizens were involved in every step of the process and concurred with every finding before the Task Force moved on to a recommendation.

D. Perhaps the most important role of the engineer/ managers was the abandonment of traditional planning concepts for water supply. Two new concepts underlay the basis for regional cooperation: risk management, whereby it was accepted that some shortages would occur and would be managed during severe drought, and regional operation of the utilities on a daily basis to maximize the available storage. The three independent water systems would be operated to maximize regional benefits, rather than individual benefits.

E. Leadership and political involvement by engineer/managers is necessary to resolve conflicts. Engineers must take a leadership role, which could be considered a political leadership role (indeed was in this case), in order to eventually resolve complex issues.

Platte River Conflict Resolution

Ann Salomon Bleed[1]

Abstract

The allocation of water in the Platte River system in Colorado, Wyoming and Nebraska presents a complex river management problem. Despite many and varied attempts to develop a mutually acceptable management plan, conflict and litigation dominate the decision making process. Engineers and other technical experts have played major roles in this process. This paper briefly describes the role played by engineers and seeks to determine how engineers could have been more effective in their attempts to help decision makers achieve an acceptable compromise.

Introduction

The Platte River system presents a complex river management problem. As both an engineer and an ecologist, I have been involved in many attempts to develop a workable decision making process. To date, these efforts have not been successful.

This paper briefly describes the Platte River problems and discusses the role that engineers and other technical experts, notably biologists, have played in trying to solve them. At the risk of over-using stereotypes, I will discuss why engineers have not been more effective and offer suggestions of how their impact could be increased.

Description of the Problem

Since the late 1800's the allocation of water from the Platte River system has been the source of controversy. Today, in spite of extensive scientific

---

[1]State Hydrologist, Nebraska Department of Water Resources, 301 Centennial Mall South, Lincoln, NE 68509

studies, in spite of innovative attempts by expert negotiators and in spite of real opportunities for compromise, the achievement of an acceptable water allocation plan for the Platte River eludes decision makers.

The Platte River system originates in the Rocky Mountains of Colorado and includes the North Platte River, which also flows through the state of Wyoming, the South Platte River, which flows through the state of Colorado, and the Platte River itself, formed by the confluence of the North and South Platte Rivers in western Nebraska. The Platte then flows across the remaining two-thirds of the state of Nebraska and joins the Missouri River at Nebraska's eastern border. Along its route, water from the Platte system has been diverted for irrigation, hydropower, municipal use and recreation. Until now the Platte system has been able to meet most of these out-of-stream demands. However, current proposals for additional out-of-stream uses far exceed the capacity of the river system.

Further complicating the problem are the increased demands for the maintenance of water instream to provide habitat for fish and wildlife. These environmental demands have been codified by the National Endangered Species Act (ESA), which prohibits any activity that would diminish the critical habitat of an endangered species, and the National Environmental Policy Act (NEPA), which requires all federal agencies to assess the impact of their projects or programs on environmental quality. Thus, a successful allocation plan must not only decide who should receive the water that is diverted but also how much water should be left in the stream for wildlife and other environmental reasons.

The allocation problem is exacerbated by the institutional structure of the decision making process. Involved in the process are several different agencies of the U. S. federal government including: (1) the U. S. Fish and Wildlife Service, through its regulatory and advocacy roles as a protector of wildlife habitat; (2) the U. S. Army Corps of Engineers and the Environmental Protection Agency which are responsible for protecting water quality; (3) the Federal Energy Regulatory Commission which regulates hydropower; and (4) the U. S. Bureau of Reclamation which traditionally has promoted, built and operated water development projects. Each agency is somewhat independent, has their own group of technical experts and has a different set of goals and constituents. In spite of laws mandating federal coordination, coordination is not always achieved.

Although the impact of federal regulation on water policy is great, and some fear may become greater at the expense of the states (Western States Engineers Conference 1988), to date the states have retained the right to allocate water within their state as they see fit. Conflicts between the states must be settled by interstate compacts that allocate water between states, or in cases on the Platte where no settlement could be reached, by decree from the U. S. Supreme Court. Engineers have and continue to play a key role in negotiating and enforcing these compacts.

Within the states, various local entities, such as cities, resource districts, or power and irrigation districts, all with their own complements of engineers, compete with each other for water. Thus, in spite of a major federal role, no single governmental entity controls water allocations along the total Platte system. Rather, conflicts among states and among local entities dominate the allocation process.

The general public and special interest groups which also employ technical experts are also involved in the process. State and local water authorities and hydropower districts have traditionally been influenced by special interest, development oriented groups. Since the 1969 enactment of NEPA, which mandates a public input process, environmental advocacy groups have also had a strong influence.

The Platte River situation affords an excellent opportunity for studying decision making processes because it is not a simple case where only one entity can be a winner and no winners can be chosen until one entity gathers sufficient power to force a solution. Rather, there appear to be numerous opportunities for compromise decisions where everyone has something to gain (and lose!).

That opportunities for compromise exist was demonstrated by a study of planning alternatives for an important reach of the river (Bleed et al. 1986). This study evaluated the impacts of over 4,000 water diversion development options and then determined optimum water development plans that would achieve the multiple objectives of state economic development, maintenance of wildlife habitat and conservation of state monetary funds. Results from the model indicated that there were many areas where compromises could be made. The trade-offs between maintaining instream flows for fish and wildlife and diverting flows for economic development was surprisingly flat indicating that, though compromises must be made, the economic sacrifices required to maintain instream flows are not as steep as generally thought. These results suggest that a creative management option could be developed that, if not ideal from all perspectives, could allow for both more development and habitat maintenance.

Attempts at Compromise

The absence of a compromise solution is not for lack of trying. Attempts at reaching a compromise solution to Platte River problems have been many and varied. Just within the state of Nebraska, compromise attempts include litigation, negotiations in private retreat settings, adaptive environmental assessment processes and the formation of a special water management board.

One of the first organized attempts to reach a compromise solution on Platte River water allocation was an adaptive environmental assessment process which became known as the Platte River Forum (Nebraska Natural Resources Commission 1985). Although this forum was sponsored by and focused on issues important to the state of Nebraska, upstream demands from other states were considered. The compromise process essentially amounted to river modeling by committee. A group of about 30 interested people, including engineers and other technical experts and interest group representatives, were appointed and charged with deciding what should be modeled, what data should be used, etc. The basic idea was that this process would facilitate compromise decisions by providing a forum for agreeing on the facts.

Although much was learned by the participants, the process failed to achieve a compromise. Adopting the assumption that agreement on the facts would lead to agreement on a management plan, the Platte River Forum focused on understanding the natural system. Little attention was given to trying to clarify and reach compromises on objectives. A limited number of project alternatives precluded a thorough analysis of alternatives. A lack of data prevented full understanding of the system. More importantly, the assumption that agreement on the facts would lead to agreement on a management plan proved to be invalid. Not only did participants fail to agree on all the facts, but even when there was general agreement on how the natural system worked, differing value systems prevented agreement on how the water should be used.

The multi-objective model described earlier (Bleed et al. 1986) was developed in part because of observed limitations with the Platte River Forum approach. The Platte River Forum used a simulation model that focused on the physical aspects of the river system. In addition, the Forum considered only a small set of alternatives. The multi-objective model, on the other hand, focused on the delineation of trade-off curves and allowed consideration of a large number of alternatives. The intent was to improve on the Platte River Forum by producing additional information for decision making and to do so without the inefficiencies associated with a committee of thirty. This study was successful in that

the most relevant trade-offs were considered and a credible operational model was produced. However, the results of the model have not been embraced by decision makers. Perhaps this is due to timing, i.e., the economic climate is not right for pursuing any kind of action at this time, or perhaps it is due to a distrust of black boxes by decision makers, irrespective of who built the box.
Another major attempt to improve the decision making process within the state of Nebraska was the formation in 1984 of a special Water Management Board. Composed of five members, its charge is to "identify, propose, support, advocate, resolve conflicts regarding, and expedite water development projects in the state in the most efficient manner possible" (Nebr. Rev. Stat. 2-15, 107, Cum. Supp. 1986). Although the Water Management Board has the authority for effective and comprehensive planning decisions, it has been inactive to date. Only time will tell if this inactivity is due to present economic and political conditions, or whether it is due to other factors which may indefinitely preclude effective action by the board.
Meanwhile a Nebraska power entity is seeking to relicense a key hydropower project with the Federal Energy Regulatory Commission (FERC). One of the requirements for receiving a license from FERC is the development of a plan to protect the habitat of endangered species. Several environmental entities have blocked the licensing attempts until license requirements for instream flows are put in place. It is likely that project sponsors will be required to provide flows for fish and wildlife, but a lack of scientific data and acceptable analysis of what the flow requirements are has created high levels of uncertainty and controversy.
Another effort at reaching a compromise, this time involving the three states, Colorado, Wyoming, and Nebraska; several agencies of the federal government, notably the Service and the Bureau; and several private environmental and water development groups, is the Platte River Management Joint Study. Initiated by the federal government in 1983, the purpose is to seek ways to develop and implement plans which will enable federal agencies associated with water project development and depletion in the Platte Basin to proceed in compliance with ESA and state water rights systems (U. S. Bureau of Reclamation 1988). Engineers and biologists were organized into hydrologic and biologic task forces. A steering committee representing the major federal agencies and the states oversees the effort. To date, a few studies have been undertaken but there is little real progress toward a final solution.
In the meantime, however, Nebraska has had to take legal action to protect its claims to Platte River

flows from out-of-state proposals for projects in the
upstream state of Wyoming. Nebraska is suing the U. S.
Army Corps of Engineers and the U. S. Fish and Wildlife
Service in federal district court for violating NEPA and
ESA by issuing a permit for construction of one of
Wyoming's proposed projects, the Deer Creek Dam, without
an adequate environmental impact statement or habitat
protection plan. The Corps of Engineers, again with the
consent of the Fish and Wildlife Service, also has
indicated their intention to issue a permit for another
Platte River project, the Two Forks Project in Colorado.
Another federal agency, the Environmental Protection
Agency, however, is considering a veto of the permit.
These permit decisions have proceeded in apparent disre-
gard of the federal Platte River Management Joint Study.
The fact that the federal government proceeded to issue
building permits has seriously undermined the govern-
ment's attempt to reach a compromise agreement.
          In part, as a result of the Wyoming project,
Nebraska has also sued Wyoming in the U. S. Supreme Court
(Nebraska v. Wyoming 1986) for violation of a 1945 U. S.
Supreme Court decree that allocated the flows of the
North Platte River.

Role of Engineers

          Clearly, successful management of the Platte
River system is complicated because the river crosses
state boundaries, multiple levels of government are
involved, decision makers are not well-defined and the
recent imposition of environmental goals has upset
traditional value systems. Piecemeal decision making,
the lack of joint consideration of a full range of
alternatives, insufficient involvement of the public, and
the inability to deal effectively with risk and uncertainty have contributed to the problem. Engineers and
other technical people have been involved in all aspects
of this process. Presumably, these experts had the tools
and expertise to alleviate some of these problems. It is
instructive to ask why these experts have not been more
effective.
          To a major extent, the engineers were a miniature
version of the larger decision making system. The engineers employed by each entity reflected the personality
and biases of that entity. Most likely selection processes that were active when the engineer was hired, both
on the part of the employer and the employee, tended to
result in agencies where the employee's goals and agency's goals were similar. People supportive of water
development work for the Bureau of Reclamation, the Corps
of Engineers, state development oriented agencies and
local project sponsors; people supportive of maintaining
ecosystem integrity are more likely to work for the Fish

and Wildlife Service, state fish and game departments or private environmental groups. Thus, engineers, who tend to be more development oriented, comprise the majority of technical experts in water development oriented agencies. The top decision makers in these agencies are also likely to have an engineering background. Biologists tend to be environmentalists and are more likely to dominate the fish and wildlife agencies.

Though trained to be objective, engineers cannot be expected to ignore their value systems and be without bias. When engineers meet with other technical people, it is usually assumed that politics and biases will not be a problem. It is assumed that the "public interest" will be represented. However, biases do intrude. If nothing else, technical experts must always be mindful of who they represent so that they don't jeopardize an agency's bargaining position. When engineers worked as a consultant in litigation, these biases were recognized. This was not the case in many of the work group sessions. In these discussions, the bias itself may not have been as much of a problem as the charade that bias was nonexistent and, therefore, did not have to be addressed. It cannot be assumed that engineers are any more representative of the public interest than any other decision maker.

Not only did engineers and other experts have different value systems, they also had different vocabularies, different types of data sets, different theoretical constructs, and different general understandings of how the world operates.

The theoretical constructs which form the basis of every discipline, though critical to an understanding of that discipline, are rarely discussed. For example, the behavior of river channels or the health of bird populations were often a topic of discourse among the technical groups, but rarely if ever did an engineer make an attempt to understand population theory or did a biologist attempt to understand the theories related to river behavior and channel morphology. Yet, at times, engineers developed their own conclusions about population dynamics and biologists set forth arguments on channel behavior. The fact that different disciplines have different theoretical constructs as well as different ways of viewing the scientific world will always be a problem. However, some acrimony among experts may have been avoided if participants had not made the assumption that an expert in one field could, without considerable effort, understand the thinking of an expert from another.

Different fundamental viewpoints held by experts also caused problems. These basic, underlying viewpoints were particularly pernicious because they are so basic and pervasive. Schwartz (1980) has characterized two

types of decision makers in today's society. Those with
Perspective I view people as being dominant over nature,
view nature as an understandable and predictable resource
and technology as an answer to society's problems.
Engineers generally fall in this category. Biologists,
on the other hand, tend to hold Perspective II which
views humankind as being a part of (not dominant over)
nature, views nature as mysterious, somewhat unpredictable and sacred and technology as the cause, not the
solution, to our problems (Schwartz 1980). Hence,
engineers tend to be open to managing and manipulating
natural systems while biologists hesitate to intrude. At
another level, engineers reject as too low coefficients
of correlation that are considered significant by biologists.

Further exacerbating the problem was the fact
that typically the engineers were not cognizant of these
or other interpersonal problems. Florman, in his book
The Existential Pleasures of Engineering, cites five
studies that indicate engineers as a group have very
similar character traits. "unlike many other occupations
where it is impossible to demonstrate any consistent
trend, the engineering profession is composed of a fairly
homogeneous group of men with a fairly narrow range of
temperamental variation" (Florman 1976). One study
states that engineers' "constricted interests are apparent in their relative indifference to human relations, to
psychology and social sciences, to public affairs and
social amelioration, to the fine arts and cultural
subjects and even to those aspects of physical science
which do not immediately relate to engineering" (Florman
1976).

If not by native disposition, at least by training and experience, engineers are not generally adept at
appreciating and coping with problems related to social
and political interactions. The lack of attention to
personal interactions has been a problem in the decision
making process on the Platte. As a rule, experts have
thought little about how to develop a cooperative work
group, insure a productive discussion in which all
participate, or even run an efficient meeting. These
problems were sometimes addressed at the level of the
decision makers but were often ignored at the technical
work group level. The result was often a poor work
product that was not supported by the work group members.

Even when there was a supported quality product,
the product was often ignored by decision makers. At
this point in the process, communication skills, both
written and verbal, were critical. Especially when
technical analyses involve complex systems, decision
makers tended to dismiss analytical results that did not
fit with their personal perceptions of the problem.
There were times when technical experts appeared to have

agreed that a mutually acceptable compromise plan could be attained. However, the decision makers appeared to ignore this information and continued to squabble. In these cases, a major effort on the part of the technical analysts is required to get decision makers to accept study results that were contrary to a previous viewpoint. This effort was not made nor were the engineers able to inspire enough confidence in the product to get by without such an effort. Again, communication was the key and, as a rule, engineers were poor communicators.

Conclusion

Basic to the solution of some of these problems is the recognition that engineers, like everyone else, are not thoroughly objective nor can they be expected to represent that amorphous entity called "the public interest." Like everyone else, they carry their personal agendas and biases and those of the agency they represent with them to work group sessions. When goals compete, these working group meeting take on the characteristics of a negotiating session. In order to cope with these problems, the myth that there can be a work session with no hidden agendas must be debunked. In some situations, hiring a skilled discussion leader familiar with techniques of how to work with groups and negotiate a settlement would significantly enhance the effectiveness of the work group.

Another solution to many of these problems, at least for the long term, is to do a better job of educating engineers in the social sciences and art of communications. However, it may be too idealistic to think that education will make all engineers into effective group participants. A more realistic solution is to recognize that only some engineers will have an interest and talent in learning how to work with disparate groups of people. When available, these are the engineers who should be assigned to sensitive task forces.

Appendix

Bleed, A. S., N. Gollehon, D. Razavian, and R. Supalla. (1986). Economic, Environmental and Financing Optimization Analysis of Platte River Development Alternatives. Nebraska Water Resources Center, Conservation and Survey Division, University of Nebraska, Lincoln, NE.

Florman, Samuel C. (1976). The Existential Pleasures of Engineering. H. Martins Press, New York, NY.

Nebraska Natural Resources Commission. (1985). Platte River Forum for the Future, State Water Planning and Review Process. State of Nebraska, Lincoln, NE.

Schwartz, Peter. (1982). "Changing Values and the Environment." in Renewable Natural Resources, A Management Handbook for the 1980's edited by Dennis L. Little, Robert E. Dils and John Gray. Westview Press, Boulder, CO. pp. 27-41.

Western States Engineers Conference. (1988). Coeur d'Alene, ID.

Water Supply Planning Model for Southwest Florida

James P. Heaney[1]

ABSTRACT

Models for water supply planning are reviewed and an object-oriented expert system is proposed for evaluating water supply alternatives. Procedures for calibrating the model are demonstrated using the results of fifteen years of water supply planning activities in Pasco County located immediately north of Tampa, Florida.

INTRODUCTION

This paper describes decision aiding techniques to help determine the most effective, long-range utilization of water supply alternatives to satisfy the projected needs of all water users within the Southwest Florida Water Management District (SWFWMD). A prototype of the procedure is presented using Pasco County, north of Tampa and St. Petersburg, as the study area.

DESCRIPTION OF THE STUDY AREA

The Southwest Florida Water Management District (SWFWMD) is one of five regional districts in the State of Florida that is charged by Florida Statutes with pro- tecting the fresh water resources (SWFWMD, 1989). Its duties include issuing permits for consumptive use of water, well construction and surface water management. It also monitors water supply and flood hazards. SWFWMD was created in 1961 in response to severe flooding caus- ed by Hurricane Donna. The District covers 10,200 square miles in all or part of 16 counties. One fourth of the state's population, or over 3.3 million residents, lives within its boundaries. The District is growing at a rate of nearly 100,000 residents per year.

----

[1]Prof., Envir. Engrg. Sci., and Dir., Florida Water Resources Ctr., Univ. of Florida, Gainesville, FL 32611

STATEWIDE WATER SUPPLY PLANNING

The first basinwide water resources plan for South-west Florida was published in 1966 (Florida Board of Conservation). Numerous state and federal agencies par-ticipated in preparing this report. With regard to water supply planning, simple needs and sources projections were made for 1980 and 2015. Significant water supply shortages are projected for the Tampa Bay area by the year 2015. The available supply is based solely upon the mean annual runoff from the rivers in the study area. No direct evaluation of groundwater is included in the esti-mate. Interestingly, waste dilution is one of the larg-est "water use" categories. This initial effort did not discuss how water could be transported from area to area. Unfortunately, similar planning studies for other areas of the state were never completed and the project was abandoned.

The next attempt to develop a statewide water plan began in the mid-1970's. The SWFWMD published a draft water use plan in 1977 as part of this effort (SWFWMD, 1977). The three primary objectives for the planning horizon through the year 2020 were:

1. Supply all needs for water and provide protection from excess water.

2. Guarantee to all areas the use of that portion of the local supply needed for their projected demands through-out the planning horizon.

3. Reserve water from consumptive use to preserve and/or maintain natural systems at an acceptable level of quality.

The proposed policies to implement the plan are list-ed in Table 1. From an operational point of view, this draft plan included county level estimates of water needs through the year 2020. Numerous sources of supply and a possible transmission network were described. However, no actual area by area evaluation of needs and sources was included. The more controversial parts of the draft plan dealt with proposals to move water over relatively long distances to serve the Tampa Bay area. As with the effort in the late 1960's, the late 1970's state water planning effort was never completed.

REGIONAL WATER SUPPLY PLANNING EFFORTS

The West Coast Regional Water Supply Authority (WCRWSA) was established in 1974 to provide wholesale

Table 1. Policies proposed in 1977 for water supply
planning in the Southwest Florida Water Management District (SWFWMD, 1977)

1. Coordinate water management planning with land use
   and water quality planning to insure the long range
   maintenance or enhancement of water quantity and
   quality.

2. Encourage the utilization of local resources to
   accommodate new development rather than transfer of
   water from other regions. However, such transfers
   are not precluded if they are in the larger interest
   of the people of the District.

3. Encourage water conservation practices and the development and implementation of reuse techniques
   throughout the District.

4. Manage the water resources in order to insure a safe,
   sustained water supply.

5. Develop the water resources in a manner that will
   minimize the overall adverse environmental impact.

6. Reserve water for essential non-withdrawal demands
   such as navigation, recreation, and the maintenance
   of natural aquatic systems.

7. Where possible, encourage the use of water of the
   lowest acceptable quality for the purpose intended.

8. All users (domestic, industrial and agricultural)
   should be informed of water resources limitations and
   should plan their growth with due consideration of
   these limitations.

9. Encourage the preservation and utilization of natural
   ly occurring storage and recharge areas.

10. Encourage multiple use systems such as the combining
    of electrical power generation facilities with
    desalination and other processes.

11. Encourage interconnection of all appropriate water
    supply systems to maximize the benefits of these
    sources.
===

water to Pasco, Hillsborough and Pinellas Counties.
WCRWSA sponsored three Needs and Sources studies that
were published in 1978 (Ross, Saarinen, Bolton, and

Wilder), 1982 (Camp, Dresser, and McKee), and 1986 (Camp, Dresser, and McKee). A similar methodology was used in each of these three reports to select and update the master plan. A 1990 revision of the master plan will be the next iteration.

The 1978 Needs and Sources report is a comprehensive 705 page water supply planning document. The 1982 and 1986 updates are also quite detailed. The planning process included, not only an area by area inventory of present and projected water needs and sources, but also a thorough evaluation of possible supply-demand interconnections. Alternative plans were evaluated according to the twelve criteria shown in Table 2.

Table 2. Decision criteria used in 1978 WCRWSA evaluation

Number	Criterion	Relative weight
1	Cost Effectiveness	10
2	Water Supply Useful Life	9
3	Public Health	9
4	Environmental Impact	8
5	Hydrological	7
6	Facility Compatibility	7
7	Water Compatibility	6
8	Reliability	6
9	Energy Consumption	5
10	Potential for Improving Water Management	4
11	Compatibility with Long-Range Plans	20
12	Ability to Serve New Customers	2

The final master plan from the 1978 study for the years 1980-2020 is shown in Figure 1. This plan is presented in four five-year phases from 1980 to 2000 and a final twenty year phase. This original plan was updated in 1982 and 1986, and will be updated again in 1990. These planning documents have provided a valuable basis for guiding the actions of the WSRWSA.

The next sections of this paper discuss how computer-based water planning models have been and could be used in such planning activities. This review will provide a brief state of the art appraisal of water planning models. The stimulus for this activity is an on-going project for the Southwest Florida Water Management District to develop a water use planning model.

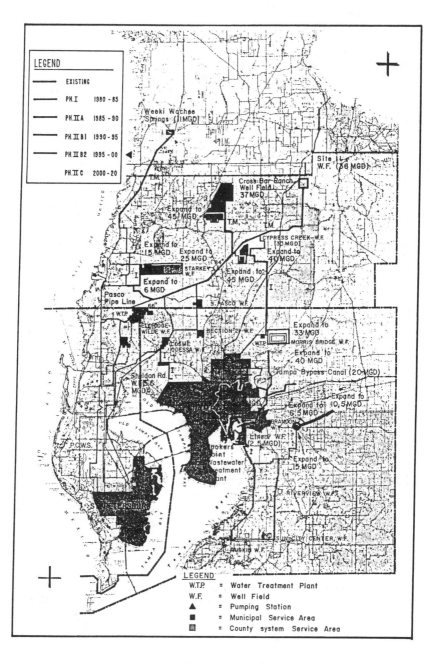

Figure 1. 1978 WCRWSA Water Supply Master Plan, 1980-2000, (Ross, Saarinen, Bolton, and Wilder, 1978).

NORMATIVE PLANNING MODELS

Normative water supply planning models are used to find the most desirable way to allocate available sources of water to meet projected needs. Allocation criteria include concern for the water resources and associated natural systems and economics. This problem can be classified as one of capacity planning. Lauria's (1983) review paper is used as a basis for this discussion. The primary water system components of interest are: (1) supply reservoirs, (2) pumping stations and treatment works, (3) transmission mains, (4) distribution networks, and (5) water storage tanks.

While the reservoir problem is of major importance in many water supply planning activities, it is of relatively minor importance in the SWFWMD since groundwater is the primary source. Thus, this issue will not be discussed further.

The hydraulic design of pumping stations and treatment works is straightforward. Much of the modeling literature in this area is devoted to the capacity expansion problem, i.e., how much should we expand now and what is the optimal planning horizon? The solution to this problem depends on the cost of capital and the expected growth rates. General results are available for a variety of assumed functional forms for growth rates (Scarato, 1969).

Models to assist in the design and analysis of transmission mains have also been developed. Deb (1978) presents a simple model to evaluate the optimal blend of pumping and a single transmission main or transmission mains in a branching network. Robinson and Austin (1976) solve the branched network problem using linear programming. Their application was to rural networks. The solution of the looped network problem is much more complicated than the branched network. Lansey and Mays (1989) summarize the state of the art and present a solution model that couples nonlinear programming techniques with widely available water distribution simulation models, e.g., Wood (1981).

Ng (1986) and Payne (1988) show that the questions of economic efficiency and equity in cost allocation are interrelated. The economic optimization is done for some assumed fixed quantity of water that is demanded by each group. After the regional solution is found and some procedure is used to allocate costs among the various groups, each demand unit then faces a charge for water. However, this charge can affect their demand for water.

Thus, it is necessary to iterate between the efficiency and equity analyses until equilibrium is reached.

Ng and Heaney (1989) compare partial and total enumeration methods for finding the optimal solution to the water allocation problem. Partial enumeration techniques such as linear programming are attractive in that they can evaluate a large number of alternatives and find the "optimal" solution. Unfortunately, these models do not usually provide realistic answers because of the necessarily restrictive assumptions regarding the nature of the cost and production functions. More importantly, the decision process is usually much too complex to be meaningfully represented by a single or multiple objective optimization model.

Another serious limitation with partial enumeration techniques is that only the optimal solution is presented. It is very difficult, if not impossible, to determine the good, or near optimal, solutions. For example, the optimal solution may require extensive interbasin transfers while a good solution, e.g., only a few percent more expensive, may require little or no interbasin transfers. Lastly, it is important to know the optimal solutions for each demand unit or subsets of demand units.

Ng and Heaney (1989) describe an efficient total enumeration technique for finding the optimal solutions for all supply-demand combinations. This approach allows all of the alternatives to be ranked from best to worst, and to use realistic cost functions. This output can be used to find efficient and equitable solutions from the point of view of the entire region, and for each affected area in the region. Ideally, all participants should benefit from the selected solution. While more robust than the partial enumeration models, this approach still requires the problem to be reduced to a highly simplified version of itself.

DESCRIPTIVE PLANNING MODELS

During recent years, research on water resources modeling has shifted to developing descriptive, rather than prescriptive models (Maher, 1987). Our first attempt to use the expert systems approach was in developing a system for evaluating and notifying hazardous waste generators (Knowles, Heaney, and Shafer, 1989). Major lessons learned from this initial effort included the value of spending significant time with the user group to understand the decision problem. For example, our initial perception was that the "problem" was one of how

to analyze the statistics of the information provided by
the generators. The actual problem turned out to be much
different. The analysis of the quantities generated was
relatively simple. The more substantive problem was to
take the results of the analysis, e.g., the monthly quantity generated is too high, and translate that into a
written response to the generator that includes the desired action item(s), e.g., sample on a weekly basis.

Another major lesson learned was the importance of
setting up a database management system that could be
queried in a wide variety of ways because the user's
needs are highly varied and cannot be reduced down to a
few uses of the information that can be hard wired into
the evaluation system. The prototype database permitted
records of interest to be extracted and displayed not
only in tabular format but also in locational format.
The database for this project was organized by hazardous
waste generators and their static (e.g., location) and
temporal (e.g., generation during July 1987) attributes.

The more recent project is an expert system for reviewing permit application for surface water discharges
as part of planned developments in South Florida (Heaney,
Potter, and Wittig, 1989). While the hazardous waste
expert system prototype contained a single file, the
database management system for this study consisted of
several relational databases. A key advantage of the
relational database approach is that knowledge can be
stored in numerous smaller databases that can be searched
through inter-file linkages. In this case, the common
attribute is the application number. In addition to the
relational databases, an interfacing program was developed that permitted the user to move effortlessly among
various work environments, i.e., spreadsheets, word processing, and simulation models written in Basic and
Fortran.

PROPOSED APPROACH FOR PASCO COUNTY

The information contained in the 1978, 1982, and 1986
master plans is being used to develop an object-oriented
knowledge base and expert system that will describe how
the system was developed including not only the standard
engineering models for doing the hydraulic and economic
analysis but also other relevant attributes of the decision problem.

This section presents the results of our prototype
development of such a system for water supply planning in
Pasco County, Florida - one of sixteen counties within
the boundaries of the Southwest Florida Water Management

District (SWFWMD) as shown in Figure 1. This prototype
model will be expanded to a model for the entire area of
the SWFWMD.

A general schema of this decision-aiding technique is
shown in Figure 2. The knowledge base is structured as
an object-oriented relational database. Object-oriented
data modeling is a recent trend in database management
wherein data modeling and database processing are merged
(Elmasri and Navathe, 1989). For engineering applications, the databases are organized by physical objects.
Thus, as shown in Figure 2, source objects include wells,
springs, and rivers; destination objects are demand centers such as a city; transmission system objects are
pipes, and so forth. Within this context, a water management system is a collection of these objects that has
been extracted from the knowledge base in response to a
query as illustrated in Figure 2 as Supply Alternative I-
1. Decision makers can then query the system to evaluate the performance of this alternative according to
several criteria. The decision model used in this case
uses the criteria shown in Table 2.

While these twelve criteria were used as a guideline
to select the master plan, the actual selection process
is much more involved. The final plan incorporates considerations well beyond these twelve criteria. Thus, the
total number of relevant attributes for each object can
be quite large and contain a mixture of physical, locational, economic, socio-political, environmental and
other properties. For example, an early version of this
model contains 51 attributes of a transmission pipe including hydraulic, physical, economic, environmental, and
other properties as shown in Table 3.

The main lesson learned from setting up this knowledge base is that it is premature to develop closed form
prescriptive planning algorithms in the early phases of
developing planning models. Rather, the initial focus of
the modeling effort should be to archive and record how
decisions have been made so that a realistic calibration
is obtained. This calibration phase provides a valuable
record not only of the selected and proposed alternatives
but also the unsuccessful ones and an explanation of why
they were not selected. Only then will the model have
credibility with the decision makers by capturing the
reality of the process. The early WCRWSA planning efforts did not rely heavily on models. However, they
appear to have done a very careful evaluation of a relatively small number of alternatives and succeeded in
providing a solid foundation for a continuing planning
process.

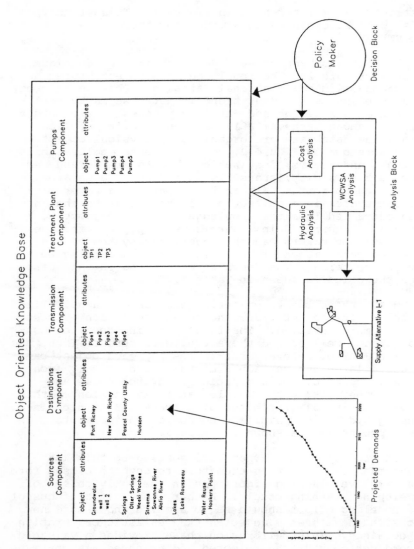

Figure 2. Expert System for Water Supply Planning.

Table 3.   Attributes of an Interconnection in the Network

No	Field name	Description	Field Type
1	Pipe_ID	Pipe identification	Character
2	Maxflow	Maximum pipe flow	Numeric
3	Aveflow	Average pipe flow	Numeric
4	Init_elev	Initial pipe elevation	Numeric
5	Fin_elev	Final pipe elevation	Numeric
6	Peak_elev	Peak pipe elevation	Numeric
7	Rough	Roughness of pipe	Numeric
8	Diameter	Pipe diameter	Numeric
9	g_valves	Number of gate valves	Numeric
10	st_elb	Number of standard elbows	Numeric
11	Msw_elb	Number of medium sweep elbows	Numeric
12	Lsw_elb	Number of long sweep elbows	Numeric
13	Length	Length of pipe	Numeric
14	P_type	Pipe type	Character
15	Land_cost	Cost of land	Numeric
16	Pipe_cost	Cost of pipe	Numeric
17	Exc_depth	Depth of excavation	Numeric
18	Trench_w	Trench width	Numeric
19	Trench_ss	Trench side slope	Numeric
20	Conc_bed	Trench bed is concrete	Logical
21	Peak_pres	Peak pipe pressure	Numeric
22	Hyd_pm	Number of hydrants per mile	Numeric
23	Soil	Soil type	Character
24	Per_open	% excavation in open country	Numeric
25	Per_nres	% excavation in new res.	Numeric
26	Per_sdres	% excavation in sparse res.	Numeric
27	Per_ddres	% excavation in dense res.	Numeric
28	Per_com	% excavation in commercial	Numeric
29	Per_city	% excavation in city	Numeric
30	Des_life	Design life of pipe	Numeric
31	Per_exc	Percent of excavation in rock	Numeric
32	Yr_blt	Year pipe laid	Numeric
33	City	City of pipe	Character
34	County	County of pipe	Character
35	Xcoord1	X coordinate of pipe node 1	Numeric
36	Ycoord1	Y coordinate of pipe node 1	Numeric
37	Xcoord2	X coordinate of pipe node 2	Numeric
38	Xcoord2	Y coordinate of pipe node 2	Numeric
39	Cost_eff	Cost effectiveness	Numeric
40	WSUL	Water supply useful life	Numeric
41	Pub_hth	Public health	Numeric
42	Impact	Environmental impact	Numeric
43	Hydro	Hydrological rating	Numeric
44	Fac_comp	Facility compatibility	Numeric
45	Wat_comp	Water compatibility	Numeric
46	Rely	Reliability	Numeric
47	Energy	Energy consumption	Numeric
48	WM_improve	Pot. for improved management	Numeric
49	Long_comp	Long range plan compat.	Numeric
50	Customers	Ability to serve new cust.	Numeric
51	Owner	Pipeline ownership	Character

FEEDBACK IN WATER PLANNING

Traditional water supply planning models optimize the design for a single "worst case" event. The next level of sophistication is to run a continuous simulation model and find an "optimal" solution over all events of interest. However, these models use static set points and are optimal only for the time series used in the continuous simulation models. Real time control techniques can be used to translate the initial planning level estimates of expected performance into an organized system for evaluating actual performance and using this feedback to improve future planning efforts.

The 1978 Master Plan of the WCRWSA represented the first effort of this new agency in a rapidly growing area. While the planning horizon was to the year 2020, the immediate decisions concerned the next decade. Reaction to the initial master plan is reflected in the 1982 Plan. Also, the 1982 Plan had the benefit of feedback from the actual operation of the system during this four year period. For example, the area of influence of the Cypress Creek Well Field in central Pasco County was estimated based on extensive testing and groundwater modeling. It was placed into production in the late 1970's. Subsequent studies indicate that the original assumptions were too conservative and that the extent   of water table drawdown is much less. This time series information can be entered into the well field knowledge base so that the original planning estimates can be updated accordingly. However, the response time to this new information may be relatively long if the original permit does not expire for a number of years.   This information is relevant not only for the Cypress Creek Well Field but also for similar areas. These facts can be gleaned by querying the knowledge base to learn the cause of the conservative estimate, be it the groundwater model, insufficient calibration data, or other explanatory factor(s).

CURRENT MONITORING ACTIVITIES BY SWFWMD

Supply Monitoring

The primary SWFWMD monitoring network consists of the 300 rain gages, 103 lake stage measurements, streamflow at 14 stations, and 16 surficial aquifer sites and 76 Intermediate and Floridan aquifer sites (SWFWMD, 1989). Data from these monitoring stations provide the basis for deciding whether to impose water shortage restrictions. For example, a "severe" water shortage was declared in the spring of 1985 in response to the following combination of shortages relative to long-term averages: stream-flow-down 81 percent, lake levels-down 1.5 feet, the water table- down 2.0 feet, and the deep aquifer-down 3.4 feet (SWFWMD, 1985).

Demand Monitoring

A major limitation of historical and present water supply planning efforts is lack of databases with measured water use. SWFWMD has made significant improvements in this area. Nevertheless, agricultural water use, the most significant water use in many areas, remains unmeasured. Viessman and Finn (1988) analyzed water use activities by the five water management districts and recommended the following improvements:

"In particular, there is a need for: on-going data collection and interpretation programs; comparisons of actual and permitted withdrawals; projections of water requirements; improved methods for estimating agricultural water use; more attention to water use by transients (tourists), especially as might relate to distinct pricing policies for this sector; better projections of land use for all sectors; improved information on water requirements of environmental systems; improved coordination of programs among districts; and the establishment of a cooperative state-wide water use data base and forecasting system."

SUMMARY AND CONCLUSIONS

An object-oriented database management system is being developed to record the past fifteen years of key information regarding the planned and actual performance of all of the relevant "objects" in the Pasco County water supply system. The objects are all of the existing and proposed physical components of the system such as pipes, pumps, treatment plants, wells, and demand centers. A water management alternative is a collection of these objects that is derived from querying the knowledge base in search of an alternative that satisfies specified conditions.

The prototype model will describe historic and proposed water planning efforts in Pasco County by various branches of government. This prototype model will then be expanded to do a regional water supply evaluation for the entire Southwest Florida Water Management District.

ACKNOWLEDGMENTS

    This effort is part of a state-wide activity to de-
velop a comprehensive water supply plan. As such, the
ideas developed in previous efforts have helped in formulating an approach for this third major attempt at state
water supply planning.

    This work is being sponsored by the Southwest Florida
Water Management District. Mr. Andy Smith of SWFWMD and
Mr. Gene Heath and Mr. Harold Aiken of the West Coast
Regional Water Supply Planning Authority have been very
helpful in providing background information on Pasco
County.

    Lastly, Mr. James Wittig and Ms. Kathleen Tomik,
graduate students in the Department of Environmental
Engineering Sciences at the University of Florida, have
helped develop this prototype model.

References

Camp, Dresser, and McKee. 1982. Regional Water Supply
Needs and Sources 1982-1995 Update Report, Engineering
Report for West Coast Water Supply Authority, Clearwater,
FL.

Camp, Dresser, and McKee. 1986. Regional Water Supply
Needs and Sources: 1985-2020 Update Study, Report for
West Coast Regional Water Supply Authority, Volumes 1
and 2.

Deb, A.K. 1978. Optimization in Design of Pumping Systems, Jour. Envir. Engg. Div. - ASCE, 104:EE1.

Elmasri, R. and S.B. Navathe. 1989. Fundamentals of Database Systems, Benjamin/Cummings Publishing Co., Redwood
City, CA, 802 p.

Florida Board of Conservation. 1966. Florida Land and
Water Resources, Southwest Florida, Tallahassee, FL, 181p

Heaney, J.P., T. Potter, and J. Wittig. 1989. Expert
System for Surface Water Permit Review, Final Report to
South Florida Water Management District, July.

Knowles, L., J.P. Heaney, and M. Shafer. 1989. Expert
System for Evaluating and Notifying Hazardous Waste Generators, Jour. of Computing in Civil Engineering, 3,2, p.
111-126.

Lansey, K.E., and L.W. Mays. 1989. Optimization Model for Water Distribution System Design, Jour. of Hydraulic Engineering, 115, 10, p. 1401-1418.

Lauria, D.J. 1983. Research Needs for Capacity Planning, Jour. American Water Works Association, 75, 1, p. 14-19.

Maher, M.L. ed. 1987. Expert Systems for Civil Engineers: Technology and Application, American Society of Civil Engineers, NY, 148 p.

Ng, E.K. 1986. Efficiency/Equity Analysis of Water Resources Problems--A Game Theoretic Approach, Florida Water Center Report No. 95, U. of Florida, Gainesville, 160 p.

Ng, E.K. and J.P. Heaney. 1989. Efficient Total Enumeration of Water Resources Alternatives, Water Resources Research, Vol. 25, No. 4, p. 583-590.

Payne, S.W. 1988. Efficiency/Equity Analysis of Water Resource Problems, Florida Water Center Report No. 105, U. of Florida, Gainesville, 100 p.

Robinson, R.B. and T. Austin, 1976, Cost Optimization of Rural Water Systems, Jour. Hyd. Division, ASCE: 102, HY8.

Ross, Saarinen, Bolton, and Wilder. 1978. Comprehensive Study of the Regional Water Supply Needs and Sources, 1980-2020, Engineering Report for West Coast Water Supply Authority, Clearwater, FL.

Scarato, R.F. 1969. Time-Capacity Expansion of Urban Water Systems, Water Resources Research, 5,5, p. 926.

Southwest Florida Water Management District. 1977. Water Use Plan, Draft II, Brooksville, FL.

Southwest Florida Water Management District. 1985. Severe Water Shortage Declared, Hydroscope, Spring, p. 1.

Southwest Florida Water Management District. 1989. Annual Report- 1988. Brooksville, Florida, 20 p.

Viessman, Jr., W. and A. Finn. 1988. Water Use Trends and Projections: Their Role in Integrated Water Management, Final Report to SFWMD, Dept. of Environmental Engineering Sciences, U. of Florida, Gainesville.

Wood, D.J. 1981. Algorithms for Pipe Network Analysis and Their Reliability, Research Report No. 127, Water Resources Research Inst., Univ. of Kentucky, Lexington, KY, 96p

Disputes Surrounding 404 Permitting in Colorado

Merle S. Lefkoff, Ph.D.[1]

Abstract

In the Spring of 1987, Albuquerque District of the Corps initiated an Alternative Dispute Resolution (ADR) process in anticipation of conflict over the special conditions of a regional permit for stream modification in El Paso and Teller Counties, Colorado, including the City of Colorado Springs. The process consisted of a series of public meetings to surface concerns, followed by the convening of a task force, carefully selected by the field office in Pueblo to represent all stakeholders in the issue. Personnel from the Corps' regulatory staff acted as facilitator of the first two meetings of the task force. The level of conflict was high, and Corps' staff recognized the need to be removed from the facilitator role in order to represent the Corps' position within the task force. A professional facilitator was hired to guide the process and enhance the possibility for consenses. This case study details that process through the eyes of the facilitator.

Issue Context

The City of Colorado Springs anchors a larger community of regional growth and development in the Front Range of Colorado. While much of the state has been notable in recent years for promotion of environmental values, the City of Colorado Springs has demonstrated a more conservative approach to environmental policy. Many in the city attribute the conservative political climate to the large number of military personnel who have retired there. The City Public Works Department typifies the resistance to change and has held fiercly to traditional

----

[1]President, ARS PUBLICA, Santa Fe, New Mexico, 1450 South St. Francis Drive, Santa Fe, New Mexico 87501.

engineering solutions for accommodating growth and development, often to the detriment of environmental quality. A growing and more vocal environmental constituency has begun to challenge "business as usual," and federal agencies which have responsibility for environmental regulation have become more aggressive in recent years.

For many years, the Public Works Department has implemented a policy of "hard lining" streams to control erosion resulting from the impact of developments. Channelization is also accepted as the preferred solution to the problem of maintaining "historic flow" under Colorado law. Developers like the policy because they don't have to worry about providing expensive grassy areas for flood plain and can build right up to the edge of the concrete channel. But a growing environmental constituency is demanding natural drainage as opposed to concrete, and traditional engineering practices have recently begun to be questioned.

In the years immediately preceding the start of the ADR process, there were numerous environmental conflicts in the city concerning drainage policies. Large developments, in particular, "Corporate Center," "Park Visits" and the "Stetson Hills" project, involved major stream modifications, leading to numerous engineering studies and law suits. Many of the conflicts centered around the competing approaches of the city Public Works Department and the county planners, but environmentalists also demanded to be heard as stakeholders in these conflicts.

Attempts at dispute resolution were typified by the "compromises arrived at during negotiations over a new city drainage criteria manual. The public was not invited to participate in the negotiations, and when the manual was presented to the City Council for approval, it was criticized for being an engineering, rather than a policy document; that is, the real conflicts were not resolved by the publication of the document.

Prior to convening the ADR process, the city was repeatedly embroiled in controversies with federal agencies involving permits for streambed jobs, because the city's criteria differed from federal guidelines. Federal agencies with overlapping interests in drainage issues were also in growing conflict with one another. Most disturbing for the Corps, as they continued to grant 404 permits for stream modification which involved hard lining, loss of wetlands and loss of aesthetic values, was

the specter of an angry EPA, which threatened to shut down
the permitting process for some time by taking the Corps
to court on the issue of cumulative impact.

While the issues of drainage policies, erosion
control, stream modification and flooding captured public
attention periodically, the issues served mainly to
highlight and symbolize the pressing public interest in
environmental quality in the Pikes Peak region. The
issues also highlighted an archetypal stand-off between
those in traditional power centers defending the status
quo and those emerging to challenge both the old
institutions and the old agendas.

Description of Process

In November 1986, the Corps' Pueblo office convened
several public meetings to surface concerns in
anticipation of a regional permit approach to streamlining
the 404 permitting process. The meetings resulted in a
long list of concerns which formed the basis for selection
of a broadly-based citizen task force to help resolve the
apparent conflicts surrounding the issues over stream
modification. The task for the new committee was to
negotiate conditions for a regional permit for stream
modification, based on consideration of the citizen
concerns surfaced at the public meetings.

The first two task force meetings were difficult and
conflicts surfaced quickly. Virtually no one at the table
had met in discussions of the issues in the past, except
in one-on-one or crisis-oriented, confrontational
meetings. The Corps' facilitator was attempting to
advocate for a regional permit, represent the Corps'
interests and facilitate the meetings, all at the same
time. Predictably, the meetings degenerated to the point
that a third meeting of the task force seemed unlikely.

A professional neutral facilitator was hired at that
point to attempt to get the task force on track. The
District Engineer, in response to conflict at the first
two meetings, had drawn up a list of the Corps' "non-
negotiable demands" and insisted that the next meeting of
the task force start from there.

The facilitator met with the regional office staff
and was impressed with the careful attention paid to
choosing task force members. Twenty-two participants were
appointed, and the Corps sought a balanced group with all
stakeholders present. After discussions, the facilitator
decided on the following course of action for the process:

1. A meeting with the District Engineer pointed out that it might be counter-productive to start the next task force meeting with a list of "non-negotiable" items. The feeling was that as convener of the process, the Corps was there to participate and listen, not make demands. An agreement was reached to abandon the list of demands and accept the consensus of the task force on the permit conditions (as long as they did not violate federal law).

2. The facilitator decided to use a "one-text process," an iterative process which allows a group to build consensus around a written document (beginning with a "straw man" draft) because: (a) a continuing critique of what would become the permit, itself, would be an aid to surfacing issues and underlying interests; (b) the "hard liners" on the task force were likely to be those with the most technical backgrounds, and this process works well for them since it involves precise wording and detail; and (c) the Corps was willing to provide excellent staff support in the arduous task of revising the text each time.

3. Continuing monthly meetings for several hours after work and before supper also appeared to work well for maximum participation. The time in between allowed for turnaround of the text without losing momentum, and more frequent meetings would probably have lost some task force members, who were donating their time. No time constraints were placed on the process until about the eighth meeting, when the process appeared to be nearing completion.

4. At the first meeting with the task force, the facilitator did a little "in-house" training, explaining the difference between positional and interest-based bargaining. Participants were asked to help the facilitator "catch up" with the issues by brainstorming a list which looked like this:

Uniformity in permitting -- shortening the process

Improve Monument Creek

Improved access to recreation

Local review

Fish and wildlife

Fewer individual permits

Public input on an ongoing basis (oversight)

Well-functioning drainage system

Consistency in approach

Cost-effective, but flexible criteria which maintains quality of life and economic development

Manageable guidelines

Environmental quality -- streams

Equity between environmental quality and economic development

Uniformity in engineering criteria as regards aesthetics

Riparian habitat

5.   The need for a "shared intent" not only to come to the table, but to want to solve a problem, is critical in this kind of a process. The facilitator felt that this stage had been bypassed in the earlier meetings, and determined to spend as much time as necessary getting a buy-in for resolution from all the task force members. In order to help establish this willingness to try to reach a resolution of the issues, each task force member was asked to submit a list of individual goals for the process, appended to their first mark-up of the working draft permit. As expected, most addressed their goals in terms of the permit, rather than the process. These were shared with the whole group. The facilitator also shared her own process goals with the group, assuring them that a permit would not be issued if a consensus -- not unanimity -- were not found. Later the facilitator helped the group reach agreement on a shared set of goals for the permit, which were as follows:

     -- To streamline the permitting process for non-controversial projects;

     -- To protect or enhance existing environmental values while providing for health, safety and general welfare;

     -- To encourage cross-disciplinary, basin-wide planning and management of basins;

     -- To encourage permit consideration at an early stage of project planning;

-- To encourage local participation and administration of the regional permit; and

-- To have ongoing review and enforcement of authorized activities and the permitting process.

6. The facilitator made very specific assignments of tasks and "homework" in between task force meetings. Some members were asked to work together on items which needed new wording to be brought to the next meeting. For example, one member early submitted a list of endangered species for the area, and another group of three participants reported to the full committee on submittal, review and reporting requirements. The work was reported both verbally to the full committee and in written form as "Working Papers" for everyone to have in hand during the task force meetings. These assignments substituted for the use of caucuses during the meetings because the feeling was that the whole group needed to work together to define the underlying interests. While "public recording" (newsprint notes hung around the room for group reference) was used as a facilitation tool during the meetings, minutes based on the tear sheets were augmented by notes taken by a group secretary.

7. Because the level of conflict was very high, particularly at the beginning, a technique which asked participants to restate what they had just heard was frequently used. If people know that they will be asked to restate the position of someone with whom they are in disagreement, they are forced to listen and feed back in an understanding manner. It is a simple, but very powerful, technique when discussion gets heated.

8. The facilitator played cheerleader more than usual, complimenting the group when they began to surface and discuss underlying interests and reminding them of how important the work they were undertaking would be to the future of the region. As the group began to trust the dialogue process and disclose agendas, they were complimented on their growing level of trust with one another.

9. Particular attention was paid to noting, clarifying and reinforcing agreement. Disagreements were not discounted, but agreements were definitely reinforced. This technique is essential to the discovery of the sense of the group," which is what good facilitators are always looking for.

10. The facilitator bent over backwards to "empower" the participants from the Colorado Springs Public Works

Department, who felt that their policies were under siege
-- and they were! -- by other task force members,
especially those representing environmental
constituencies. Frequent deference was paid to the
communications from the public works representatives,
which were carefully recorded and reframed, giving them
opportunity to respond to attacks.

     11. The public works representatives tried to seat
the City Attorney at the table late in the process. The
facilitator shared her feelings that it would be a
violation of the task force intent to allow attorneys
representing stakeholders to sit at the table at this
point in a non-adversarial, consensus-building process.
The attorney agreed to be seated away from the table and
to take questions from the task force members as needed.

     In addition to continued resistance to the process
from a beleaguered Public Works Department, other actions
of key actors influenced the process and the process
outcomes. Those participants representing environmental
interests, including some local and state officials,
quickly coalesced as a sub-group with the committee, which
forced the public works folks into a defensive posture.
EPA and the Corps, traditional adversaries over the
issuance of 404 permits, found themselves in more
agreement over environmental criteria than they would have
supposed, lending support to the environmental side of the
table. The League of Women Voters representative assumed
a cautious, mediation role within the group, assisting
them in moderating the dialogue as the process progressed.
And the "business representatives," including the Home
Builders Association, surprised their historic
environmental foes with both their willingness to listen
and their artful presentation of the issues.

Issues, Positions and Interests of Key Actors

     For purposes of analysis, key actors in the process
may be grouped in the following way:

     1. The Army Corps of Engineers

     2. The U. S. EPA

     3. Environmentalists (including federal and state
wildlife representatives and citizen groups)

     4. Developers

     5. Local and county planners and engineers

6. City of Colorado Springs Public Works Department

The Army Corps took a neutral position in terms of the permit conditions and the issues under discussion, although the Corps was clearly in favor of the permit, itself. The Corps had several interests, though, which should be stated: neutralizing EPA's threat to bring the Corps to court on cumulative impact; avoiding elevation of the permit from either EPA or U. S. Fish and Wildlife; and getting a handle on the issues and where the balanced public interest lay in terms of streamlining the permitting process. As the process proceeded, there was also a sense that another underlying interest of the Corps -- unstated except by inference -- was to give notice to the City of Colorado Springs that business as usual could no longer be tolerated in a regulatory framework. This last interest developed into a shared consensus of the task force and, indeed, was acknowledged in the Permit Evaluation and Decision Document as follows:

"Many of the task force members were intensely dissatisfied with the way the COE and various local governments were handling drainage issues. About half (I believe it was more) of the task force members felt that sending a message to the entities who governed drainages was a valid purpose of the regional permit and was still needed. (p. 26, CWSWA-CO-R, CO-OYT-0423)

A traditional rivalry with the Army Corps resulting from the shared 404 permitting responsibility brought the EPA to the table reluctant to trust the concept of a regional permit. But as the dialogue progressed, and trust in the process itself began to take hold, the EPA entered the negotiations with gusto, taking a variety of positions favoring strict environmental controls. Water quality and water supply issues and issues of biological character and change were paramount. An important issue seemed to be the use of refuse, old tires, construction debris, etc., for use as protection against erosion, common practice in the past. As expected, cumulative impact was a big issue for EPA. At the time of the ADR process, EPA was in litigation against the City of Colorado Springs and shared the underlying interest of "sending a message" to the city.

Three "citizen representatives" were appointed to the task force, and each took strong positions in terms of environmental quality. Combined with the two "environmental" representatives, the Colorado Division of Wildlife, U. S. Fish and Wildlife and various municipal interests which joined the "environmental side" at different points in the process, the task force comprised

an unusual balance of environmental and traditional
engineering and development interests. The absence of
trust for local jurisdiction over drainage ways was
quickly evident, and one of the issues was how to insure
federal control and oversight of the regional permit, with
local administration. Another issue was the lack of trust
due to the absence of citizen participation in land-use
decisions. Preservation of habitat and mitigation were
the issues emerging from the position for more natural
stream regimes. But the underlying interest, once again,
was stated well by one of the "environmentalists" in
response to the facilitator's request for written goals:
"Create an attitude change that indicates that aesthetics
and environmental preservation are important."

The developers were consistent in articulating their
one basic issue: reconcile the conflict between the local
jurisdictions' philosophy, policies and criteria with the
goals, policies and regulations of state and federal
environmental agencies who have jurisdiction over the 404
permitting process. Their position was that the conflicts
were causing them intolerable delays. If the issues
surrounding this conflict could be addressed and the
disputes resolved, it would meet the underlying interest
of the business and development community for a timely and
less expensive permitting process.

Another important issue which the developers had was
that large as well as small projects could be developed
under the regional permit. Without this assurance, there
was concern that the permit would not be useful. This
interest that the permit be usable was in direct
contradiction to an interest of the environmentalists and
EPA that the permit be designed to minimize environmental
impacts only on minor projects, keeping open the option to
take a closer look at the larger projects on an individual
basis. The basic interest of the developers for a useful,
streamlined process was at odds with the bottom line
environmental preservation interest of the
environmentalists.

The local and county planners and engineers, while
not monolithic in their thinking, were trying to meet
local concerns for more aesthetic stream channels, while
providing adequate flood control and erosion control
without increased engineering costs. So their issues were
quality of life, safety and keeping costs down. They took
strong positions against the too stringent limiting of
authorized permitting activities when they thought these
might slow down development or cost local jurisdictions
more money, but their real interest appeared to lie in
finding a way to appease a growing environmental

constituency in suburban areas under heavy pressure from growth and development.

The City of Colorado Springs appeared to be uncomfortable at the table from the beginning of the process. The city could not reasonably be expected to take a position that decades of engineering activities had been detrimental to the environmental quality of Colorado Springs. Instead, they positioned themselves quickly as the defenders of past and present policies.

The most important issue was the integrity of the city's local zoning ordinances and drainage criteria. The underlying interest was retaining historic power over drainage decisions and maintaining the status quo. To quote from a letter to the Corps from the City Engineer "From my perspective, there were no compromises ... only minor movement away from strict environmental issues. No consideration was given to the requirements of the local ordinances." (February 11, 1988) From another earlier letter: "At best, the proposed regional permit is an exercise in paperwork and construction by committee which accomplishes nothing. At worst, it represents an unsuccessful and highly objectionable attempt to intrude on the domain of local land use authority." (September 9, 1987)

As the task force proceeded to draft an environmentally-sensitive permit which was in direct conflict with the city drainage ordinances, in order to meet what had become a commonly held interest by many on the task force to "send a message" to the city, the city began to shift its strategy to damage control. At one point, the city drafted an alternate permit and presented it to the Corps on their own, stating:

"The City Engineer's version addresses the construction techniques in a manner which can be accepted into today's drainageway management procedures, while at the same time addressing the protection of (the environment)."

Only late in the process when, after almost a year of meetings, the city began to understand the depth of resistance among a broad constituency represented at the table to the historic and present drainageway practices, and began to offer some concessions. Some on the task force suggested to the city that an ultimate solution to the conflicts was not a regional permit, but an "updating" of the City of Colorado Springs' 21 basin plans, a revision which would involve public participation and integrate the environmental interests reflected by the

growing community consensus. The city seized on this idea
to slow down the building consensus on the permit,
suggesting some "compromises" which in the end were
unacceptable to the remainder of the task force. As the
end of the ADR process approached, no one on the task
force has offered a creative way to meet the interest of
the city to preserve local land-use controls and also
issue the regional permit. Unfortunately, if the local
ordinances could not be reconciled with federal
imperatives, there was also no way to meet the interest of
the developers in a coordinated, streamlined process.

The Outcome

     First, the apparent bad news, to quote from the
Permit Evaluation and Decision Document:

"(e) The comments received at the 14 December public
hearing represent two views: that the proposed regional
permit is valuable because of its environmental
considerations and should be issued, and that the proposed
regional permit is unworkable and conflicts with local
MDPs and should not be issued. ... The ... process may
have aided the general public in their formulation process
of consensus, but it would not determine the final
outcome. ..." (p. 48)

     This is a very honest, very succinct analysis of the
final outcome of this ADR process. At the end, the task
force was divided: the City of Colorado Springs remained
opposed to the permit, which was in conflict with their
local basin plans; and they were joined by the developers
for whom the permit was not much use, since the original
conflict remained and the permit only applied to small
projects.

     But there is good news, as well, in terms of the
outcome. The permit was issued. No law suits have been
filed. The permit was not elevated. The City of Colorado
Springs has promised to revise its basin-wide planning
process, using citizen input and looking at environmental
criteria in a new way. They have, in fact, set up a
Citizen Advisory Committee for the first time, to move in
these directions, and initial meetings have been held.
Some members of this committee were people on the ADR task
force who, through dialogue, built a trusting relationship
with the public works representatives. The city is also
willing to allow the Corps to be part of their process, an
important outcome of the process. EPA and the Corps built
a new working relationship on several levels as the result
of the meetings. And, finally, the environment of the
region has benefited directly. Under the new permit,

which will be used by surrounding communities, if not by
developers in the city, there will be less hard-lining,
and no net loss of wetlands and habitat.

"The city intends to restudy the most urgent master
drainage basins in 1988 and incorporate into the basin
study environmental issues in an attempt to mitigate the
environmental concerns of the 404 requirements. ... I wish
to work with your staff in developing these master
drainage basin restudies so that we can eliminate as many
of these conflicts as possible. I also am intending to
work with the local citizen groups through the planning
study revisions so that I can assemble a good measure of
input from these groups. ..." (Letter from Gary R.
Haynes, City of Colorado Springs Engineer to Lt. Col. Kent
R. Gonser, February 10, 1988)

A public hearing on the permit was requested by the
city, and the District Engineer pointed out that neither
the task force process nor the permit, itself, was
intended to tell the city "how you wish to develop your
community. ... That's kind of your business, and I'm not
going to get into that." (Proceedings, Public Hearing
Regarding Application No. CO-OYT-0423, p. 27) But in
fact, ADR processes often encourage a community of
individuals to grapple with those very basic issues, and
the regulation under consideration becomes a secondary
consideration at best.

As one of the task force participants stated at the
public hearing:

"We spent a lot of time (on the permit issues), but
they are not the true issue. I think the true issue is
the purpose statement. ... It took us months to come up
with that purpose statement. I believe the citizens ...
involved in the task force thought that that purpose
statement was a victory in itself because we felt that
environmental concerns were not being addressed in the
local community, and the purpose statement gave that to
us. ..." (Proceedings, p. 19)

In a letter to EPA, another task force participant
provided a final summary:

"COE and its task force developed a ... permit which
... was not acceptable to the city. ... However, the task
force did strike a bargain concerning all future basin
plans including the three that will be re-studied
beginning this year. Wildlife habitat, recreational
potential and aesthetic considerations will become

integral to the basin planning process.   The goal is to
secure a 404 permit for each of the 22 basins in the urban
area and draft a General Permit covering small projects
for the balance of the COE study area.   In my view, the
above   agreement   is   a   landmark   event   of   lasting
significance. ..."   (Letter from John Covert to Gene
Reetz, January 8, 1988)

Some Final Thoughts on the Process

    Third-party intervenors who assist parties to reach
resolution in a public dispute often do not have the
opportunity to design the process from the beginning.   For
example, they may be brought in late after positions have
hardened.   This was the case here, where intervention
began after a process was already in motion.   As Carpenter
and Kennedy have pointed out:

    "In   the   complexity   and   uncertainty   of   public
disputes, the more attention given at the beginning to
preparing a conflict management program, the better the
chances of a successful outcome.   The preparation stage
involves all the activities that occur prior to bringing
parties together for face-to-face discussion."   (Managing
Public Disputes, Jossey-Bass, 1988, p. 68)

    Even though neutral third-party assistance was late,
however, the process that emerged resulted in a powerful
and positive outcome for the future of the city and the
way it plans for protection of its resources.   The issues
were ripe for discussion in a new forum; there was a broad
range of detailed technical issues involving engineering
criteria which were available for tradeoffs; there were a
manageable number of actors involved in the process; and
a consensus emerged that the status quo would have to
change in light of new environmental realities.

    Power at the table was perhaps more equal than it had
ever been in a public dialogue in Colorado Springs.
Citizen representatives felt empowered by the process in
a new way.   However, because the outrage of the growing
environmental constituency pervaded the discussion, the
city did not feel either procedural or substantive, and
certainly not psychological satisfaction.   They felt that
it had been unfair not to allow their attorney at the
table.   They thought that they had offered a "compromise"
which would allow the permit to go forward exempting the
City of Colorado Springs (no one else on the task force
remembers agreeing to the "compromise" and there is no
record of such in the minutes).   The developers certainly
felt no substantive satisfaction or ownership in a permit
which substituted stricter, more expensive environmental

criteria for a less restrictive nationwide permit, and
which neither applied to larger projects, nor streamlined
the process.

One of the most important outcomes, as expected in
all similar processes, was the opportunity for mutual
education. The new advisory committee to the city on the
drainage plans updating is concrete (excuse the pun)
evidence that the city -- while defiant to the end -- has
learned much. New alliances and communication networks
have been formed at several levels. And participants
learned much about the way human relationships mature in
an atmosphere of candid discourse and mutual respect.

THE CHANGING ROLE OF THE ENGINEER IN INTERSTATE WATER DISPUTES: FROM DESIGNER TO MANAGER

Charles T. DuMars
University of New Mexico
School of Law[1]

ABSTRACT

The role of the engineer in water matters has perhaps more traditionally been that of a problem solver involved in the construction of irrigation works such as dams and reservoirs. That role has changed, and, in the future, engineers must become an integral part of the water management process. The days of the great new water project are probably gone. In its place, management is paramount. In interstate water issues we can see the merger of the policy/engineer role. The Pecos River Compact is a case in point that graphically shows the complexity of this new role.

INTRODUCTION

Beginning with the Desert Land Act of 1877 and through the Reclamation Act of 1902, the policy of the federal government was consistently to promote water development by harnessing the untamed rivers of the West. The rivers in their natural state brought a paradox of feast or famine. In the spring they rushed bank full with great momentum down the hillsides toward their outlet. By midsummer, however, they were reduced to a non-usable trickle. The solution to this problem

---

[1] Professor of Law, University of New Mexico, School of Law, 1117 Stanford, N.E. Albuquerque, New Mexico, 87131

was reservoir construction. These reservoirs could regulate the flow and provide usable quantities of irrigation water throughout the growing season. The federal government in partnership with the states promoted these projects and provided funding through the familiar local irrigation or conservancy district created under state law. Many projects, however, were even more grandiose, involving construction of reservoirs on the greatest of rivers thirsty growing cities. The canal systems across the great deserts of California and into the center of Arizona are other examples of engineering accomplishments.

The desire to "Make the desert bloom" sometimes caused decision-makers in Washington to look the other way when cost/benefit ratios were being measured and produced substantial federal subsidies in the form of low interest and long pay back periods. Nevertheless, the projects were completed and have provided substantial benefits throughout the West. These projects, and their private counterparts, use approximately 70% of the water in the Western United States.

During the administration of President Carter, however, the bubble of federally developed water development projects burst, probably to never rise again in the grandiose form it has known in the past. New projects are unlikely for a number of reasons. First, there are not a large number of realistic sites available, and second, the competition for federal dollars has grown to the point at which projects with questionable cost/benefit ratios can no longer compete. The States must come up with local matching funds and these are not often forthcoming. The net result has been that there has been a great push to ensuring that existing projects operate efficiently. This concept is rarely understood, or at least understood differently by different persons who use the term.

For example, an agricultural scientist might evaluate a project and determine that the project is efficient because it is consuming the minimum amount of water because of laser leveling techniques and an optimum system for ensuring the maximum return flows to the river. An economist, on the other hand, might evaluate the same project and conclude that it is not efficient at all because it is not growing the crops that could return the maximum return on the investment. An ornithologist might conclude that the project is inefficient because the highest and best use for the land would be a wetlands for rare birds that need to be protected for the enjoyment of future generations.

The issues discussed above probably come under some general definition of project management. If the politics of today are a predictor of the future, the Engineer's of the future are not going to be involved in constructing new projects, but aiding in the management of existing ones. It is one thing to calculate irrigation efficiency in the abstract and return on investment of projects before they are constructed. Who, after all, can prove a prediction wrong before it comes to pass? It is another, however, to take the vagaries of an existing river system on which a project is constructed and work with tangible on the ground materials to achieve a result. When a project is being constructed, one can talk in the abstract about "externalities" such as environmental objections, political pressures and lack of understanding. It is quite another to guide a project through such a mine field after it is constructed.

Perhaps nowhere is the marriage of engineering and water management more difficult than in the interstate allocation of water resources. To avoid shouldering the responsibility for error, engineering choices are often masked as policy and policy choices are masked as engineering. A full understanding of this concept requires an evaluation of the methodology employed for allocating water between states.

If a river begins in one state and passes into another downstream of it, the interstate management issue is joined. Some questions that immediately arise include the following:

1.   Does the fact the water originates in one state mean that the downstream state has no right to it?

2.   Does the first state to put the water to beneficial use have a better right?

3.   Do the relative efficiencies of existing projects in the two competing states dictate who has the better right?

4.   Does water conservation play a role? Why should one state conserve if the fruits of its conservation will only aid the downstream state.

5.   What about non-economic values in water, are they entitled to weight?

These factors are of course only a few of the diverse set of questions that arise in interstate water circumstances. Since wars between the states are not permitted under the United States Constitution, only three different institutional contexts are available to answer these questions. Congressional acts may apportion the water between the States. The Supreme Court itself may make the decision in the exercise of its original jurisdiction or the states with the approval of congress may enter into a compact to apportion the river.

In the case of congressional apportionment, engineer's play a critical role in developing the studies for projects that form the basis for the apportionment. These apportionments are rare and occur only as an adjunct to a proposed project as in the case of the Boulder Canyon Project Act or the Animas-La Plata project.

Equitable apportionment decisions are often made by the judiciary outside the context of a particular project. While the engineers play an important role, it is not as direct as in the case of congressional apportionment.

In the context of compact drafting and adoption, the role of the engineer has been paramount. First, many of the Western States traditionally have required that the chief water administrator be a professional engineer. These "State Engineers" have often served as the chief negotiator for the state and as the principal designers of the water compacts. These individuals, along with chief legal counsel in water matters for the states, have hammered out many of the various compacts in the West.

Actual operation of the compacts have, as mentioned above, married the role of engineer and policy manager in a series of extraordinarily complex ways. A few of the policy/engineering issues that must immediately be considered in compact cases include the following:

Most compacts require delivery of a specific amount of water at the border. To achieve delivery of the specified amount, one must regulate wells extracting stream related groundwater. If the well is a great distance from the river, the impacts may not be felt for fifty to one hundred years. To what degree should these impacts be regulated? Is an impact that will not occur in one hundred years, one which should be con-sidered so distant as to be non-existent? Should the problem of stream overdraft be shifted to future generations? The quantum of the overdraft is an engineering question and whether it should be allowed is a policy question. The questions cannot, however, be answered separately. To answer the second question, issues of probability arise which also turn on engineering issues.

What is the engineering feasibility in the future of designing imported water conveyance systems to replace the groundwater impacts? What is the possibility of removing phreatophytes to replace water taken from the system and of creating a river channel lined with rock? What is the possibility of shifting to less consumptive irrigation systems or pumping water back into the river from the pumps that have begun to draw surface water from the stream? All of these are questions of engineering feasibility and policy bound together. The person who makes them (the engineer of the future) must understand both the technical complexity of the issues and the full breadth of their policy implications.

For example, if extensive groundwater pumping is allowed in a stream-related aquifer, the water table will drop and the phreatophytes may die as a direct result of the dewatering of the basin. However, this loss of phreatophytes may have great implications for the bee-keepers and will undoubtedly be of concern to the fish who no longer have sufficient flow in-stream. In addition, the very irrigation pumpers who are dewatering the aquifer may find that their extensive pumping has caused their drains to cease to work properly and that salt loading may occur because of the failure of the land to drain properly.

Thus, in interstate water management, delivery of a quantity of water at the border is an incredibly complex combination of engineering and policy issues inextricably intertwined. The Pecos River Compact provides an excellent example of this phenomena.

The Pecos river rises in the north-central mountains of New Mexico and flows southward for 435 miles in New Mexico until it joins the Rio Grande 320 miles into Texas near Comstock, Texas. The river can be divided into three basins. The Upper Basin comprised of the headwaters and tributaries above Alamogordo Reservoir. The middle basin is comprised of the portion of the river that flows from Alamogordo Reservoir to the New Mexico-Texas state line. The Lower Basin, consists of the river drainage in Texas, and extends from Red Bluff Reservoir, which regulates the river in Texas, to the

Rio Grande. The annual flow of the Pecos is largely composed of flash flood water. This water carries a large quantity of topsoil that contributes to the declines in reservoir capacity by silting and increases the salinity of the water in the lower reaches of the river. After it leaves the mountains, the Pecos may be completely dry for a period of weeks as it makes its way through Central New Mexico. Groundwater aquifers supply much of the Pecos in the middle reach. The flow received by Texas varies greatly as a function of beneficial consumption in New Mexico, evaporation, precipitation and phreatophyte consumption resulting in transpiration into the air.

The Pecos River Compact grew out of New Mexico and Texas' hope to equitably divide the river and increase water conservation. Although a commission was appointed in the early 1920's and a compact was drafted, it was vetoed by New Mexico's governor. Real negotiations did not start again until 1939 when an engineering study committee provided new data. A second compact commission authorized a study of the river and a manual of inflow-outflow methods of measuring changes in streamflow depletion was developed. This engineering study called the (Inflow-Outflow) manual formed the basis for the Pecos River Compact which was signed by the states and ultimately approved by the Congress in 1949.

The purposes of the compact include to equitably divide and apportion the use of the river's waters; to encourage interstate harmony and prevent controversies; to protect development existing within the states; to facilitate construction for water salvaging, efficient water use, and flood protection. Provisions of the Compact designate methods and means for apportionment of flood waters and salvaged water. Most importantly, however, the compact allocates a share of water for New Mexico and a share to Texas.

Compacts make these allocations in various ways. They can allocate a flat amount of water to the lower basin, such as 7.5 million acre feet, which is the amount contained in the Colorado River Compact. Or, they can allocate a percentage of the annual flow, as in the case of the Upper Colorado River Compact. Compacts can contain debit and credit provisions (can arrive at a method of allowing the down stream state to incur water debts from the upstream states) as in the case of the Rio Grande Compact, or they can be silent. The Pecos River Compact contains no debit and credit provision and it allocates the water in a manner that is an engineer's nightmare. The compact simply states that

New Mexico shall not deplete by man's activities the flow of the Pecos River at the New Mexico-Texas state line below an amount which will give to Texas a quantity of water equivalent to that available to Texas under the 1947 condition. Man's activities is defined as man's beneficial consumptive use of water in New Mexico.

The compact was fatally flawed from the start. First, it has three compact commissioners - one from Texas, one from New Mexico and one U.S. commissioner. The U.S. commissioner has no vote. Thus, there was no way to have a majority rule on any disputed issue. Second, while the compact clearly provided that it wished New Mexico to deliver the same amount of water as it was delivering in 1947 (under like conditions of withdrawal), it did not state whether it meant the withdrawals were to be measured on January 1, 1947 or December 31, 1947. The differences are substantial. Third, the method for calculating impacts in the Inflow-Outflow model was incorrect, but formed the basis for the calculations of delivery for the first 15 years of the compacts operation. Fourth, the compact made no reference to credits or debits, so the parties could not agree whether mistaken delivery amounts under the incorrect Inflow-Outflow model could have accrued a debt against New Mexico in favor of Texas. Fifth, the language depletion by man's activities is an extraordinarily difficult quantity to calculate affirmatively. The computer model developed calculates "man's activities" by what is known in logic class as the classic fallacy of affirming the antecedent. "If the river is providing less water than under the 1947 condition and it is not phreatophytes, evaporation, or channel loss,it must therefore be man's activities."

When the original error in calculation was discovered fifteen years into the compacts operation, a new inflow-outflow manual was drafted. However, Texas argued the original (although erroneous) method should be used to calculate shortfalls by New Mexico, therefore, New Mexico owed them 1.1 million acre feet of water. New Mexico argued the erroneous method should be rejected even though it formed the basis of the compact and the correct method should be used. Under the new inflow-outflow manual, the amount of shortfall was only 53,000 acre-feet. Texas filed suit in the mid 1970's and the Supreme Court made a number of rulings. A few of these included a holding that the Supreme Court would not solve the problem of political gridlock by appointing a tie breaker to join with either New Mexico or Texas or any vote that came up. It did, however, resolve the issue as to the date from which the 1947 condition was to be calculated. Furthermore, it found that the shortfall should be measured by the correct engineering methodology and that the error in the first manual was not a part of the compact. This left the following question: If the river has been in a short-fall circumstance, how much of the shortfall was due to "man's activities?" This obviously was key since any non-man's activities shortfalls were not caused by New Mexico and New Mexico owed no debt on these amounts.

The case was remanded to a special master who found the following: First, even though the compact did not contain any debit or credit provisions, these should be implied and New Mexico could owe, in effect, a water debt. Second, the proper method for calculating man's activities was to follow the methodology offered by a computer model developed by engineer's for Texas. This model accounted inter alia for evaporation, carriage loss, transpiration and other non-man's activities. Therefore, if the shortfall exceeded these, it must be due to man's activities. Using this method, the special master found New Mexico had under-delivered 340,100 acre-feet of water over the previous 34 year period and New Mexico would have to pay this back. He also found that in the future, after a three year grace period, New Mexico would have to increase its deliveries by 10,000 acre feet a year to avoid future shortfalls. He sug-gested "water interest" be charged to New Mexico if she were delinquent in the future. In calculating the shortfall, he did conclude that New Mexico should be given credit for lands taken out of irrigation since 1947 and under the new manual, when there were excess deliveries, New Mexico would be given credit.

The Supreme Court upheld the special master's rulings as to the implied debits and credits but remanded for a hearing on whether the shortfall could be paid in dollars rather than water. At a subsequent hearing the parties took widely varying positions as to how much cash would have to be paid in lieu of water to compensate for Texas loss. New Mexico testimony sug-gested a range of six million dollars, whereas Texas argued for an amount in the range of from fifty million to close to a billion if New Mexico farmers were forced to disgorge all of their profits allegedly made from the use of water that should have been delivered to Texas. The parties settled the case prior to a decision by the special master for a total of $14 million.

One of the results of the litigation has been the appointment of a river master who will deal with the issue of how New Mexico will make up the additional

10,000 acre-acre feet of estimated future annual shortfalls. New Mexico faces the problem that it follows the
prior appropriation doctrine. Under this rule, (incorporated expressly in the compact), the junior water
rights must be retired first to offset any compact
shortfall. The junior rights are far upstream from the
border, such that it takes seven acre-feet of water to
deliver one at the border. Retiring these upstream
rights is a very unattractive prospect for New Mexico.
Alternatively, New Mexico could perhaps buy rights in
New Mexico near the border and retire them, but these
are extraordinarily productive lands. Ironically,
between the New Mexico border and the irrigation
district where Texas users use the water, there is a
naturally occurring brine inflow and extensive carriage
loss, estimated at between fifty-five and seventy
percent. Thus, complying with the compact could mean an
extremely high net loss in irrigation efficiency in the
region. It would mean taking out the most productive
lands to support the least productive.

An even more serious problem may remain. The Pecos
is a very pernicious river that can perplex mathe-
maticians with its flood flows. For example, between
1940 and 1941, without any change in man's activities,
there was an over delivery of 28,100 acre feet. Furthermore, the river seems to over deliver in trends.
For the past five years since the Supreme Court decision, the river has over delivered, but no one seriously
argues that "man's activities" have created this over
delivery. Yet, under the manual, New Mexico is given
credit. But what if the trend swings the other way? In
the fourteen year period from 1919-1932 (12 three-year
mean periods), the accumulated shortfall was approximately 90,000 acre feet. However, from 1933 through
1946, the accumulated credits amounted to 114,000 acre
feet.

What these numbers show is that while Texas and New
Mexico may have entered into a compact and agreed to use
"man's activities" as a measure of the river's annual
variations, the river never signed. Thus, notwithstand-
ing some excellent engineering work by experts from both
states, the initial standard for measurement given the
engineers may be a completely unworkable one.

CONCLUSION

The Pecos River Compact demonstrates beyond perad-
venture that the engineering problems of today are
inextricably tied to problems of river management. If

the Pecos River Compact is ultimately redrafted, engineers must ultimately be involved in arriving at a standard which fits the tools they have available to them. If New Mexico must make the hard choices to deliver by removing some existing uses, engineers must be involved in the choices relating to on-farm and basin-wide efficiency. The engineering tasks of the future will not be constructing new works, but helping policy makers decide mixed questions of a technical and policy nature.

REFERENCES

Texas v. New Mexico, 421 U.S.927 (1975)

Texas v. New Mexico, 423 U.S. 942 (1975)

Texas v. New Mexico, 462 U.S. 554 (1983)

Texas v. New Mexico, 467 U.S. 1238 (1984)

Texas v. New Mexico, 482 U.S. 1284) (1987)

Pecos River Compact, N.M. Stat. Ann. § 72-15-19 (Supp. 1978)

Congressional Ratification of Pecos River Compact Act of June 9, 1949, Ch. 184, Pub. L. No. 81-91, 63 Stat. 159 (1949)

LINKED MODELS FOR INDIAN WATER RIGHTS DISPUTES

William B. Lord[1], Mary G. Wallace[2],
and Rose M. Shillito[3]

ABSTRACT

Information is a key factor in the resolution of water-related disputes. The type of information required depends upon the type of conflict involved, whether over facts, social values, or interest impacts. Formal models are efficient means of organizing and analyzing information.

INTRODUCTION

Although not the only requisite for success, "better information" is often a key factor in the resolution of water-related disputes. But what is better information, and how can it be used for dispute resolution? In this paper we will attempt to deal with these issues, both conceptually and through presenting a case study. Our approach employs linked models for producing the kinds of information which may be strategic to dispute resolution efforts.

We begin by observing that the type of information needed depends upon the type or types of conflict which lie at the heart of the dispute. Lord (1979) identified three types of conflict. The first, social value conflict, occurs when the disputants hold and pursue different, or differently weighted, social values. The second, interest conflict, is also a conflict over values, but in this case the values are the more utilitarian ones concerned with the direct receipt of goods and services by the disputants themselves. The third, cognitive conflict, is disagreement about the facts of the case. It is concerned with the beliefs of the disputants,

----

[1,2,3,] Director and Research Assistants respectively, Water Resources Research Center, The University of Arizona, Geology Building, Room 318, Tucson AZ 85721

Research supported by the U.S. Geological Survey, Department of the Interior, under USGS award number 14-08-0001-G1320. The views and conclusions contained in this document are those of the authors and should not be interpreted as necessarily representing the official policies, either expressed or implied, of the U. S. Geological Survey.

not directly with their values. (We know, of course, that what we believe to be true can be influenced by what we want to be true.) Resolution of social value-based conflict is facilitated if the disputants have good information about their own values and those of the other parties. Resolution of interest conflict is easier to achieve if the disputants understand which options will provide the basis for constructive bargaining and which will be unacceptable to some parties. Resolution of cognitive conflict requires that the disputants share the best available factual information.

Analytic aids for conflict resolution may be used to provide any or all of the three types of information just delineated. Few, if any analytical models yield information of all three types. Linking several such models, however, may satisfy the information needs for the resolution of complex disputes which involve all three types of conflict.

Most disputes will include all three conflict types, with correspondingly complex information needs for dispute resolution. An example of such a complex conflict can be found in the Indian water rights disputes which now exist throughout the western United States. These disputes involve value conflict, interest conflict, and cognitive conflict. They involve other factors, as well, such as cultural differences on how decisions are made, strong emotional elements, and a well-developed set of positions to which many of the parties are already committed.

BACKGROUND

Water rights throughout the western states are most often allocated pursuant to the doctrine of prior appropriation. In principle, this doctrine is a far more effective method of resolving water rights disputes than is the older eastern riparian doctrine because it assigns rights unambiguously and according to an explicit method for responding to shortage situations. Simply stated, a water right is acquired by diverting water from a stream and putting it to beneficial use. The water right so acquired has at least two essential dimensions, quantity, expressed as a rate of diversion, and seniority, expressed as the date when the water was first diverted. The rule for allocating water when there is not enough to go around is that the diversions of appropriators are shut down in increasing order of seniority until the rights of all remaining senior appropriators are served.

Non-Indian water users have acquired rights to the water in western streams since the middle of the last century. By now, many of those streams are fully appropriated, which is to say that rights to the full mean annual flow of the stream have already been assigned. All that remains are the appropriable rights to the flows in abnormally wet years; rights which are of little value because they seldom produce wet water and are so costly to develop.

In 1908 in the landmark *Winters* decision the Supreme Court decreed that Indian tribes were entitled to water in quantities sufficient to achieve the purposes for which Indian reservations were created, that such rights were effective on the dates when the original reservations of land from the public domain were executed, and that they were not lost since those dates just because they had not been exercised. Many of the treaties through which Indian reservations were established predate most of the water rights acquired by non-Indian water users.

The Supreme Court's *Winters* decision was ignored in practice for many years, but its implication was that heretofore unexercised and potentially vast quantities of water could be claimed by Indian tribes even though to do so would displace many long-established non-Indian water users. In 1963, however, the Supreme Court revisited the *Winters* decision in *Arizona v. California* and advanced the practicably irrigable acreage standard for quantifying the water rights of tribes. This decision gave operational meaning to the earlier *Winters* decision through implying that the purpose of the creation of the Indian reservations was to provide the tribes with a land base sufficient to support an agricultural life style and that, by inference, the amount of water simultaneously reserved was that amount sufficient to irrigate all of the reservation acreage which was practicably irrigable. Subsequent judicial explorations of the meaning of practicably irrigable need not be reviewed here. Suffice it to say that the amount of water involved could be great indeed (Western States Water Council, 1984).

Indian water rights claims are presently being adjudicated in almost every Western state. Such claims are usually very senior and are still unquantified. They create an atmosphere of uncertainty for both Indians and non-Indian water users alike. Indians look to the acquisition of senior water rights as a major way of increasing tribal resources and improving the possibilities for achieving tribal goals. Non-Indian water users fear the possibility of weakened priority, increased uncertainty of water supplies, and economic losses. Federal authorities pursue conflicting objectives, responsive as they must be to trust responsibilities to tribes, political pressures from states and organized water constituent groups, and the fiscal responsibility to control federal outlays.

There are three ways in principle to resolve disputes over Indian water rights. The first is litigation, in which the courts are relied upon to determine the quantity and seniority of the rights of all claimants. General stream adjudications, a subcategory of litigation, are now in progress in several western states. Adjudication can be an accepted way of resolving such disputes when there is enough water to go around. But in fully appropriated streams an adjudication must take each drop of water awarded to Indian claimants from non-Indians who already are using that water and who may have made heavy capital investments predicated upon the expectation that such use could continue unhindered. This is an example of a zero-sum game, the most difficult kind of interest conflict to resolve.

Litigation has never been used alone to resolve Indian water rights disputes in a fully appropriated basin. It has always been necessary to resort to legislation as well, to expand the range of options and convert the zero-sum game to a positive-sum game, in which no player need lose. Federal legislative action has always been used to expand the options, most usually by providing (and paying for) augmented supplies of water, and also by providing the financial assistance necessary to permit development of water allocated to the Indians.

The terms of the federal legislation to resolve Indian water rights disputes are never self-evident. In fact, the objectives of the federal government are usually at least partially in conflict with those of other disputants, and often with each other. In particular, the federal government's fiscal obligation to the nation's taxpayers in this era of budgetary stringency prevents it from freely providing all of the funding which might make dispute resolution among the other parties relatively easy to accomplish. The distributive political mode of aggregation, mutual non-interference, and accommodation (Lowi, 1964), which historically has been the political way of resolving so many large scale western water disputes, is no longer easy to implement.

The task of dispute resolution becomes more difficult when the federal government is unwilling to bankroll a distributive solution in which each disputant's demands are met without impinging upon others. Negotiations among the disputants become essential to determine how the necessary sacrifices will be apportioned. Negotiations between the parties, including the federal government, have been a prominent feature of every recent Indian water rights settlement when the setting was a fully appropriated basin.

The typical pattern, then, in a fully appropriated basin will be for litigation to be initiated, for litigation to lead to a general stream adjudication, for the parties then to begin negotiations among themselves, leading to a tentative agreement which is submitted to the administration and the Congress, further negotiations to determine the terms of the federal participation, settlement, and then resolution of the adjudication through stipulation.

It is just such negotiated settlement of Indian water rights disputes, as a complement to litigation and legislation, that is becoming increasingly important throughout the West. Many water users and Indian tribes are finding that their objectives can best be met, and conflicts over water rights resolved, through negotiated settlements. Such negotiations have not been easily initiated, conducted, or implemented, however. Affected parties have not always grasped the potential benefits of negotiation, and have not always been able negotiators. Better information about the possibilities of negotiated settlements, about the objectives of other parties, about the hydrologic and social realities which constrain both negotiation and litigation, and about available settlement options and their potential consequences can help to facilitate the negotiation process.

THE CASE STUDY

Our Indian water rights research project, conducted from 1986 to 1989, was broadly interdisciplinary, reflecting the fact that the problem of negotiating settlements of Indian water rights claims cannot be subsumed within the subject matter of any single discipline. The dispute which was studied had hydrologic, environmental, anthropological, economic, legal, political, and psychological aspects. Consequently, the methodology employed was multidisciplinary and relied upon the concept of linked models. Linked models are commonly used in hydrology, where surface and ground water models are sometimes linked, and in economics, where programming models and demand models are sometimes linked. Seldom, however, have so many models, from so broad an array of disciplines, been linked as has been attempted in this study. The linkage of these diverse models, is the chief theoretical and methodological contribution of the study.

Three of the linked models were formal mathematical ones, as shown in Figure 1. A hydrologic-institutional-economic network optimization model described the workings of the system in which the conflict was embedded. A multiple regression preference elicitation model described the objectives of the disputants. Finally, an n-person non zero-sum cooperative game theory model described the conflict itself. The approach was applied in a case study situation which is a part of the massive on-going Gila River Basin adjudication, in which the rights to use most of the surface water and some of the groundwater in Arizona will be determined. We chose the San Pedro Sub-Basin, one of the six sub-basins of the Gila adjudication.

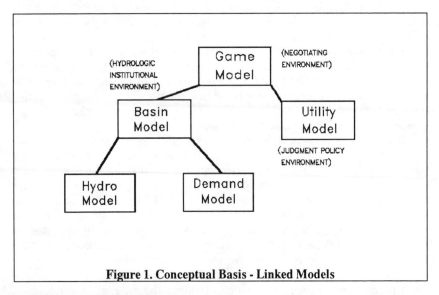

Figure 1. Conceptual Basis - Linked Models

FACTUAL INFORMATION

Achieving stable and long-lasting negotiated settlements of Indian water rights and other water-related disputes depends heavily upon obtaining the best possible information about the natural and social environment in which the dispute is located. Hydrologic, biological, institutional, economic, and other types of information may be needed, depending somewhat upon the characteristics of the specific dispute. Preparing a conflict map, a descriptive account of the dispute including its strategic features, is a good way to start.

Two main sources of information were used for detailed mapping of the case study conflict. They were the San Pedro Hydrographic Survey Report (HSR) and interviews with disputants. A hydrographic survey report is a document compiled by the Arizona Department of Water Resources as a basic information source for the Court and the participants in the Gila River adjudication. It contains a listing of all claims filed with the Court and as complete a description of the hydrology of the basin as available data permit (Arizona Department of Water Resources, 1987). The interviews provided essential information not included in the HSR, such as the goals of the parties and their ideas about possible options for resolving the conflict.

In the case of the San Pedro dispute, the conflict map revealed that a model of the hydrology of the basin would be required. The necessary features of such a model were the capability to represent inflows to the system, outflows, natural depletions, and the hydrologic relationships between these parameters. Similarly, it was necessary to model the institutional system of water rights in place, the various demands (anthropogenic depletions) placed upon it, and the economic value of water at the margin in the various uses to which it could be put. Figure 2 presents a schematic diagram of the San Pedro Basin, showing the features which were to be included in the basin model.

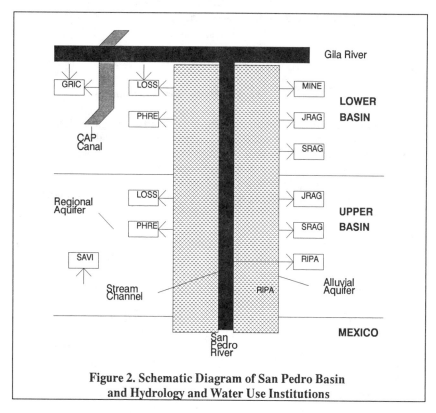

Figure 2. Schematic Diagram of San Pedro Basin and Hydrology and Water Use Institutions

MODSIM (Labadie, 1987) was chosen to model the hydrologic and economic system of water allocation within the San Pedro basin. It is a network optimization model employing the out-of-kilter algorithm and specified for a conjunctive surface and groundwater management system. The general network optimization model, which is a variant of the transportation model, in turn a special case of the linear programming model, is shown as Figure 3.

Minimize

$$\sum_{i=1}^{n} \sum_{j=1}^{n} c_{ij} q_{ij}$$

Subject to

$$\sum_{i=1}^{n} q_{ij} - \sum_{i=1}^{n} q_{ji} = 0 \qquad , \quad j = 1, n$$

$$l_{ij} \leq q_{ij} \leq u_{ij} \qquad , \quad \text{all } i, j$$

where

q_{ij} = flow along arc_{ij} (i.e., from node i to node j)

c_{ij} = unit cost associated with flow along arc_{ij}

l_{ij} = lower bound on flow along arc_{ij}

u_{ij} = upper bound on flow alnog arc_{ij}

n = number of network nodes

Figure 3. Network Optimization Equations

An analytical optimization model was chosen instead of a numerical simulation model to represent the basin because it is tractable and computationally efficient. This choice implied some sacrifice of detail and realism. The ability to change the configuration of the model and run it repeatedly to explore different scenarios was considered to be an overriding advantage.

MODSIM not only models the typical dendritic hydrologic system efficiently but also permits water allocation to be responsive to a set of generalized criteria which may be specified to simulate the prior appropriation doctrine, water markets, or other institutional options. Water may be introduced to the system and withdrawn from it at any point (node), subject to availability and cost.

A variety of data were collected in order to specify the MODSIM model for the San Pedro Basin. Hydrologic and water rights data were obtained from the HSR. A ten year period of record was chosen, encompassing both wet and dry periods. Water demand projections were constructed from current use data and municipal growth projections for urban areas. Economic estimates of the marginal value of water in alternative uses, including irrigation on the Gila River Indian Reservation, were formulated from farm budget data and from opportunity cost data for urban and industrial water supply sources.

A description of the natural and social setting for a water-related dispute is not the only factual information required for its resolution. The disputants also must be aware of the options available to them. The options available to each party are not the same as the possible outcomes of the negotiation. A disputant may make demands or offers (typically, a combination of both). Any combination of such demands and offers, on the part of all parties, will yield an outcome to the dispute.

The conflict mapping exercise yielded one set of suggested possible outcomes for resolving the Indian water rights conflict in the San Pedro Sub-Basin, namely that set suggested by the participants themselves. However, another method was employed to enrich the range of possible outcomes to be evaluated. Researchers collected information about the outcomes of each of the Indian water rights conflicts which were resolved in recent years. There were seven such settlements. An explicit analytical framework was designed and employed to reveal the strategically important aspects of their outcomes. From this, the research team was able to identify common elements, as well as differences, and deduce those features which seemed to be necessary for conflict resolution. They were awards of water rights to tribes, no uncompensated diminution of water rights of non-Indian water users, and federal financial responsibility for all or most of the costs incurred, with the federal contribution limited to about fifty million dollars per settlement. Another common feature was federal water supply augmentation in those instances where appropriable water resources were insufficient to support the award of rights to tribes.

Twelve possible outcomes were identified. They differed in several respects. First, the amount of San Pedro water awarded to the Gila River Indian Reservation could range from no new awards to the undepleted virgin flow of the river at the upstream boundary of the reservation. Second, imported water could be awarded to the Indians in place of San Pedro water, up to the same virgin flow constraint. The imported water in this case would consist of Central Arizona Project water, which can be delivered to the reservation. Third, the costs of making this water available to the Indians could be borne in various ways. The entire burden might be borne by the junior appropriators on the San Pedro (through loss of water rights), the burden could be spread more generally among all of the San Pedro water users, or the burden could be borne by the federal taxpayer. Combinations are also possible. Fourth, the Indians could be awarded monetary payments or subsidies to permit them to develop new water. Again, the burden of doing so could be spread in various ways. Fifth, the Indians could be awarded monetary payments in lieu of new water, and be permitted to use these funds for economic development purposes on the reservation. This burden could also be assigned in various ways. Sixth, water marketing could be permitted in order to allow limited water supplies to flow to their highest uses, and thus to minimize the social costs of any award to the Indians.

In addition, the research team projected three possible outcomes of a failure to reach a negotiated settlement. Failure to negotiate successfully in this case meant that the Gila River Adjudication would proceed to its conclusion unassisted and that the court would then face the more limited options of awarding available San Pedro water to the claimants without the flexibility to consider imported water, to compensate the Indians monetarily, or to specify cost-sharing arrangements. Since no one can foresee how much San Pedro water the court might award to the Indians we defined three different possibilities and assigned probabilities to them. This probability assignment was highly arbitrary, so that provision was made for changing it easily in subsequent analytical efforts. Failure to reach a negotiated settlement was taken to imply that a probability-weighted combination of the three possible adjudication outcomes would have to be considered by the parties.

SOCIAL VALUE INFORMATION

Negotiations aimed at settling Indian water rights disputes are essentially bargaining transactions to resolve interest conflicts. However, elements of social value conflict and cognitive conflict can be found within them and must be resolved through appropriate means.

The primary expressions of social values within Indian water rights negotiations are located within the domain of the federal policies which permit and constrain the positions which the executive and legislative branch representatives may take in the bargaining process. There have been persistent calls for the Congress to enunciate a clear national Indian policy which could be applied in water rights and many other situations. The Congress has been unwilling and unable to do so, primarily because the underlying social value conflicts remain unresolved (Burton, 1989).

Negotiations to resolve specific local disputes are not the appropriate settings for resolving national social value conflicts, although a succession of such negotiations may establish the precedents which inadvertently yet effectively do so. Support for specific local negotiations should include an attempt to elucidate federal policy objectives so that options for dispute resolution can be formulated and evaluated to achieve consistency with federal policy.

A comprehensive review of federal Indian policy, reservation establishment and maintenance, and issues of social equity in Indian affairs, was conducted as a part of this research project (McGuire, 1988). Its aim was to elucidate the federal Indian policy objectives which must be considered in Indian water rights negotiations. It provides a recapitulation of the stated purposes of the reservation policy when it was established, of the evolution of those purposes during the implementation period of the past century, and of alternative purposes which were advanced by the executive, legislative, and judicial branches throughout this period. McGuire identified economic self-sufficiency, tribal sovereignty, and cultural pluralism as the principal objectives of federal Indian policy.

Additional matters of federal policy concern include the fiscal responsibility to minimize budgetary impacts and diverse concerns which may arise from other federal activities on a site-specific basis. Site-specific environmental concerns are apt to be present, for example, whenever water rights affecting national parks, forests, wildlife refuges, or natural areas are at stake. In the San Pedro, a prominent feature of the dispute is the existence on the upstream portion of the river of the nation's first Riparian National Conservation Area. Maintenance of adequate instream flows and groundwater levels within the alluvium is essential to perpetuating the riparian ecosystem.

INTEREST IMPACT INFORMATION

Consideration of a possible negotiation outcome by a potentially affected party depends not only upon the objective or factual characteristics of that outcome (its potential impacts upon water distribution and use, monetary exchanges between the parties, etc.) but also upon how the affected party assesses the importance or value of any impacts to it. In order to model the negotiation, then, it is necessary to model the preferences or values of the negotiators. There are several ways to do this. One way is to let the disputants themselves choose among the possible outcomes. Fisher and Ury (1983) call this positional bargaining, and provide a strong argument against it. They do not mention yet another objection, which is that disputants may have mistaken factual beliefs about the characteristics of possible outcomes. Bargaining over facts is inappropriate, and such cognitive conflict should be resolved by appropriate means before bargaining takes place.

In a real dispute resolution effort the information on the values of the disputants would come directly from the disputants themselves. We did not want our research project to intervene in the actual dispute so we chose the indirect method of role-playing. Research team members interviewed representatives of the parties and achieved a sense of what was important to them. As a result, team members were able to play the roles of the negotiating parties with some degree of knowledge and empathy. Intensive discussions among the research team members were used to identify the variables which were strategically important to the negotiators' preference functions (their underlying values). These values then became the pertinent impact categories for evaluating possible negotiation outcomes. The identities of the disputants and the objectives established for them are shown in Table 1.

GILA RIVER INDIAN COMMUNITY
          Economic Self Sufficiency
          Tribal Sovereignty
          Cultural Pluralism

FEDERAL GOVERNMENT
          Economic Self Sufficiency
          Tribal Sovereignty
          Cultural Pluralism
          Environmental Concern
          Minimize Impact on the Federal Budget

MINES
          Minimize Cost

AGRICULTURAL INTERESTS
      (Upper and Lower San Pedro Basin)
          Maintain Rural Lifestyle
          Maximize Income

Table 1 Objectives for Case Study Disputants

Next, instead of attempting to represent the underlying preference functions directly we employed a model of the preference or utility functions of the disputants. We asked each role playing team member to evaluate a series of profiles which were characterized by randomly chosen levels of attainment of the relevant impact categories. Although randomly chosen, the values of these variables fell within what we estimated to be the relevant range of impacts of the available outcomes. Multiple regression analyses were performed on the resulting data sets, thus yielding linear representations of the preference functions, together with estimates of the internal consistency of the respondents' judgments. A variant of this technique, known as social judgment analysis, has been applied also in the Bureau of Reclamation's MATS approach for water planning and conflict resolution. We have used MATS in subsequent iterations of the analysis.

Also included in the social judgment analysis was a stochastic variable, the response to which permitted us to estimate the respondent's risk preference. Quantification of risk preference was necessary because the three potential adjudication outcomes, each of which was characterized by a stated probability of occurence, had to be combined into a single weighted outcome which represented the potential consequence of unsuccessful negotiations.

MODELING THE NEGOTIATING ENVIRONMENT

The twelve potential negotiation outcomes identified above, and the thirteenth outcome arising out of failure to negotiate successfully, constituted only theoretically possible outcomes, in the sense that they incorporated the hydrologic and economic reality constraints which any settlement would have to accomodate. They did not reflect or imply anything about the negotiation process, and it was not clear whether any or all of them were possible of attainment within the context of that process.

The next step, then, was to specify the possible strategies available to each of the disputants. Indians, for example, could demand all of the San Pedro water to which they could conceivably be entitled (the reconstructed virgin flow) and refuse to settle for less. Alternatively, they could agree to accept a lesser award. They could demand monetary compensation, either in lieu of water or in addition to it. They could agree to accept imported (CAP) water in lieu of San Pedro water. The possible options available to each disputant were studied and systematically recorded by the research team. There were five to eight such strategies for each disputant.

At this point it was necessary to select an analytical technique for identifying the outcome which would result from each combination of player strategies and which of those outcomes would be desirable to all of the disputants and could thus form the data base for subsequent negotiations. N-person nonzero-sum cooperative game theory was the model chosen to represent the negotiating environment.

Each possible outcome was characterized by its potential impacts upon the objective set of each of the disputants. Next, this impact matrix was transformed into a payoff matrix by multiplying it by the vector of regression coefficients produced by application of the Social Judgment Theory model. The elements of the payoff matrix are real numbers ranging from zero to one. They provide an ordering of the settlement outcomes for each player. The higher the utility index, the more desirable that outcome to the player. The utility indices have absolutely no meaning for interplayer comparisons.

The resulting payoff matrix would contain many thousands of elements, and would be very difficult to construct element by element. However, the great majority of those elements would consist of the thirteenth outcome, since the options selected by the players would be mutually inconsistent, with the result that negotiations would fail and the adjudication would proceed unassisted.

A procedure of "outcome removal" (Fraser and Hipel, 1984) identified those elements which consisted of some outcome other than the thirteenth. This meant that subsequent analytical steps could be based solely upon the thirteen settlement outcomes.

The final analytical step was to assess the prospective consequences, or outcomes, of the several settlement options (and, by implication, the players' options which led to their realization) to determine which were valid conflict resolution possibilities. A valid conflict resolution possibility is an outcome which produces impacts which are superior to the impacts of failing to negotiate from every player's perspective. In other words, all the parties will continue to negotiate rather than drop out and rely on the adjudication. The set of all such outcomes is called the negotiation set (Luce and Raiffa, 1957). If there are no such possibilities then negotiations are doomed from the start. If there is only one such possibility then negotiations are theoretically unnecessary since all will agree immediately upon it. In the more usual case that multiple possibilities are found one would expect negotiations to occur between the players to find a single solution, and that those negotiations could proceed with the assurance that a successful conclusion was likely.

Finally, the elements of the payoff matrix for each outcome were compared to the payoffs of the thirteenth (adjudication) outcome. Any outcome for which each player's payoff was higher than the payoff of the adjudication outcome for that player can be said to dominate the adjudication outcome (it is preferred to it by all players), and is therefore a member of the negotiation set and a settlement possibility. Three of the twelve possible negotiation outcomes were found to lie within the negotiation set. Table 2, on the next page, shows the thirteen possible outcomes, the payoff to each disputant associated with each outcome, and the acceptability of each when compared with the adjudication alternative. Finally, it shows the three outcomes which comprise the negotiation set. Each of these outcomes was characterized by provision of imported water to the Indians in lieu of San Pedro water.

The three models, MODSIM, which models the hydrologic and institutional environment, MATS, which models the preference environment and evaluates the outcomes to yield specific payoffs, and the game theoretic model, have now been linked through a speadsheet in a way which permits exploration of the consequences of changing hydrologic, economic, institutional, psychological, and

| STRATEGY | UTILITY PER PLAYER | | | | | ACTIVITY SUMMARY | | | | | ACCEPTABLE |
	I	II	III	IV	V	I	II	III	IV	V	STRATEGY?
1.	.673	.392	1.000	.992	.240	1	0	1	1	0	0
2.	.673	.516	.283	.926	.207	1	1	0	1	0	0
3.	.673	.516	1.000	.180	.655	1	1	1	0	1	0
4.	.602	.560	.283	.926	.207	1	1	0	1	0	0
5.	.602	.560	1.000	.180	.655	1	1	1	0	1	0
6.	.673	.379	1.000	.992	.978	1	0	1	1	1	0
7.	.673	.516	.204	.919	.942	1	1	0	1	1	0
8.	.602	.423	1.000	.992	.978	1	0	1	1	1	0
9.	.602	.560	.204	.919	.942	1	1	0	1	1	0
10.	.615	.634	1.000	.992	.978	1	1	1	1	1	1
11.	.615	.702	.605	.955	.960	1	1	1	1	1	1
12.	.615	.668	.802	.974	.969	1	1	1	1	1	1
13.	.575	.532	.717	.179	.655						
14.	.077	.444	.717	.991	.978						p(13) = .6
15.	385	.432	.000	.926	.103		1 = yes 0 = no				p(14) = .2
											p(15) = .2
adj.	.44	.49	.57	.49	.61						

PLAYER

Player I = Indians (GRIC)
Player II = Federal Government
Player III = San Pedro Basin Mines
Player IV = Upper San Pedro Basin Farmers
Player V = Lower San Pedro Basin Farmers

Table 2. Strategy Selection Table

other data collected for the San Pedro Basin. Such exploration leads easily and quickly to a better understanding of the natural and social environment and of the conflict resolution process itself. This understanding, more than the identification of the members of the negotiation set, represents the real value of the use of analytic aids within the dispute resolution process.

Additional information, no matter how good and how complete, cannot resolve complex water-related disputes. However, the careful examination of the elements of the dispute, the identification and generation of pertinent information, and the use of a methodology which can bring this information to bear can aid the dispute resolution process.

REFERENCES

Arizona Department of Water Resources, Preliminary Hydrographic Survey Report For The San Pedro River Watershed, Volume I: General Assessment, January 1987.

Burton, L., "Improving the Prospects for Negotiated Settlement of American Indian Water Rights Disputes, Proceedings of the Symposium on Indian Water Rights and Water Resources Management, American Water Re-sources Association, Missoula, MT, pp. 115-125, June 1989.

Fisher, R., and W. Ury, Getting to Yes, Penguin Books, New York, NY, 1983.

Fraser, N.M. and D.W. Hipel, Conflict Analysis: Models and Resolutions, North-Holland, New York, NY, 1984.

Labadie, J.W., "River Basin Network Flow Model: Program Modsim, Unpublished draft manuscript, Department of Civil Engineering, Colorado State University, April 1987.

Lord, W.B., "Conflict in Federal Water Resource Planning," Water Resources Bulletin, American Water Resources Association, Minneapolis, MN, Vol. 15, No. 5, pp. 1226-1235, 1979.

Lowi, T.J., "American Business, Public Policy, Case Studies and Political Theory," World Politics, Vol.16, No. 4, pp. 677-715, 1964.

Luce, R.D. and H. Raiffa, Games and Decisions, John Miley & Sons, Inc., New York, NY, 1957.

McGuire, T.R., "The Definition of Federal Policy Toward Indian Reservations," unpublished draft manuscript, Feb. 17, 1988.

Western States Water Council, Indian Water Rights in the West, Study prepared for the Western Governors' Association, 1984.

Dispute Resolution Experiences:
The Engineer's Role

by
Charles L. Lancaster, J.D. **

"Justice has many ingredients, of which
the truth is only one."

<blockquote>
Donald T. Weckstein in "The Purposes
of Dispute Resolution: Comparative
Concepts of Justice"
</blockquote>

Abstract

     In this short paper, I will try to do a number of
things. I will describe some of the U.S. Army Corps of
Engineers experiences and in using Alternative Dispute
Resolution (ADR) to resolve conflicts. I will also
briefly describe the Corps effort to establish a
program to promote ADR within the Corps. These
experiences will raise some issues of the preconcep-
tions about dispute resolution which people of varying
backgrounds bring to their involvement in managing
conflict. I will make a generalization about how
engineers solve problems, which raises some issues
about the attitudes engineers may have toward dispute
resolution. Understanding these attitudes may help
engineers to be better conflict managers.

**Charles Lancaster is Assistant Program Manager for
the Crops of Engineers Alternative Dispute Resolution
Program, Institute for Water Resources, Fort Belvoir,
Virginia. He is on special assignment to the Corps
from the University of Virginia's Institute for
Environmental Negotiation under provisions of the
Intergovernmental Personnel Act. The views expressed
in this paper are those of Mr. Lancaster and do not
necessarily reflect the policy of the Corps of
Engineers.

Introduction: The Corps of Engineers and ADR

The Corps of Engineers is the acknowledged leader among federal agencies in using ADR to resolve disputes which would otherwise be headed for the courtroom (Crowell and Pou, 1988; ACUS, 1987).[1] Implicit in that statement is the role that ADR plays; that is, ADR procedures are intended to serve as alternatives to litigation, our traditional dispute resolution method. ADR is not intended to replace or be an alternative to negotiation. The non-binding ADR procedures that the Corps favors (as contrasted to binding methods such as arbitration, where a third party makes a decision) are intended to be either forms of structured negotiations or a prelude to negotiations between the parties to the dispute. An important aspect of the Corps ADR program is the philosophy that Corps managers should be making dispute resolution decisions where possible, not third parties such as judges. Who better knows the Corps, its goals and policies, than a Corps manager?

The principles of the Corps ADR philosophy that have just been mentioned represent guiding concepts of what is really the second phase in the effort to use ADR. The Corps effort began in the early 1980's with a period of ad hoc experimentation in using ADR techniques. The success of these experiments has now led the Corps to establish a coordinated program to try to institutionalize ADR in the Corps as an everyday management tool. The program includes training in ADR and technical assistance to Corps divisions in using ADR. Another important element of the program is the effort to record and evaluate the Corps experience in using ADR. This effort to look at the Corps experience and benefit from it has led the agency to commission case studies by Endispute, Inc., a group specializing in conflict management consulting. The first five of these case studies have been published by the Corps both as separate cases (Susskind, 1989b-f), under one cover along with Endispute's suggested framework for managerial dispute resolution decision making (Susskind, 1989a). I will draw on the Endispute case study material for the following review of two cases which illustrate aspects of the engineer's role in conflict management.

---

[1]The Corps has also been recognized by the non-profit Center for Public Resources as an innovator in promoting the use of ADR.

Case Studies in Alternative Dispute Resolution

The following mini-trial experience is perhaps the Corps' most famous success. The case involved a claim for additional payment due for construction of a significant portion of the Tennessee-Tombigbee Waterway, a massive construction project. The Corps case study describes the background of the case as follows (Susskind, 1989a: 8-9):

" The U.S. Army Corps of Engineers contracted with Tenn Tom Constructors, Inc. (TTC) to excavate an eleven-mile stretch of the Tennessee Tom Bigbee Waterway. A five year, fixed-price contract for $270 million, it required the removal and disposal of ninety-five million cubic yards of earth. Prior to soliciting bids for the contract, the government performed extensive studies to determine subsurface soil conditions, including a test excavation of a 1500 foot wide section of the project area. The government provided potential contractors with the test results to help them calculate cost projections.

During the excavation process, TTC claimed they encountered more drainage inhibiting clay zones and higher moisture levels in the soil than pre-bid specifications suggested. This resulted in severe "trafficability" problems and increased travel time per truckload of earth. For these reasons, TTC filed a differing site conditions claim and requested an equitable adjustment of $42.8 million. After negotiations reached impasse, the Corps established an in-house task force to evaluate the merits of the claim. The project was extensively monitored and documented by both the government and the contractor...

The major issues in dispute centered on subsurface soil conditions and the difference between the contractor's expectations based on pre-bid specifications and the actual conditions encountered. According to Corps tests, the soil was expected to drain well with normal trenching operations so that the contractor's equipment would not be adversely affected by excessive moisture. TTC found that the soil retained a high level of water. This reduced the speed at which trucks could travel to and from the site, thereby causing significant maintenance and repair problems for TTC's de-watering equipment. The Corps contended that geological tests performed prior to awarding the contract clearly identified subsurface soil conditions that were not significantly different form those experienced by the contractor."

The ADR procedure chosen to try to resolve the dispute was the mini-trial. In brief, a mini-trial is

a settlement procedure that includes three elements: a
summary presentation of the case by lawyers for each
side, before representatives of each side with
authority to settle, followed by settlement
negotiations. Mini-trials are designed to provide a
structured prelude to negotiations between
representatives of the disputants who have authority to
settle the case. The procedure has a definite
structure but the decision makers have the flexibility
to improvise if the situation demands. The mini-trial
in the Tenn-Tom case was held on June 11-13, 1985, with
negotiations between the principals to begin
immediately. In this case, however, the principals
felt there was a need for more information which had
not been provided in the initial presentations. This
additional data was gathered and presented to the
principals on June 27, 1985, and the principals, with
the help of the neutral advisor, reached an agreed
settlement of the claim on June 28, 1985. The $55.6
million claim was settled for $17.25 million.

The technical staff for both TTC and the Corps
played critical roles in this dispute. The case study
describes the positions of each side in the dispute
(Susskind, 1989a: 9):

"In appealing the contracting officer's decision
[denying the claim], TTC claimed they deserved an
equitable adjustment of $42.8 million. After an
extensive investigation, the government found no
justification for a differing site condition claim. By
the time TTC and the Corps were considering ADR, the
claim amounted to $55.6 million including interest.

At the start of the project, TTC informed the
Nashville District of its problems associated with the
high moisture content of the soil. Since it was clear
this would prove to be a very large claim, both sides
carefully documented all aspects of the project as it
unfolded. The Corps alone had more than 10,000
photographs and twenty hours of video.

Technical field staff on both sides were deeply
entrenched in their positions. TTC claimed they had
great difficulties during excavations and had ruined a
lot of their equipment. The Corps refused any
responsibility for the problems and argued that soil
conditions were nothing different from what should have
been expected."

The technical staff for the Corps held such strong
opinions of the correctness of their position that they
were very dissatisfied with the settlement. An
anonymous call was made to the Department of Defense
Inspector General complaining about the case, and an

investigation followed. The Inspector General found
that the government did have significant potential
liability and that the settlement was justified in the
best interests of the government.

        Given this conclusion by the Inspector General,
how should the technical staff dissatisfaction be
viewed? Were they merely unable to see the other
side's position? Did some element of professional
pride keep them from acknowledging that there might be
another "reality," or another "truth" other than their
own conception which they had invested with so much
effort and thought? Were they merely too close to the
case and unable to maintain any objectivity? During
the presentation at the mini-trial, the geo-technical
expert witnesses for both sides were asked to explain
how they reached different conclusions. The case study
describes what happened: "During the mini-trial, the
geo-technical experts for each side were asked to
explain their differences, and in effect, debate the
issues. It became clear that they agreed on the facts,
but held different interpretations. The decision-
makers then questioned the reasoning behind their
interpretations." (Susskind, 1989a:14)

        Some further questions come to mind. Were the TTC
experts unscrupulous, i.e., was their loyalty bought in
some way? Did the outcome of the mini-trial, a
negotiated settlement, mean one interpretation was
right and the other wrong? Were there considerations
other than the "truth" or validity of the claim in the
minds of the decision makers when they reached a
settlement?

        Similar questions are prompted by a second mini-
trial from the Corps experience. Unlike the Tenn-Tom
case, however, this mini-trial involved a decision on
the allocation of costs for the cleanup of
environmental contamination. This is case study number
five in the Corps ADR series, entitled "Goodyear Tire
and Rubber Company." It represents the first use of
ADR to resolve the cost allocation question at a
Superfund site. It is described as follows (Susskind,
1989a: 52-53):

        "The Phoenix-Goodyear Airport (PGA) Superfund site
is located approximately 17 miles west of Phoenix,
Arizona. The southern half of the site consists of
adjoining properties: the Phoenix-Goodyear Airport,
formerly the Litchfield Park Naval Air Facility, now
owned and operated by the City of Phoenix; and the
Loral Corporation plant on land owned until 1986 by
Goodyear Tire and Rubber Company through a then
subsidiary, Goodyear Aerospace Corporation.

The adjoining Navy and Goodyear facilities had been established during World War II to modify, repair and service Navy aircraft. After the War, Goodyear left the site and the Navy stayed on to preserve decommissioned military aircraft. When the Korean War broke out, Goodyear returned to its former site and manufactured airplane parts, largely under government contract, until the facility was sold in 1986. The Navy operated its facility until 1968, when it was transferred to the City of Phoenix.

In 1981, Goodyear and the Arizona Department of Health Services discovered volatile organic compounds (VOC), principally trichloroethylene (TCE), in the groundwater and soils at the PGA/Litchfield site. (TCE is a human carcinogen.) EPA added the site to the Superfund National Priorities List in 1983.

From 1983-1987, EPA conducted a Remedial Investigation and Feasibility Study (RI/FS) at the site. Following the Study, Special Notice Letters were delivered to the Department of Defense and the Goodyear Corporation identifying them as Potentially Responsible Parties (PRPs) in the cleanup of the site. The U.S. Army Corps of Engineers, through its Omaha District Office, was assigned by DOD the responsibility of acting for DOD in the investigation and negotiations. In September of 1987, EPA issued a Record of Decision (ROD) calling for remediation of the groundwater problem as the first phase in cleaning up the site. The ROD triggered a regulatory timetable for remedial actions by the PRPs. They then had 60 days to respond to EPA with a proposal for financing and undertaking the necessary remedial action. By request of the parties, this was extended to 90 days. During this time, the first attempts to negotiate a settlement were made.

The major issue in contention was the relative responsibility of each of the PRPs (DOD and Goodyear) for the TCE contamination. The resolution of this issue depended upon determination of the source and timing of the contamination. Each side conducted extensive investigations of its own, but the results were controversial and inconclusive. There were also few witnesses still available . Little detailed documentation remained, because the site was used for military purposes and some of the records had been destroyed or "sanitized" by Naval Security after World War II...

The Corps evaluation was that their relative responsibility for clean-up was small. In fact, their initial offer to Goodyear when negotiations began was that the Corps would pay only 6% of the clean-up cost.

They did increase their offer during the negotiations, but still maintained that the Corps responsibility was much less than 50%.

Goodyear argued that, because they were operating as contractors to the Navy and proceeding according to government specifications, the government should share equally in the responsibility for the contamination. Because of this, Goodyear claimed that they and the Corps should split the costs 50/50. But they also felt their position was weak because "the government is the government"; i.e., even though DOD is not EPA or DOJ, they are all "the government" and by definition on the same side. This put Goodyear at a disadvantage, or so they thought, in any battle with DOD."

When a mini-trial was suggested as a possible way to resolve the percentage of responsibility for cleanup costs, there was reluctance from some of the Corps staff: "the technical staff at the District level were not initially in favor of ADR. They felt that their case was strong and that an ADR procedure would reflect dissatisfaction with their analysis and force the Corps to make concessions that were inappropriate. They eventually supported the ADR process." (Susskind, 1989 a:54)

The negotiation of the ADR agreement which would govern the conduct of the mini-trial was lengthy, perhaps due to the uncertainty of the costs of cleaning up groundwater contamination. The problem of determining the underground hydrology of the site was also the most contentious technical issue at the mini-trial. As in the Tenn-Tom case, the experts for both sides came to very different conclusions from the same set of facts. Prof. Richard Collins of the University of Virginia was the neutral advisor at the mini-trial. He had a suggestion for dealing with the apparent conflict (Susskind, 1989a: 58): "Collins contributed in another major way as well. At the end of the second day [of the mini-trial], the disagreement of the expert testimony from each side was still hard to reconcile. Collins suggested that the experts from both sides discuss the technical information (primarily the hydrology of the site) before the principals as a panel, without the interference of Counsel. This allowed Collins [and the principals] to focus attention specifically on these different viewpoints and have the experts themselves explain their disagreements."

The mini-trial presentation was concluded within the allotted three-day time frame. It took the principals approximately a day and a half to reach agreement on a cost allocation formula. The principals settled on a cost allocation which called for the government to pay 33% of the cleanup costs and Goodyear to pay 67%."

Once again, as in the Tenn-Tom case, two features stand out about the input of the technical staff. First, there was an initial reluctance on the part of the staff to use ADR because they felt that it somehow betrayed a distrust in their technical judgment. Secondly, the neutral advisor found it useful to have the experts from both sides talk together about the bases of their disagreement in the presence of the principals. In this way, the principals could better understand the cause of the apparent discrepancy.

What is going on here? In two of five ADR cases which have been examined by Endispute, technical staff have initially opposed the use of ADR because they thought their positions were unassailable. Then, during the mini-trial, we see the all too familiar courtroom scene of a battle of the experts where opposing interpretations from presumably objective, technically trained people are presented to the decision makers. In the flexible mini-trial setting, the decision makers were able to call the experts into the room and have them explain their differences. This can't be done in a trial, and it has been said therefore that judges and juries frequently make up their minds on which position to favor based on the believability of the expert. Perceptions of expert witnesses may be more influenced by the appearance or demeanor of the witness than the soundness of the `scientific truth' that is the basis of the testimony. (Meehan, 1984: 64)

Clearly, the reasons for the objections of technically trained professionals to settlement using ADR is a complicated issue. Wrapped up in the issue are questions of the management attitude toward perceived mistakes in professional judgment and the very real disincentives that may exist in terms of professional advancement, and the understandable reluctance of any human being to concede any validity to an opponent's point of view. Each of these reasons is part of the problem. However, I think there is also another reason that may make engineers oppose ADR which is related to the way that technical professionals view the truth of their technical opinions, and the way that they view the goals of the dispute resolution process as a truth discovering process.

Concepts of the Goals of Dispute Resolution

Donald Weckstein, Professor of Law at the University of San Diego, has written an article for the American Business Law Journal which explores concepts

of truth and justice as they relate to the way
societies resolve disputes. He points out that the
concept of justice in dispute resolution may involve
much more than the search for objective truth. As
Prof. Weckstein puts it, "in many [disputes] a 'search
for truth' and an assignment of rights and
responsibilities based thereon, is not necessarily the
predominant purpose." (605) What other purposes are
there? Weckstein says that the purposes of dispute
resolution reflect the values of the society.
Therefore, such values as social harmony, and human
dignity, along with accuracy, may also be purposes of a
society's dispute resolution system.

Therefore, there may be differing objectives which
are included in the dispute resolution system. As an
example, Weckstein (606) cites Thibaut and Walker
(1978: 543-44) who say that there is a fundamental
dichotomy between the potential dispute resolution
objective of 'truth,' and the idea of 'justice':
"Truth, they state, is the objective in 'cognitive'
conflicts, as in scientific inquiries, when the
resolution of the dispute according to an objective
standard is to the common advantage of all interested
parties. Where, however, there is a conflict of
interests between the parties in that an outcome will
maximize the interest of one party only at the expense
of the other, no solution will be recognized as
'correct' by all parties. These conflicts about the
apportionment of outcomes are considered the main
business of the legal process, and 'from the time of
Aristotle the objective in resolving this kind of
dispute has been characterized as 'justice.'" Thus, in
the realm of scientific/technical inquiry, the concept
of truth as the ultimate goal is appropriately central.
But when there is a question about the distribution of
finite benefits, as in a lawsuit, then truth or
accuracy may not be the only concern; it may not even
be the central inquiry.

Scientists and engineers, coming from the world of
cognitive conflicts and technical solutions to
construction problems, may have a difficult time
dealing with a dispute resolution system which has
different values than accuracy and objective truth.
They also may have a difficult time dealing with the
servants of our prevailing dispute resolution system:
lawyers. Prof. Weckstein notes that our court oriented
system of dispute resolution seeks justice, not
necessarily through a search for truth, but in adhering
to a just process of reaching a decision: "The
assumption is that a just process will yield a just
result." (607) Lawyers are primarily guardians and
servants of the procedures of the law (due process),
and by being servants of a just procedure, they seek to

serve the truth as well. It may be frustrating, then, for someone whose profession prizes objective truth to be told that the truth doesn't mean anything if it is inadmissible under the rules of evidence or it can't be related to the court persuasively.

Many of these points are made by engineer Richard Meehan in his book, The Atom and the Fault (1984), which considers the "prototypical hybrid scientific-legal controversy" of nuclear power plant siting in earthquake-prone California. Meehan was a consultant who testified at the Nuclear Regulatory Commission hearings and observed the way that the hearing process worked, modeled as it is on the adversarial legal system. He comments tellingly on his reaction to the dueling experts he observed: "During these hearings, I looked across the room at other experts, other scientists and engineers; it seemed they were representing the other side. How could this be, I asked myself. There's a geologist over there who is accusing me and my associates of telling lies or, at best, grossly distorting the truth, all for the sake of self-aggrandizement. How can there be this kind of advocacy when the subject is supposed to be a matter of scientific fact? Isn't there only one set of "facts," one reality? or are there several realities out there, each differing, depending on our individual - or is it professional? - background or motives, our personal or collective politics?" (Meehan, 1984: xi-xii).

Meehan is describing his reaction to the collision between the concepts of truth and the system of adversarial justice. The adversary system creates the conflict among the experts because its primary emphasis is not on a rigorous scientific search for the truth. Truth is discovered through a clash of adversaries. Though we no longer expect the intervention of divine providence as our medieval forebears did in trial by combat, this ancestor of our present day litigation process is clear. And just as a victory in combat didn't really mean a cause was just, we find that persuasiveness in the courtroom does not always relate to the accuracy of expert opinion. In the adversary system, the impact of expert witnesses (scientist and engineers) may be more influenced by the appearance or demeanor of the witness than the soundness of the scientific truth that is the basis of the testimony. Meehan describes the process as adversarial reasoning: NRC board proceedings use a "composite style of adversarial reasoning: a trial-like legal procedure is used to extract a consensus from the testimony of several different scientific and technical disciplines. A sort of legalistic reasoning prevails even though the objective is not to prove a site or facility guilty or innocent, like a criminal suspect, but to determine

whether it meets some standard of acceptable risk."
(142) This legalistic reasoning is foreign to the
concepts of scientific reasoning, creating a
fundamental problem when scientific/technical people
are involved in the legal process.

Meehan believes that to some degree all experts
are influenced in their opinions by a variety of
factors and they should be aware of these influences.
So, when asked for testimony, "[t]he experts respond,
'This is the truth, in accordance with the precepts
that have evolved over a long and honorable history of
my peers.' Each expert finds truth by invoking an
officially sanctioned social process. To the lawyer,
truth is what emerges from correct legal procedure. To
the engineer or scientist, truth emerges from certain
methods, which sometimes (but not always) include
observational verification but almost always involve
phone calls, attendance at conferences, cultivation of
associations with senior practitioners, and pursuit of
funds or fees. It is surprising that in this unlabora-
tory like process there is room for issues - whether
nature should be worshipped or put to work, for example
- that underlie the differences among the opinions of
experts." (156) He concludes that technical experts
should not decry this situation, but should recognize
its value and decide to compete ethically in the public
policy arena. For Mr. Meehan, this also means making
an internal ethical bargain: " The technical expert
can, and should, take a role beyond that of simply
reporting the truth and the facts to his client and the
court. The technical expert may be in a position to
collaborate in building a strong case, of in seeking
flaws in the opposing case, In doing so, of course, he
too becomes an advocate of his client's position. This
idea makes many experts, especially scientists,
uncomfortable, for they believe that they should limit
themselves to presenting the "unbiased" testimony, they
should be indifferent to winning. they worry about
being whores, about science for sale.

These concerns arise from a belief in the sanctity
of scientific truth. The burden of concern about
advocacy is much lightened if one accepts science as a
power-seeking enterprise, not a religion. After all,
Francis BAcon looked at it that way. I decided that my
job was to collaborate in the effort to build the
strongest possible case, consistent with the facts, for
the safety of [the power plant]. But I also saw that
what I saw as fact, someone else might see as
interpretation. The truth of the matter lay in
contest. I made a deal with myself that I would devise
only those arguments that could be competently
scrutinized by NRC staff or other experts." (Meehan
1984: 118.) Mr. Meehan acknowledges that the cost of

such adversarial policy development is great in time
and money, not to mention the delay in making important
public policy decisions. Nevertheless, he concludes
that the crucible of adversity has not caused us to
make bad decisions in the siting of nuclear power
plants. We have on the whole been able to muddle
toward an appropriate (though unwritten) definition of
the risk from earthquake faulting that we are willing
to accept.(Meehan 1984: 156). We have not gone too far
in requiring undue safety features nor have plants been
put at unsafe sites.

     Mr. Meehan's point is well taken if we are talking
about large public policy issues with potentially
enormous consequences. Such issues may require the
expense of a court-like proceeding. However, in most
"ordinary" cases, even where policy issues are
concerned, there is no need to spend so much time and
money. Alternative dispute resolution offers benefits
in making efficient informed decisions that should
appeal to engineers.

Conclusion - ADR Benefits

     One of the principle benefits of ADR, mentioned in
the introduction, is the fact that ADR procedures allow
the parties to make the settlement decisions rather
than turning decisions over to someone else. Those
decision makers, whether they be engineers, managers or
policy makers, will want the advice of technical
experts in developing a position for negotiation. The
engineer who chooses not to participate in a process
because it seems designed to reach some settlement
which will compromise the purity of a technical opinion
has missed an opportunity. ADR offers the opportunity
to avoid the time, expense and uncertainty of a court
decision, to participate effectively in shaping the
position of the organization, and to be a strong
advocate for a technical opinion. Technical experts
needn't be wimps about their opinions to participate in
ADR. They must present their opinions forcefully, and
even passionately, as a part of the decision making
process. They must also recognize, however, that one
person's fact is another's interpretation.

     ADR can be a better vehicle for considering
technical questions because ADR procedures are flexible
to meet the needs of the decision makers. If a dispute
involves a significant issue of technical or scientific
interpretation, an ADR procedure can be devised which
will place objective accuracy as a priority. For
example, a process could be devised which would allow
additional evidence to be gathered and analyzed. The
technical expert who rejects ADR will have no part in

deciding how technical questions can best be
determined.

    ADR should be viewed as empowering decision making
by those who have the information to make the best
decision, considering all of the many factors which
shape the alternatives. Turning a dispute over to a
third party, such as a judge, does not make the outcome
a better decision (though it may be easier to have a
decision imposed than to accept the decision making
responsibility). The best decisions will be made by
the parties to the dispute, including engineers, policy
makers, and managers working as a team to balance all
the factors of a good dispute resolution decision.

    Participating in ADR means that the technical
expert must be willing to recognize that there may be
other issues and practical considerations that keep
absolute objective accuracy from being the standard for
decision making. Other values may be in the minds of
the decision makers, such as social harmony, risk,
policy questions, party satisfaction and protecting
important relationships. Absolute accuracy may not
even be possible to achieve given the limits of time
and expense. The battle of the experts proves the
lawyer's first rule of case preparation: For every
expert Ph.D with an opinion there is an equal and
opposite Ph.D available for testimony. Given these
limits on discovering the "truth" of a case, technical
experts should involve themselves in reaching for
justice, recognizing that "Justice has many
ingredients, of which the truth is only one."
(Weckstein 1988: 606)

References

Administrative Conference of the United States,
                Sourcebook: Federal Agency Use of
                Alternative Means of Dispute
                Resolution, 1987.

CDR Associates, Participant's Workbook: The Executive
                Seminar on Alternative Dispute
                Resolution (ADR) Procedures, U.S. Army
                Corps of Engineers, 1989.

Crowell, Eldon and Charles Pou, "Appealing Government
                Contract Decisions: Reducing the Cost
                and Delay of Procurement Litigation,"
                Report to the Administrative
                Conference of the United States,
                January 1988.

Meehan, Richard L., *The Atom and the Fault*, Cambridge, MIT Press, 1984.

Susskind, Lawrence, Susan Podziba and Eileen Babbitt, "Using ADR in the U.S. Army Corps: A Framework for Managerial Decision-Making," U.S. Army Corps of Engineers, 1989a.

Susskind, Lawrence, Susan Podziba and Eileen Babbitt, "Case Study 1: Tenn-Tom Constructors, Inc.," U.S. Army Corps of Engineers, 1989b.

Susskind, Lawrence, Susan Podziba and Eileen Babbitt, "Case Study 2: Granite Construction Company," U.S. Army Corps of Engineers, 1989c.

Susskind, Lawrence, Susan Podziba and Eileen Babbitt, "Case Study 3: Olson Mechanical and Heavy Rigging, Inc.," U.S. Army Corps of Engineers, 1989d.

Susskind, Lawrence, Susan Podziba and Eileen Babbitt, "Case Study 4: Bechtel National, Inc.," U.S. Army Corps of Engineers, 1989e.

Susskind, Lawrence, Susan Podziba, Eileen Babbitt, and Richard C. Collins, "Case Study 5: Goodyear Tire and Rubber Company," U.S. Army Corps of Engineers, 1989f.

Thibaut and Walker, "A Theory of Procedure" 66 *California Law Review*, 541 (1978).

Weckstein, Donald T., "The Purpose of Dispute Resolution: Comparative Concepts of Justice," *American Business Law Journal*, vol. 26, pp. 605-624 (1988).

UTILIZING NEGOTIATIONS TO RESOLVE COMPLEX ENVIRONMENTAL DISPUTES

Christopher W. Moore, Ph.D.[1]

Abstract

This paper explores a variety of procedural considerations necessary for the implementation of negotiations over complex water issues. The author outlines a variety of strategies for each stage of the negotiation process, and describes how third party neutrals may be helpful in reaching a settlement.

Introduction to Complex Disputes

Complex public disputes abound in U.S. society. This is particularly true in cases relating to the environment and involving water issues. Parties argue over water rights, the proposed site and methods of constructing dams, and stream flow necessary for the spawning of fish. They struggle over water quality, issues related to hydropower generation and permitting, the operation of flood control dams and subsequent impacts on recreation. Conflict arises over wetlands management and preservation, flood control and drought management strategies, hazardous waste and its impacts on groundwater, forest and land use as they impact water, non-point pollution attributable to the use of agricultural fertilizers and pesticides and innumerable other water-related topics. All of the above disputes have in common their complexity--complexity regarding the number and technical nature of the issues involved, the number and organizational structures of concerned stakeholders, and the diversity of procedures and solutions that are available to address the conflicts.

---

[1]Christopher W. Moore, Ph.D is a Partner in CDR Associates, a decision-making and conflict management firm located at 100 Arapahoe Avenue, Suite 12, Boulder, Colorado, 80302.

Given the nature of complex disputes, what are the procedural alternatives for busy decision makers, technical experts, and the public for making decisions on these tough issues? Over the past twenty years, a body of expertise has emerged in the area of public dispute resolution. New professionals have also emerged who assist parties to implement these procedures. Roughly falling under the designation of "Alternative Dispute Resolution" or "ADR," these procedures assist contesting parties to overcome relationship barriers to settlement, procedural obstacles, or substantive problems (Marks, Johnson and Szanton). Among these procedures are negotiation, conciliation, facilitation, mediation, mini-trials, disputes panels, fact-finding and settlement conferences. What the majority of these alternative dispute resolution procedures have in common is that they promote and enhance the voluntary negotiated settlement of disputes.

Whenever one of the alternative means of dispute resolution is proposed, the first question that usually arises is, "But do they work?" While conclusive answers to this question are still being investigated, and no one dispute resolution procedure is appropriate or applicable for every situation, current research indicates that alternative dispute resolution procedures have a high rate of success and have saved the parties who have used them significant time, money, and organizational resources. A study of negotiated settlements of environmental cases conducted by Bingham (1986), the most quantitative and complete to date, found that in 132 disputes involving both site-specific and policy issues, parties reached negotiated agreements with the assistance of mediators or facilitators in 103 cases (78 percent). Bingham found little difference in the settlement rate between site-specific and policy level disputes. However, when the parties at the table had formal decision-making authority, they were able to reach agreement in 82 percent of the cases, as opposed to a 73 percent rate of settlement when they had only advisory authority.

Given the success rate of negotiated settlements and the alternative dispute resolution procedures which have been used to enhance them, it is clear that these processes deserve further study and application to complex disputes. In the remainder of this paper considerations that should be taken into account by decision makers, engineers, planners, and legal staff when deciding upon an approach to resolving complex environmental or public policy issues will be explored. Critical factors will be outlined for several stages of the negotiation process and several roles for third parties will be presented.

Defining the Source of the Conflict, Identifying Interests, and Framing the Issues

Once a party perceives that a conflict exists, a definition of the source of the conflict is the first significant step toward determining which conflict management procedures will be appropriate. There are few major sources of public conflicts. Conflicts can be caused by problems in the interpersonal relationships between the parties which makes them unable to solve problems jointly; by problems involving the adequacy, accuracy or interpretation of data; by problems of competing interests where the parties have perceived or actual incompatible needs which they believe can only be addressed at the expense of another party; by problems over competing values and beliefs; or by problems caused by the structural relationships of the parties such as the definition of roles, delegation of authority, or geographical proximity.

Once the source of the conflict has been defined, the interests of each contending party, also needs to be identified. Interests are the desires or needs that a party wants to have satisfied. Interests fall into three categories: substantive, procedural, and psychological/relationship needs. Substantive interests refer to concrete and tangible exchanges that are desired by a party. For example in a dispute over hydro power generation, the utility wanted to have a certain amount of generation capacity available at the time of peak power demand. The amount of power generation capacity which was needed was their substantive interest.

Procedural interests refer to needs or desires that a party has about the way that a dispute is resolved or its solution implemented. For example, in several recent negotiations over Indian water rights, the involved legal teams determined that the tribes could indeed win legal cases which would grant them badly needed water. Unfortunately, it was projected that legal victory via litigation would take many years to accomplish. The tribes had immediate needs for water and were willing to negotiate settlements which gave them earlier access to less water than might be attained through litigation. Their procedural interests were a settlement procedure that would result in a rapid agreement and one that was less costly than a judicial decision.

Psychological interests refer to how the individual
parties expect to be treated, and the type of relationship which is desired by the parties both during and
after the negotiations. For example, in a recent water
dispute, one of the parties attended a public meeting
to discuss the issues in question. During the public
meeting the party was verbally attacked by another. The
relationship between the parties was damaged and the
abused party had its interests of a relationship
characterized by trust and respect dashed.

Once the source of the conflict has been determined, and
interests identified, parties have to determine how they
will frame the issues in dispute. Issues are the topic
areas to be addressed by the parties. Framing refers
to the process of naming, describing or defining the
issues. Generally, parties tend to frame issues or
conflicts in an egocentric manner with little concern
regarding the perceptions or definitions of other
parties (Thomas, 1976). Thus one party in a Colorado
water dispute involving trans-mountain diversion framed
their problem as: "How to stop the rape and plunder of
agricultural interests by speculative pro-growth
elements who have no end to their greed"; while another
party framed the problem as: "How to get badly needed
water to urban areas and have it used in a more socially
responsible manner than supporting subsistence ranchers
who are going out of business anyway!"

Often the issue or problem is defined in terms of a
solution as opposed to framing it in terms of underlying
interests to be satisfied. For example, when negotiations were proposed to address the possible construction
of the Two Forks Dam and Reservoir, the problem was
initially framed by two of the key interest groups as:
"Should the dam be built at all?" or "What will be done
to mitigate potential impacts when the dam is built?"
Both of these framings of the problem immediately
maintained the polarization between concerned conservation and development interests. It was only when the
problem had been re-framed to: "How can the water needs
of the metropolitan Denver area be met, while protecting
the environmental quality and economic opportunities of
the regions from which the water is drawn?" that the
parties were able to make some headway in negotiations.
The parties, while unable to settle the issue regarding
the specific construction of Two Forks Dam, were able
to reach agreements regarding the need for Front Range
water storage and a conservation and metering plan for
the city of Denver.

Framing serves not only to define the problem, but also
to delineate what is, or is not negotiable. Framing

often involves the "too large/too small problem definition," or the "too general/too specific" dilemma.
Defining a problem in too narrow a way may preclude the
creation of innovative options, or may leave only
either/or options on the table; while defining an issue
or problem too broadly may lead to an unmanageable
number of issues or result in agreements which are too
superficial or general to be of use to the parties.

Often the process of issue identification and initial
framing is conducted by individual parties alone or in
interest groups.   However, in order for effective
problem solving to progress, it is often important for
parties with opposing viewpoints to consult each other
in the problem-defining process.   Ultimately, mutual
agreement and framing of the problem is an important
step toward convening a joint problem-solving session.

Identifying the Principle Parties

Identifying the principle parties to a dispute often
occurs concurrently with the identification of the
source of the conflict, key interests, and issues.
Generally parties can be identified by their past
involvement in decision making on similar issues, their
position as an institutional authority responsible for
handling the issues in dispute, or because they have a
reputation for involvement on the particular issue in
question.   Parties can be grouped into primary and
secondary categories, with primary parties being those
individuals, groups, or organizations which must be at
the table for an agreement to be reached; and secondary
parties, those individuals, groups or organizations
which will be affected by a decision but who probably
will not have the resources or power to directly
influence or block an outcome or its implementation.

Once key parties are identified, the party or parties
initiating an ADR procedure must decide what form of
representation is most desirable. In some disputes one
individual may directly represent an interest group and
have the authority to settle, while in other cases
interest group representation is accomplished through
a delegate who represents a party's views but must check
back with his or her constituency before final approval
of an agreement.

The organizational structure of parties and their
internal procedures for decision making should also be
taken into consideration when structuring negotiations.
Organizations, such as corporations, often have the
power to delegate authority to settle to an individual
decision maker; associations or public interest groups,

on the other hand, may require constituent approval or ratification. Anticipatory planning may prevent after-the-fact ratification problems and minimize structural constraints on the decision-making authority of the parties' representatives.

Deciding which Dispute Resolution Procedure to Use

Once the issues and interests are defined, the parties have to select a dispute resolution procedure which will help them to attain their goals (Moore and Delli Priscoli, 1989). Parties can select either a judicial/administrative settlement, a political settlement, or a voluntary negotiated settlement with or without the assistance of a third party impartial. In determining which approach to take parties must answer a series of questions (Creighton, 1988):

> 1) What is the relative power of the parties and how important is this dispute to each party? 2) Taking into account the relative power and commitment of each party, if this dispute continues on its present course, what is the most likely procedure by which it will be resolved? 3) Taking into account the relative power and commitment of each party, if this dispute continues on its present course, what are the most likely substantive outcomes and what are their relative probabilities? 4) Taking into account (the) predictions in Questions #2 and #3, what are the potential benefits/costs of the current procedure by which the dispute will be resolved? 5) Is the use of the current procedure justified? 6) Which ADR procedures are most suitable for this dispute? 7) What are the benefits/costs of using the most suitable ADR procedure? 8) Is the use of the ADR procedure justified?

If the parties determine that they do not have adequate power to assure a unilateral decision in their favor, the costs or risks of using an adversarial procedure are too high, the outcome of a dispute is unpredictable and predictability is important, a future relationship between the parties is desirable or necessary to implement a settlement, or the potential substantive outcomes of an adversarial process do not address underlying interests, then the parties may decide to initiate some form of negotiated settlement, with or without the assistance of a third party.

Unassisted or Assisted Negotiations

Early in the planning process of any alternative dispute resolution procedure the decision as to whether
third party assistance will be desirable or needed must
be addressed. Third party assistance is generally
useful in helping parties accomplish some of the tasks
described above, such as party/issue/interest identification; or in helping to overcome specific kinds of
barriers to settlement previously described such as:
relationship, procedural or substantive problems.

If the parties have extremely antagonistic relationships, there may be a need for a third party to play a
conciliatory role to convene the meetings, act as a
referee to prevent actions which could further damage
relationships, or to promote a positive working relationship.

A third party may be needed to either coach or train
the parties in how to set up and use a cooperative
problem-solving process; or a more directive procedural
intervention may be needed, in the form of facilitation
or mediation to help guide parties through the cooperative problem-solving or negotiation process (Moore,
1986b). Facilitators or mediators are neutral and
impartial third parties who assist disputing parties to
voluntarily arrive at acceptable agreements to issues
in dispute. These intervenors accomplish this by
providing a variety of procedural suggestions which
enhance negotiations. They do not make any substantive
decisions for the parties.

If there is a disagreement over data or the substance
of the discussions is the problem, the parties may need
third party assistance in obtaining more data or assessing the relevance of information. Disputes panels,
fact-finding, mini-trials, and settlement conferences
are procedures which provide parties with additional
information or third party evaluations of technical or
legal data (Moore and Delli Priscoli, 1989).

Securing third party assistance is usually a joint
effort of all parties, although one party may take the
lead. In a variety of water disputes the lead party in
securing third party services has been a governmental
agency--federal, state or local--within whose jurisdiction the dispute falls.

Convening: Background Data Collection, Bringing Parties to the Table, and Process Design

Regardless of whether a third party is used, the functions of convening, data collection, and process design are important considerations. Convening generally refers to the process of party and issue identification, agenda building, and bringing the parties to the table to discuss their differences. Convening should be distinguished from the later role of the mediator or facilitator in managing the on-going process of negotiations; or the role of the substantive neutral, such as the chair of a mini-trial or disputes panel member, who may assist the parties with data problems.

Convening involves not only identifying the appropriate people who should be at the bargaining table, but also persuading them that they should be participants and issuing invitations to be involved. In some conflicts the convening role and function entails only a brief education of the parties about the process for them to willingly and enthusiastically participate in negotiations, while in other disputes the convener may need to engage in aggressive persuasion to encourage the involvement of reluctant or recalcitrant parties.

Convening can be done by a third party, an independent and neutral organization such as a concerned foundation, one of the parties who is trusted by the majority of others, a governmental agency, or a public figure. In the Colorado Metropolitan Water Round Table, the convener was the governor and the governor's office. Governor Lamm was the only party in the state that had the influence necessary to bring all concerned parties to the table.

In addition to individual conveners who are in influential positions of authority, more and more government agencies are performing a convening role or function. The U.S. Army Corps of Engineers, the U.S. Environmental Protection Agency, the Bureau of Reclamation, the Forest Service, and the Minerals Management Service, and numerous state and local governments have convened meetings to negotiate settlements to environmental disputes.

Rarely does the third party alone convene a dispute resolution process. Generally the convening function is shared by the convening individual or agency and the third party conflict manager.

Convening may also involve obtaining relevant technical data or experts to assist the negotiators in making wise and informed decisions. Technical consultants, external to the dispute, may be brought in on an issue-by-issue basis, or one may be secured to provide information on all technical issues that arise during the negotiations.

Convening may also involve holding preliminary meetings, or "talks about talks," to discuss the viability of formal negotiations or to design procedures to be used to resolve disputes. These meetings allow primary parties to meet each other, explore alternatives for resolving the dispute and, if appropriate, develop procedures and protocols for formal negotiations.

Organizing the Parties For Concerted Action: Plenaries, Caucuses, Mixed Interest Working Groups and Technical Assistance From Substantive Experts

A variety of formats and procedures have been found to be effective in structuring the work in negotiations over environmental and water-related disputes. For some groups, the majority of the work can be conducted by discussion in plenary sessions. This approach is appropriate when the group is not too large, generally under 24 people; where highly polarized teams are not present; and where the group as a whole is able to work as a joint problem-solving team.

Another model involves the use of caucuses, or private meetings, among the members of a party or interest group. This format is often used in highly polarized disputes where the parties are formally organized into teams. In caucuses, issues are discussed, proposals are generated, and options evaluated. Caucuses are generally used in the context of periodic plenary sessions, but in some highly polarized disputes, caucuses may be the major working format. Caucuses may also be the medium which the mediator uses to separate hostile or antagonistic groups so as to minimize negative exchanges that inhibit the parties from reaching agreement.

A third model for processing issues is one commonly referred to as "small group to large." In this model, the members of the plenary session as a whole define the issues to be discussed and the interests to be satisfied, delineate general parameters which would be acceptable for settlement, and then delegate the process of working out concrete and detailed proposals to a series of small groups. The small groups, usually composed of representatives from diverse interest groups, work outside of the plenary session to develop integrative proposals which addresses all parties' interests and which will be "saleable" to the group as a whole. Tentative solutions or draft proposals are brought by the small working groups to the plenary session for discussion, consideration, modification or fine tuning, and approval. If the plenary is not satisfied with the results of the small groups' work, the problem or proposals may be sent back to the working group for further consideration, refinement, or revision.

Educating the Parties About the Issues and Interests

Generally environmental and water issues involve complex technical or legal information--data which is often not easily understood by the general public or information which is not widely accessible to diverse audiences. Experience with past environmental disputes indicates that numerous barriers to productive settlement negotiations may be avoided by providing parties with an early opportunity to educate each other about technical and legal questions and to address data problems.

Assessing data needs can be accomplished by several means. Parties at the beginning of negotiations can be asked to indicate the kinds of data that will be necessary for wise and comprehensive decision making. The parties can then proceed to devise means by which the requisite information can be obtained.

In disputes where the knowledge base between the parties is very diverse, the negotiations may begin with an extensive educational phase in which substantive experts acceptable to the various parties make presentations regarding the information which is needed. This model not only provides disputants with a common information base regarding issues in dispute, but also frequently develops the common perception that "we are all in this together" and builds the esprit de corps of the negotiating group.

Often the question arises as to who can provide acceptable data that will be perceived by all parties to be accurate and complete. Several models have been successfully used to address this concern. In some disputes, where some parties hold specific technical expertise, they may make special presentations to the negotiating group as a whole. This model works when all parties believe that an objective presentation of technical data by a partisan can be separated from the position or preferred solution of the presenter.

A second model is to have a technical consultant who is hired by the negotiating group as a whole, and therefore has all of the parties as his or her client. This technical resource can provide information requested by the group to address specific issues, may be used as a data arbitrator to evaluate the technical data presented by opposing sides, or may be asked to render an advisory opinion as to how the data should be interpreted.

An example of the third party expert in the arbiter role was illustrated in a Colorado water dispute. Opposing parties differed as to how to assess the amount of water that was available to a water provider to meet the demands of its customers. The provider had data that it believed was privileged information, which if revealed would greatly increase the cost of future acquisitions. However, without baseline data on potential water resources and reserves, environmentalists could not participate in negotiations. The parties, with the assistance of a mediator, worked out a procedure whereby the public interest groups would develop a computer model of the region which would calculate the amount of available water in various drainages. This model along with the confidential data of the water provider would be submitted to the review of an impartial water expert who could compare and contrast the models and data, verify their accuracy, provide the negotiators with acceptable baseline data, and protect the confidentiality of the information.

Another model for dealing with disagreements over data is to establish a procedure for sharing and evaluating data. The mini-trial, a procedure used by the Corps of Engineers to resolve the clean-up of a hazardous waste site in Phoenix, Arizona, where materials had leaked into the groundwater, involved a formalized procedure whereby each party's legal and technical staff made "best case" presentations of their data to decision makers from both sides. These key individuals subsequently used the data to negotiate a settlement (Collins, 1989).

Other procedures where competing data can be collected and evaluated, and where an advisory opinion of respected third party experts can be obtained are fact-finding and disputes panels. In these procedures a respected third party or panel of neutrals, collects or hears information regarding a dispute and issues an advisory opinion regarding liability or provides a range of possible settlement options. The parties can

then take this information and use it to guide further
negotiations.

Approaches to the Option Generation and Problem-Solving Process

Once data necessary for wise decision making has been
developed and exchanged by the parties, the negotiators
are ready to proceed with joint problem solving. The
first phase of this process is a joint framing, or if
necessary a re-framing, of the problems to be addressed. Problem definition or framing usually involves
the development of a joint problem statement--a
mutually acceptable description of the problem to be
addressed. The problem statement generally must include a description of the interests of each party
which are to be satisfied in a settlement.

The option generation phase of negotiations, mediated
negotiations, or cooperative problem solving is often
one of the most critical and problematic, for it is in
this phase that the parties may become the most positional and locked into untenable solutions that do not
meet or address all of the parties' interests. It is
in this phase that two maxims regarding option generation presented in Fisher and Ury's, *Getting to Yes:
Reaching Agreement Without Giving In (1981)*, are most
important. These authors argue for the generation of
multiple options and separation of the generation from
the evaluation process. This, they believe, will help
to prevent the parties from prematurely committing to
untenable solutions and will help produce higher
quality decisions. The identification of at least
three realistic options will provide the parties with
a genuine opportunity to make creative choices and to
make comparisons between a range of possible solutions.
With only two options, as is common in more traditional
negotiations and positional bargaining, the range of
choices is extremely narrow and the parties generally
have an opportunity to make only an "either/or" decision between opposing parties' proposals.

The option generation phase of the negotiation process
is often greatly enhanced by developing solutions
through a series of increasingly specific agreements
(Zartman and Berman, 1982). First the parties generate
a set of general principles, criteria, or standards
which will guide or shape the broad terms of settlement. Once these criteria have been identified, the
parties discuss them and reach some general levels of
agreement. This framework of general principles provides the criteria and parameters for subsequent option
generation efforts and more specific agreements.

In addition to the general-to-specific option generation procedure described above, parties may also want
to use several others. This author has previously
identified a variety of other means by which parties
can generate options (Moore, 1986). These include an
elaboration process, whereby parties identify a kernel
of an idea to which they can all agree, and then elabo-
rate upon it until such time as a complete settlement
has been reached; brainstorming, generating possible
solutions in rapid succession without evaluating them;
modification of "model" procedures which have been
developed in other settings to address similar problems; exploring trade-offs in which parties exchange
benefits on issues which they value differently; frac-
tionation or breaking a large problem into smaller sub-
problems that are more easily discussed and for which
solutions are more easily formulated; and the development of package proposals in which a composite settlement is developed which addresses all parties needs and
shares gains and losses.

**Assessing the Options and Evaluating Alternatives to
the Negotiated Settlement**

Once several viable settlement options have been
developed, the parties to a dispute have to evaluate
them and determine if they adequately address all
relevant interests. It is at this phase of the negotiations that the parties often reach impasse. Faced
with several options, some of which are less desirable
than others, the parties often are unsure as to whether
to settle or pursue a more litigious path to accomplish
their goals. Unfortunately parties often select the
latter course without considering the costs which may
accompany it. It is in this phase of the negotiations
that the parties need to consider their best alternative to negotiated agreement, or BATNA (Fisher and Ury,
1981). If the alternative to a negotiated settlement
is worse than the option on the table, a negotiated
settlement may be the preferable solution.

A premature leap to a settlement which is unacceptable
to one or more of the parties can often be delayed or
avoided by asking parties to review all of their interests, setting up a matrix chart to compare satisfaction
of interests with specific settlement options and
assessing probable consequences and costs of selecting
each option. Use of a structured comparison process
often enables parties to reach an agreement on available options, facilitates the construction of integrative settlement packages or enables parties to modify
options so as to make them more acceptable.

At this stage of negotiations the skills of a third party may be needed. The third party may be called upon to do some hard reality testing with parties who are rigidly adhering to untenable solutions.

Final Bargaining, Implementation, and Monitoring

The last stages of the negotiated problem-solving process involves final bargaining, construction of a consensus regarding the final settlement, and the development of implementation and monitoring plans. Final bargaining involves the modification and tailoring of proposals so that they are jointly acceptable to all parties. In some disputes this work may be done in a plenary session; while in other cases the work will be done in caucuses, mixed interest task groups, in meetings with constituencies, or via shuttle diplomacy with the assistance of a mediator. It is critical at this time that all negotiators focus on the broad areas of settlement and state explicitly all points of agreement, as well as making final adjustments and reaching closure on the areas of disagreement. Written transcription of settlements by a recorder in each group who reads back the settlement with final language or agreements and posts these on wall charts for all to see, often helps parties to identify the explicit areas of agreement as well as the areas remaining to be worked upon.

Conclusion

Negotiated settlements, either unassisted or assisted by a third party using an alternative dispute resolution procedure, have been proven to be effective means of resolving complex environmental disputes. Careful attention to the implementation of specific dispute resolution strategies at various stages of the negotiation process may greatly enhance the probability of success of cooperative problem-solving ventures.

APPENDIX

Bingham, Gail, *Resolving Environmental Disputes: A Decade of Experience*. Washington, DC: Conservation Foundation, 1986.

Collins, Richard, *The Goodyear Mini-Trial: Corps ADR Case Study #1*. Fort Belvoir, VA: Institute for Water Resources, 1989.

Creighton, James, "Deciding to Use an ADR Procedure" in *Alternative Dispute Resolution Procedures*. Christopher Moore and Jerome Delli Priscoli (Eds.), Washington, DC: U.S. Army Corps of Engineers, 1988.

Fisher, Roger and William Ury, *Getting to Yes: Negotiating Agreement Without Giving In*. Boston, MA: Hougton Mifflin Co., 1981.

Mark, Jonathan, Earl Johnson and Peter Szanton, <u>Dispute Resolution in America: Processes in Evolution</u>. Washington, D.C.: National Institute for Dispute Resolution, 1984.

Moore, Christopher W., *Decision Making and Conflict Management*. Boulder, CO: Center for Dispute Resolution, 1986a.

Moore, Christopher W., *The Mediation Process: Practical Strategies for Resolving Conflict*. San Francisco, CA: Jossey-Bass, 1986b.

Moore, Christopher W. and Jerry Delli Priscoli, (Eds.), *Executive Seminar on ADR Procedures* (Participant Workbook), Army Corps of Engineers, 1989.

Thomas, Kenneth "Conflict and Conflict Management," in *The Handbook of Industrial and Organizational Psychology*. Marvin D. Cunnette (Ed.), Chicago, IL: Rand McNally, 1983.

Zartman, I. William and Maureen R. Berman, *The Practical Negotiator*. New Haven and London: Yale University Press, 1982.

Managing Conflict Over a Dam Safety Problem

Curtis A. Brown[1]

Abstract: Structural analysis of the Bureau of Reclamation's Jackson Lake Dam, in Teton National Park, Wyoming, determined it would likely fail under expected earthquake loadings. A 1982 proposal by Reclamation to resolve the safety problem by constructing a new dam downstream met with strong opposition from local and national environmental and recreation groups, as well as other federal agencies. An intensive, short-duration, public involvement program was undertaken to resolve these conflicts and arrive at an implementable solution. A decision was reached to modify the existing dam. This modification was completed in 1988. Lessons from this and other conflict management situations are discussed.

INTRODUCTION

In the late 1970's, structural analysis of Jackson Lake Dam, built by the Bureau of Reclamation in 1916, indicated that the dam would likely fail under an earthquake of Richter magnitude 5.5 or greater. The dam, located on the Snake River in Teton National Park, had been built with construction techniques which left its foundation subject to liquefaction and slumping during strong earthquakes. It sits adjacent to the Teton fault, which is capable of generating a Richter 7.5 earthquake, and within 60 miles of the

[1]Head, Decision Analysis Section, Bureau of Reclamation, PO Box 25007, Denver, CO 80225

site of the Richter magnitude 7.1 earthquake on the Hebgen fault in 1959. Earthquakes of this magnitude in the vicinity of the dam were judged likely to lead to the dam's collapse. Several geological studies led to the conclusion that the chances of a dam failure in the next 100 years are about 40%. Failure of the dam would place 2,000 permanent residents and up to several thousand recreationists at risk, and cause over $100 million in damages and economic losses (Bureau of Reclamation, 1984a, 1984b).

In 1977, Reclamation lowered the maximum reservoir level by nine feet to reduce the chance of failure, and began investigating options for a permanent solution to the safety problem. In 1982, design engineers for Reclamation completed a report recommending that the preferred solution, from the standpoint of cost, engineering confidence, borrow required, amount of area impacted by construction, and time of construction, was to construct a "detention dam" approximately four miles downstream of Jackson Lake Dam which would catch and release slowly any flood resulting from the failure of the existing dam (US Bureau of Reclamation, 1982).

When this report became public, groups responded strongly to the possibility of a new dam being constructed in the National Park, criticizing Reclamation's "beaver mentality", and suggesting that the proposed solutions to the dams safety problems were worse than the problems themselves. National environmental and recreation organizations began taking positions against the proposal. However, other options, such as rebuilding the existing dam, at much greater cost, or greatly reducing the storage in the reservoir, also had their critics. The conflict quickly became intense between Reclamation, who had a statutory responsibility to protect the public from possible dam failure, environmental groups, who opposed a new dam in the park and feared the environmental effects of any construction activities at the existing dam, the irrigation districts, who depended on storage in the reservoir for their crops and who would likely have to share the cost of any solution, the downstream residents and businesses who would be inundated by a dam failure, river recreation interests who depended on regulation of flows out of Jackson Lake to maintain a long river running season, lake recreation concerns who benefited from a high, stable, lake level for their marina and boat ramps,

and the National Park Service, who would likely oppose a new dam in their park.

MANAGING THE CONFLICT

Conditions were not ideal for conflict resolution.
Because a restriction had already been placed on the
reservoir, limiting water storage, there was great
pressure to find an implementable solution as soon as
possible. On the plus side, the urgency to find a solution ensured high level agency support for the effort. Substantial resources were immediately committed to implementing an intensive public involvement
program. This included a very dedicated staff, the
principals of which were Max Van Den Berg, Jim
Mumford, Marilyn Collins, Don Tracy, Doug James,
Elaine Van Stelle, and Steve Wade for the Bureau of
Reclamation, and Dr. Marty Rozelle, a public involvement consultant.

Also important were the good relations developed
over the years between the Reclamation staff operating the reservoir and the principal users of Jackson
Lake and the upper Snake River, which included the
irrigators, lake recreationists, river
recreationists, and the National Park Service. This
had created a level of trust with some of the key interest groups that was critical to the program.

Long-standing relationships did not exist with some
of the other key interest groups, principally the
various environmental interests. To establish better relations, a more intensive public involvement
program was initiated immediately. In 1983, the period covering most of the major study decisions,
there were 8 mailings to 915 groups and individuals,
11 briefings for groups and agencies, and 12 public
meetings.

PUBLIC VALUES ASSESSMENT

To facilitate identifying an implementable solution
in a short period of time, a decision-analytic technique known as a public values assessment (PVA) was
employed. Details of this technique can be found in
Bureau of Reclamation, 1983, and another example of
its application in Brown, 1978. A public values assessment approaches this type of public controversy
as a decision problem. What option or solution best
meets the values or preferences of the involved

groups and agencies?   What are the critical decision
factors?   How does each group weigh the various factors in their own decision?   How does each alternative perform on those factors?

This approach explicitly recognizes the role of
values in guiding decisions. It provides a framework
for discussing values and goals separate from specific proposals. It distinguishes between value judgments and technical judgments, and   provides a clear
and retraceable process for combining the two to
reach a decision -- particularly helpful when trying
to document the basis for a government decision. (See
Arkes and Hammond,   1986, for recent readings and applications of decision analytic methods to public
policy disputes.)

For the Jackson Lake program, a simplified public
values assessment was employed. Decision factors were
defined reflecting the goals and concerns of the
various interest groups. These were the criteria
against which the performance of each alternative
would be evaluated. Each group's values were represented by their "weighting" of the decision factors.
Alternatives were developed, and evaluated against
each decision factor.   Overall scores were then calculated for each alternative, for each of the various
groups involved in the conflict.

Decision Factors. Based on public comment and discussion, eight critical factors were identified which
seemed to describe the range of benefits and impacts
of the alternatives, as shown in Table 1.

Definitions of these factors were drawn up. These
definitions described both the type of benefit or
loss that was of concern and the range of impact that
could be expected on that factor across all of the
alternatives.   These materials were provided to participants for the weighting portion of the PVA.

Weights. Forty-nine groups and organizations par-
ticipated in the PVA, in June, 1983. Through a rank-
ing and rating exercise, each participant developed a
set of numeric weights describing the relative importance they would attach to each decision factor.
Participants identified their predominant area of
concern and based on this they were clustered into
eight value groups (Table 2).   An average set of
weights was developed for each group.

Table 1. Decision factors for the Jackson Lake Safety of Dams Study

---

Construction impacts
Losses from dam failure
Water storage in reservoir
Flood control benefits
River recreation
Lake recreation
Oxbow Bend impacts[1]
Wildlife and fishery impacts
Local economy
National Park preservation[2]
Construction costs

---

[1] The Oxbow Bend is an area immediately downstream of the dam which, due to the regulation of river flow by the dam, has developed into an unusually stable and productive riparian habitat.

[2] This factor addressed concerns over the possible precedent-setting effect construction of a new dam would have on the institutional integrity of Teton and other National Parks

---

Table 2. Value groups for Jackson Lake Safety of Dams Study

Irrigation interests
Environmental groups
Flood control interests
Safety interests
Lake recreation interests
National Park interests
River recreation interests
Park visitors

As an example, the weights are shown for the Environment and Irrigation groups in Table 3. Not surprisingly, the Environment group emphasized impacts to the Oxbow Bend area, consequences for wildlife and fisheries, and preserving the National Park as an area free from construction of major structures. Irrigators were most concerned with maintaining storage in the reservoir and the dam's flood control benefits, avoiding possible losses from dam failure, and minimizing cost of a solution.

Table 3. Average Percent Weights for the Environment and Irrigation Groups

	Environment	Irrigation
Construction impacts	5.3	6.3
Losses from dam failure	9.7	13.3
Water storage in reservoir	7.2	17.5
Flood control	9.2	14.9
River recreation	8.8	5.9
Lake recreation	6.3	5.3
Oxbow Bend impacts	15.5	5.3
Wildlife and fishery	15.4	6.1
Local economy	7.4	6.1
National Park preservation	13.7	6.0
Construction costs	1.5	13.3

Alternatives. The set of alternatives was defined, as shown in Table 4. The compressed schedule required shortchanging some of the time and effort that would normally be spent "scoping" issues and possible solutions. Instead, a list of issues and options was drawn up from previous public input and engineering analyses as a starting point for the program. This restricted range of options was the most common source of public complaints, which led to inclusion of an additional option (alternative E), suggested by the public, which involved reducing the reservoir's storage by half and adoption of additional water conservation measures by irrigators.

Table 4. Alternatives for the Jackson Lake Safety of Dams Study

---

A. Reconstruct existing dam
B. Construct a new storage dam downstream, breach existing dam
C. Construct a "detention dam" downstream to catch a failure flood
D. Restrict reservoir to natural lake level (no regulated storage)
E. Lower reservoir to 76% of present capacity
F. Lower reservoir to 34% of present capacity
G. No action

Technical Performance Ratings. Each alternative was evaluated by appropriate technical specialists to determine how it performed on each decision factor compared to all other alternatives. An alternative received a score of 100 on a factor if it attained the highest benefit as described in the factor's definition. For example, Alternative A received a 100 on the River Recreation factor because it produced the highest number of river recreation days annually with flows above a level defined as minimally acceptable by the river running community.

Overall Scores for Alternatives. The overall performance for an alternative depends both on how it performs on each decision factor and the importance a particular group attaches to that factor. Therefore, scores differ across groups. To calculate a group's score for an alternative, the alternative's technical performance ratings on the decision factors are multiplied by that group's weight on the corresponding factor, and the products are summed across all decision factors. The overall scores for the alternatives, for each group, are graphically summarized in Figure 1.

Value Group

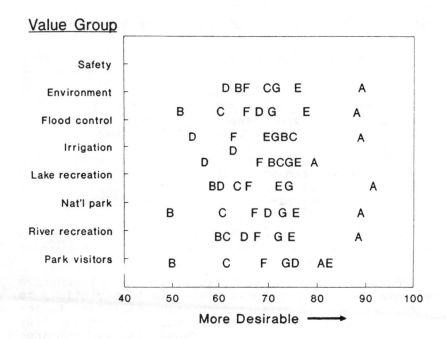

Figure 1. Jackson Lake alternatives, overall scores by interest group.

Surprisingly, there was considerable agreement in the overall scores across groups. Alternative A, modifying the existing dam, was the highest rated option for all groups. This suggested that although some interests had expressed strong concerns about the environmental and visitor impacts of reconstructing the existing dam, and other interests had been concerned about the high cost and uncertain construction procedures for this option, the possible advantages of dam modification appeared to outweigh these concerns and present a basis for compromise.

Further, only for the Flood Control Group did either of the options involving a new downstream dam rate in the top three alternatives. This suggested that it was unlikely that broad enough support could be developed for either of these alternatives to be implemented.

One of the advantages of the PVA approach is that it facilitates exploring "what-if" questions. One of the significant unknowns during the Jackson Lake study was whether impending Congressional legislation

would require that beneficiaries of a water project
share in the cost of bringing a dam up to modern
safety standards. To cover this possibility, a
"cost-sharing" decision factor was included in the
PVA, representing the amount of money the irrigators
would have to contribute to each alternative solution. Given the wide range of costs for the various
alternatives, this could be a critical factor. Since
it was not known if cost sharing would be required,
this factor was addressed in a sensitivity analysis.
Figure 2 shows the overall ratings of the alternatives for the Irrigation group, with and without cost
sharing included. It can be seen that a requirement
for cost sharing greatly reduces the attractiveness
of alternative A, which was the most expensive solution, and shifts this group toward non-structural options. As it turned out, the final 1984 Safety of
Dams Act amendments did not require cost sharing for
the Jackson Lake modifications. Several other sensitivity analyses were conducted, examining the effect
of changes in weights or technical ratings.

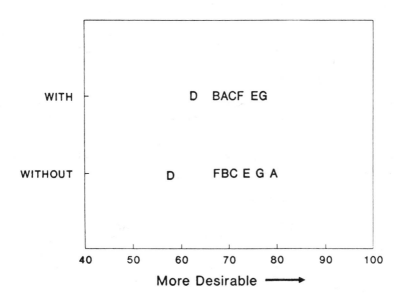

Figure 2. Jackson Lake alternatives, overall scores
for the Irrigation group, with and without the Cost
Sharing decision factor included.

SELECTION OF A PREFERRED ALTERNATIVE

In July, 1983, the results of the PVA were presented to the various interest groups for refinement
and discussion, and to use as a framework for identifying areas of agreement and possible compromise.
The participants generally confirmed that the results
reflected their values and preferences for the alternatives. Suggestions were made for refining the alternatives. Three additional public meetings were
held in September, 1983, before Reclamation and the
National Park Service jointly recommended alternative
A, modification of the existing Jackson Lake Dam, as
the preferred alternative to the Secretary of the Interior. The final environmental impact statement was
filed in November, 1984, and construction authorized
by Congress in June, 1985.

Modification of the dam, to increase the density
and stability of its foundation, was initiated in
May, 1986 and completed in October, 1988.

LESSONS IN CONFLICT MANAGEMENT

Several principles in conflict management were illustrated by the Jackson Lake case. Presented first
are some of the elements that contributed to the initially intense conflict.

Unilateral actions. Even though the engineering
analysis recommending construction of a new dam as
the "technically preferred alternative" was not intended to be a final agency recommendation, it was
perceived by many interest groups as a unilateral decision without their input or comment.

Restricted range of criteria. Partly because of
the limited interaction with interest groups, the engineering analysis employed a limited range of
evaluation criteria, mostly cost and engineering factors, and therefore lead to a recommendation that did
not consider all of the factors necessary in reaching
a broadly supportable decision. In this case, the
best engineering solution was not the most feasible
solution.

Next are described some of the positive elements in
the study that helped reduce conflict and arrive at

an implementable solution.

Believable threat to safety. This case reaffirmed that a critical prerequisite to reaching a solution amongst multiple interest groups is a shared belief in the existence of a problem that must be solved. Such a belief creates a mutuality of goals without which a solution may not be achievable. Reclamation spent considerable time and money enlisting many of the world's top experts in analyzing the threat to the dam from earthquakes. When the several reports were completed, very little doubt existed in the public's mind that such earthquakes could occur in the near future, and that a dam failure would very likely result. Several briefings and extensive newsletters described the many technical issues bearing on the decision.

Personal trust. Studies have shown that public acceptance of risk information is a function not only of the clarity of data, but also of public trust in the messenger and associated institutions (Fessendon-Radon, Fitchen, and Heath, 1987). While federal agencies and national organizations are involved in these types of conflict, trust must be developed at a personal level. The willingness of the study staff and top management to talk or meet with interest groups at any time, to consider and evaluate their proposals seriously, to address their questions and concerns, built the basic familiarity and trust needed to begin working toward an acceptable solution.

Flexibility in engineering standards. There is little question that construction of a new structure downstream of Jackson Lake dam, at Pacific Creek, was a more attractive engineering option than rebuilding the existing structure. It took advantage of a far superior location, geologically and topographically, and utilized fairly standard design features and construction methods. (The Pacific Creek site was sometimes referred to as "where Jackson Lake Dam should have been built".) Alternatively, modifying the foundation of the existing dam required use of new techniques which were little used in Reclamation, and which could not be guaranteed ahead of time to completely solve the problem. Thus, a critical element in resolving the conflict, was a willingness on the part of Reclamation design and construction engineers to explore, test, and verify new approaches to dam

modification, and implement as best as possible something less than the best engineering solution.

A range of options. As mentioned earlier, Reclamation was criticized for not involving the public earlier in the development of possible alternatives. In
this respect, the Jackson Lake study, because of the
compressed schedule, violated one of the cardinal
rules of public involvement. One step toward addressing this concern was the adoption and evaluation
of an additional option, alternative E, suggested by
the public.   The public also played an ongoing role,
helping to refine the preferred plan all the way
through final implementation.

Sufficient resources for public involvement.   Public involvement for studies involving substantial
conflict requires an amount of staff time and resources that is almost always surprising to managers.
It is not uncommon for a study manager to spend half
of his or her time on public involvement.   For support staff it can be a full time job.   And in conflict situations, a little public involvement can be
worse than none at all.   If management decides that
no implementable decision can be reached without resolving the conflict, then a commitment must be made
to provide a sustained, adequate program.   The worst
situation is to start a program without the resources
to carry it through, thereby raising expectations for
an open, comprehensive process, only to frustrate the
public when channels of communication are inadequate
or get closed off.

Some additional suggestions can be derived from the
Jackson Lake study and others.

**Remember that the process of arriving at a decision
is as important as the technical studies themselves.**
Particularly for technical professionals, it is hard
to keep in mind that the best technical analyses will
not, by themselves, lead to an implementable solution
if the parties to the conflict feel that the planning
and decision process has been unfair or arbitrary.

**Strive to reduce uncertainty about the facts, with-
out hiding true uncertainty.** In almost all conflicts, basic agreement about the facts, including
the nature and the seriousness of the problem to be
solved, is prerequisite to a solution. Developing
credible descriptions of both the problem and

possible solutions is therefore critical. However, the credibility of the technical studies can be undermined if, possibly in an attempt to eliminate disagreement about the facts, the results are presented as completely certain, without margins of error or qualification.

Don't propose anything until you've talked to the major interest groups. During preliminary technical studies, some options may seem obviously appealing and appear to dominate all other alternatives. However, before proposing such options unilaterally, "sensing" discussions should be held with the major interests to check that critical factors or impacts have not been overlooked, and to avoid the appearance of a "closed" process.

Always remember how long you've been working on the problem, and all the stupid ideas you had earlier. By the time most issues have become public conflicts, technical studies have been underway for quite some time, often years. In these cases it is easy for technical professionals to forget that the issues are new to the involved publics, to forget how long they themselves have been grappling with the issues, and how many bad ideas they have already screened out. This can lead to impatience with the public, and attempts to push too fast an unavoidably lengthy process of public education and participation.

Resist all attempts to make policy debates into technical debates. Public conflicts are almost always a tangled web of both technical problems and policy or value conflicts. In many cases our institutions are relatively less able to deal with the policy and value conflicts. There is, therefore, constant pressure to turn what are policy questions into technical questions, to search for a technical answer to questions like, "how safe is safe enough?" At the same time there is a natural tendency for technical professionals to want to make contributions in all areas of a conflict and therefore to accept these policy debates as a technical problem. This is a trap. Value and policy conflicts are not resolved until policy issues are recognized as such, and dealt with by the public, interest groups, and the political process. Trying to solve them technically puts the technical professional in a no-win situation, attempting to solve a question with the wrong tools, and suffering the wrath of the involved parties for "dictating policy" and trying to "force an engineering solution on a social problem".

Develop skills and experience for risk negotiation. In many conflicts, the set of solutions is limited by the need for all solutions to meet various engineering and other technical standards. These standards define the level of safety or performance the solutions must provide. Design standards are critical safeguards of the public health and well-being, as evidenced by the consequences of two recent earthquakes of the same magnitude; the San Francisco earthquake with less than 100 lives lost, versus the Armenian earthquake with 25,000 fatalities, primarily due to the collapse of buildings. However, in some cases, adherence to existing design standards may provide levels of safety or performance that society cannot afford. Some relaxation of standards may open the door to feasible solutions to an otherwise intractable conflict. For such an approach to be both productive and responsible, technical professionals must engage in an open-minded, thoughtful dialogue with officials and the public, evaluating the benefits and the consequences of various modifications to standards. At the same time, we must develop the political and institutional mechanisms to recognize and facilitate these "risk negotiations" and protect the involved parties and agencies from unreasonable liability.

Promote training relevant to conflict management. Expanding the role of technical professionals in conflict management requires emphasizing new types of training. Technical professionals can play many roles in conflict management, including the role of a technical specialist evaluating alternatives, as a participant in negotiation settings representing agencies or interests, as a mediator or facilitator in conflict situations, and as a convener of a negotiation group to resolve conflicts. Each role requires special skills, most of which are not addressed in traditional technical curriculums.

If you are a study manager for a controversial study expect half of your time to be spent on public involvement. In many cases, technical professionals who are managing controversial studies are surprised and frustrated by the amount of time they must spend speaking with interest groups, arranging meetings, preparing public information materials, etc. Much of this frustration can be avoided if these demands on time and resources are accurately anticipated, and properly budgeted and staffed.

Expect half of your budget to be spent on technical studies requested by the public. In this same vein, managers are often surprised to see their budget being diverted to unanticipated studies requested by interest groups and other involved agencies. Again, this is a common cost of business for resolving conflicts, to ensure that all parties feel that their concerns are being addressed.

References

Arkes, R., and Hammond, K.R. (1986) Judgment and Decision Making: An Interdisciplinary Reader, Cambridge University Press, 1986.

Brown, Curtis A. (1983). The Central Arizona Water Control Study: A Case for Multiobjective Planning and Public Involvement. Water Resources Bulletin, Vol. 20(3).

Fessendon-Radon, J., Fitchen, J.M., and Heath, J.S. (1987) "Providing Risk Information in Communties: Factors Affecting What is Heard and Accepted", Science, Technology, and Human Values, 12, 94-101.

Bureau of Reclamation (1982). ACER Technical Memorandum No. JL-222-5, Modification Decision Analysis for Jackson Lake Dam.

Bureau of Reclamation (1983). Public Values Assessment Appendix: Jackson Lake Safety of Dams Project, November.

Bureau of Reclamation (1984a). Modification Report: Jackson Lake Safety of Dams Project, October.

Bureau of Reclamation (1984b). Public Involvement Summary Report: Jackson Lake Safety of Dams Project, October.

Conflict Management and the Urban/Rural Watershed

Harold J. Day, Member ASCE

Abstract

The changing character of water resources management in the urban/rural watershed is described. An overview analysis of implementable public sector projects indicates that three elements are needed for success--knowledge, mandate and money. The trend towards including more of the stresses causing degradation of the water resources in studies of urban dominated watersheds is reviewed. The potential for increased conflict and, therefore, conflict management is reported. The paper is concluded with the prediction that the civil engineer can be expected to play a larger role in conflict management of water resources in the future.

Introduction

The problem of regional water resources management is well known and has been addressed by many investigators. The literature is rich in technical papers and books on the subject. Few journals are published without at least one paper on the subject. Many papers include both hydrologic and economic analyses. They also include formal systems analysis procedures. More recently the concepts of ecosystem analysis and sustainability have been introduced to the literature (Caldwell, 1988; Anonymous, 1987). Our knowledge of the complex interconnections of land, water and air systems in urban dominated watersheds has expanded significantly during the past decade, e.g. the role of toxic chemicals through bioaccumulation in the aquatic food chain. Yet we have little evidence of significant progress in management of these de-

----

Professor of Environmental Sciences, Room ES 317, University of Wisconsin-Green Bay, Green Bay, WI 54311-7001.

graded systems. Droughts and floods certainly are important factors in these systems but they often do not
dominate the analysis of a particular degraded watershed. Rather, cultural factors such as toxic chemical
discharges from both agricultural fields and urban industrial plants and overfishing in downstream receiving waters dominate the analysis.

Most large urban areas of the US are located in
watersheds that have these problems today. This is
true in spite of the massive public/private sector investment in waste water treatment plants during the
past two decades. Has our understanding of the
urban/rural watershed changed recently? If so, from
what to what? Has the role of the civil engineer
changed? If so, from what to what? While others have
recently addressed the broader question of a changing
role for civil engineers in water resources management
in general (Viessman, 1989), this paper is written to
focus on the urban/rural watershed and the emerging
role of the civil engineer in conflict management as
one new approach to regional water resources management.

Fundamental Requirements for Implementation of a Complex Public Policy

Solutions to water resource management issues in
problem areas like the urban/rural watershed are dependent upon a combination of technical, economic and
political activities. It is often the case that civil
engineers discount or sometimes neglect to consider
the non-technical parts of the implementation effort.
This brief section is presented to emphasize the other
requirements for action.

It may be useful to think about three key
actions/activities that are necessary prior to a successful completed project. They are knowledge, mandate and money. Adequate technical knowledge of the
problem is necessary first. It may take many years to
gain this knowledge and the scientist/engineer has the
dominant role in this effort. A complete understanding of the problem is not necessary; only enough information to have confidence that the solutions proposed are appropriate ones and that they include
corrective actions that are implementable.

Once there is adequate technical knowledge, it is
necessary to develop public support for the project.

This is the mandate. A clear mandate is not
necessary, only the perception of a mandate by decision makers (usually elected officials). With adequate knowledge to generate a sound base of alternative actions and a mandate for action, money is the
remaining factor needed.

These three steps are an oversimplification, of
course. Legal intervention, lack of sufficient equipment and lack of trained staff would all prevent
implementation. There are few examples of completed
public programs, however, that have not included this
combination of knowledge, mandate and money. The effort to develop a mandate is usually underestimated by
engineers involved in these watershed problems. Sometimes the community becomes very polarized and nothing
happens. Other times, higher priority public sector
projects such as education, public safety, or drugs
intervene and direct the watershed project to a second
order listing. Skills of conflict management can
serve in a valuable manner during the effort to build
a mandate. It is important for all of these activities to be considered and resources directed toward them appropriately during the development and
implementation of water resource management programs
in urban/rural watersheds.

Regional Water Resource Management - An Evolving Con-
cept

The basic ideas associated with planning and
implementation of regional water resource projects
have expanded during the past half century. Early on,
single purpose water quantity projects such as flood
control, irrigation or municipal water supply
dominated. Later, a shift to include multiple use,
water quantity projects occurred. Complex regional
water quality issues were initially modeled during the
1960's with the Delaware River study (Jacoby and
Loucks, 1972) and attempts to address them nationwide
were made a few years later in Section 208 of P.L.
92-500, Amendments to the Water Pollution Control Act
of 1972. Most Section 208 studies were directed primarily to biodegradable waste waters from point
sources.

During the late 1970's, attention was directed to
the analysis and management of the same regional set
of water resource problems in a more holistic manner.
In the Great Lakes, this attention resulted in the

drafting and adoption of the Great Lakes Water Quality
Agreement of 1978 by the International Joint Commission. Called the ecosystem approach, this holistic
effort was organized to integrate the analysis of a
number of stresses present in a given watershed, e.g.
municipal and industrial point sources, urban and rural non point sources, toxics and exotic fishery
(Francis, et. al., 1979 and Harris, et. al., 1982).
Today this approach is the philosophical basis for a
massive planning effort throughout the Great Lakes.
The US and Canadian governments, stimulated by the International Joint Commission, have begun ecosystem
planning efforts in 42 parts of the Great Lakes, those
areas where the surface water pollution problems are
judged to be most severe. Called Areas of Concern,
the planning effort leads to preparation of a Remedial
Action Plan (RAP). These RAP's are, with few excep-
tions, being prepared with little or no attention to
the principles of regional planning used in the 60's
and 70's, i.e. alternatives with benefit and cost estimates for each. The ecosystem approach has also
been used elsewhere in the US to address complex
regional water resource problems, e.g. Chesapeake Bay,
Tampa Bay, and Puget Sound.

More recently the concept of sustainable development has been developed (Anonymous, 1987). Sometimes
called the Brundtland report, this publication contains the suggestion that the integrity of the ecosystem is a necessary part of the long-term economic,
technologic and institutional development plan for the
natural resources of the world. Sustainable development tends to include the ecosystems approach as a
necessary element.

A trend in the planning and management of
urban/rural watersheds during the past twenty-five
years or so seems apparent. The trend is toward the
inclusion of more stresses present, e.g. point
sources, non-point sources, exotic fishery, navigation, droughts, floods, toxics and shoreline erosion.
It is also toward the inclusion of more interested
groups in the planning process. It is away from the
principles of planning based on economics and engineering. The role of the engineer has changed. It is
still important but is less dominant. With planning
and management activities less dominated by the engineer and the economist, there is an emerging role for
the engineer: conflict management. This new role is
likely to grow for several reasons.

- The increased demand for the limited land and water resources in the urban/rural watersheds. More and more people are expected to seek access to these resources.

- The continued involvement of more interested parties in the planning process e.g. industrialists, conservationists, environmentalists, homeowners, farmers and fishermen.

- The increasing demand and decreasing supply of public money to pay for the proposed additional facilities and institutions.

Conflict Management and the Civil Engineer

Conflict management may be considered as the alternative to the formal court process for resolution of complex disputes. Sometimes called dispute resolution, it has been more formally defined to be "a variety of approaches that allow the parties to meet face to face to reach a mutually acceptable resolution of the issues in a dispute or potentially controversial situation. Although there are differences among the approaches, all are voluntary processes that involve some form of consensus building, joint problem solving, or negotiation. Litigation, administrative procedures, and arbitration are not included in this definition" (Bingham, 1986).

What are the conflict management opportunities for civil engineers in urban/rural watershed situations? Three seem to be readily identifiable. 1) serve as an appointed or elected public official with policymaking responsibilities. As such the civil engineer can be expected to use his or her training as one member of the conflict management group. 2) serve as a member of the interdisciplinary technical team retained to analyze the watershed problem. The most likely role for a civil engineer in this team would be to participate in the creative effort to identify alternative solutions and make cost estimates for those alternatives. Further, civil engineers could be expected to play a major role in the use of microcomputers to provide dynamic visual displays of the results from analyzing alternatives to policy makers. 3) The civil engineer could serve as a citizen participant in the problem identification and review of proposed solutions to alternatives.

Conclusions and Recommendations

Conclusions

- There will be more conflicts in the future as efforts are made to manage water resources in the urban/rural watershed. Some will be resolved in the courts but increased efforts will be exercised to resolve them in the conflict management manner. Civil engineers and the rest of society will become increasingly aware that conflict management is a normal and necessary part of water resources management.

- The role of the civil engineer has changed over the past twenty-five years. Today, it must adapt to the present societal approach--seek to understand the watershed system as a multiple stressed system with multiple causes and effects using the ecosystem perspective. Expect a diverse and active group of participants in the planning and implementation process.

Recommendations

- Encourage the development of an urban/rural watershed planning process that includes a structure conducive to systematic analysis, i.e. identify, analyze and evaluate the effectiveness of alternatives while maintaining the concepts of ecosystems analysis. This process will, naturally, involve civil engineers and will set the stage for effective conflict management using a broad technical information base.

- Develop educational opportunities (at the undergraduate level, the graduate level, as well as in continuing education) for civil engineers and other professionals to learn more about planning and management in this new era. Focus part of the educational effort on conflict management.

References

Anonymous, Our Common Future - The World Commission on Environment and Development, Oxford, New York, 1987.

Bingham, G., Resolving Environmental Disputes, Conservation Foundation, Washington, DC, 1986.

Caldwell, L. K., Perspectives on Ecosystem Management of the Great Lakes, State University of New York Press, Albany, 1988.

Francis, G. R., Magnuson, J. J., Regier, H. A. and
    Talhelm, D. R., "Rehabilitating Great Lakes
    Ecosystem," Tech. Report No. 37, Great Lakes
    Fishery Commission, 1979.

Harris, H. J., Talhelm, D. R., Magnuson, J. J. and
    Forbes, A. M., "Green Bay in The Future - A Reha-
    bilitative Prospectus," Tech. Report No. 38,
    Great Lakes Fishery Commission, 1982.

Jacoby, H. D. and Loucks, D. P., "Combined Use of Op-
    timization and Simulation Models in River Basin
    Planning," Water Resources Research, Vol. 8, No.
    6, December 1972.

Viessman, W., Jr., Unpublished Address given at the
    Annual Meeting, Amer. Soc. Civil Engrs., Water
    Resources Planning and Management Division, May
    22-24, 1989, Sacramento, CA.

Conflict: A Stimulant for Action

Jonathan W. Bulkley   F.ASCE[1]

Introduction

It is important to establish a reference point for this examination of conflict in water-related projects. Historically, governmental units at the local, regional, state, federal, and international level have had specific responsibilities to plan and implement water-related projects for the benefit of society. One may consider that water projects being developed as a consequence of governmental action are an output or product of the associated political system. In the most general sense, the primary role of a political system is to facilitate interactions through which societal values are authoritatively allocated (Easton, 1966). In the context of water resources, the political systems operating at the federal, state, regional, and local level act to allocate societal values in the use of water for a range of purposes and uses. Also, as a consequence of shared water resources between the United States and Canada and Mexico, international political systems exist to facilitate the management of these shared resources in ways to reflect national values.

Political systems operate, in part, through a process which includes a number of interacting and related elements. This process includes demands/support for action, authoritative decisions, outcomes/ policies, and subsequent feedback in the form of altered demands/support. Political systems function as a continuous activity that responds to the needs/desires of the society and reflects the particular values operative in the society and culture at specific points in time. For example, the 1902

[1]Professor of Natural Resources, Professor of Civil Engineering, The University of Michigan, Ann Arbor, MI 48109.

Reclamation Act committed the U.S. Federal Government to building irrigation projects in the arid and semi arid regions of the West. It had taken nearly twenty-five years for the Congress to develop the policy and program to have the federal government undertaking water development projects in the West (McCool, 1987).

It is clear that sufficient resources needed to satisfy all societal desires are simply not available; hence, a competitive situation exists in which the political system acts to rank and provide those outcomes/policies which respond to the demands and support being felt at the particular moment. Conflict is an essential aspect of the political system since it functions in part to assure that a particular policy or a project is considered from a variety of perspectives and viewpoints. The presence of conflict acts to illuminate the full dimensions of a policy/activity such that decision-makers become aware of the implications of choosing a particular project or policy. Finally, the political system is dynamic and provides for change as values evolve and different societal priorities emerge.

Theoretical Foundation

It is a major thesis of this paper that conflicts can serve a positive role in water management situations. This positive aspect of conflict arises from the fact that human societies reflect a multiplicity of values which are non-universally held. Political systems exist in order to make authoritative allocations of values for societies. The positive role of conflict is thus to assure that all facets of a policy, project, issue, or program are illuminated. As a consequence of such illumination, one may observe new and innovative solutions being conceived and implemented to resolve the conflict situations.

At the level of the individual, evidence exists that humans when confronted with conflict will undertake unconscious but often creative behavior (Vaillant, 1977). For the individual, this creative behavior may take the form of adaptive or coping mechanisms which enable individuals to function in productive ways as they experience the living of life. At this level, the individual is not conscious of the adaptive behavior; these adaptive styles of defense reflect the adaptive and executive aspects of the brain. (Vaillant, 1977).

In the field of water management, as in every field of human endeavor, individual human behavior is certainly important. In addition, agencies or special interests acting in collective ways are critical players in the water planning and management arena. The nature of water management is complex, and there is need for professional expertise to plan certain elements of a water development program. However, this water planning and implementation process is basically a political process since there are limited resources available and different perspectives (values) on how the resources should be developed, who should receive the benefits from the water projects, and who should pay for the cost of building and operating the project. In essence, water policy and planning is a generalized resource allocation problem and needs the functional impact of conflict between interacting agencies, groups, and interests.

Conflict serves as a stimulant to action within any political system. For example, Easton observes that support or energy in the form of orientation which may either promote or resist both demands and decisions within the political process are necessary ingredients to keep the system operating (Easton, 1965).

The positive role of conflict is seen as a stimulus for establishing new rules, new norms, and new institutions. As a consequence of conflict, readjustment of relationships to changed conditions becomes possible (Coser, 1956). Coser also points out that conflict serves to maintain both identity and boundaries between groups. Furthermore, conflict may activate the energies of members of a group which finds itself in conflict with others and this enhances the internal cohesion of a group. It should be noted that in pluralistic situations, conflicts often are noncumulative, that is, if agencies or interests are in conflict over one issue, they are not necessarily opposed over another issue (Dahl, 1965).

In the field of water planning and policy there are many areas in which conflicts may arise. For example, conflicts arise over the allocation of water between consumptive and non-consumptive uses; conflicts arise over standard setting with regard to water quality (How safe is safe?); and conflicts arise over implementation priorities and user charges. A number of case examples will be cited to illustrate these conflicts and mechanisms utilized to resolve the conflicts. In certain examples--the conflicts are continuing and are not resolved.

Water Conflicts

Conflicts between agencies and interests regarding water resources reflect regional differences in our country. In the humid riparian East, the conflicts are more likely to focus upon quality issues excepting those situations where transbasin diversions are limiting or potentially limiting water related activities in the basin of origin. In the semi-arid and arid West, both quantity and quality issues serve to focus upon water conflicts. Often the water related disputes are complex from a technical perspective, and they require multidisciplinary approaches. The stakes are high--a major change in existing or future quality of life may be involved. The proposed activity may in fact be irreversible. The economic costs are often high; the economic benefits may be significant as well, but in the past those who paid and those who gained the greatest benefit were not necessarily the same. In some cases there may be a high degree of uncertainty present with regard to the probabilities associated with an unwelcome outcome. As a consequence of society's need for water, there are multiple stake-holders impacted by water decisions. It is often the case that multiple technical agencies interact as well. Questions arise as to who represents public and how do different people value different aspects of the water decision. In the balance of this paper, five examples will be discussed which illustrate conflict resolution completed and conflict resolution ongoing in the water arena.

The Detroit Rate Case: Conflicts Over User Charges

In April 1977 the U.S. Environmental Protection Agency filed suit against the City of Detroit and its Water and Sewage Department for failure to implement secondary treatment at its wastewater treatment plant. A related aspect of this case was a suit brought by the seventy eight (78) communities and agencies under contract with the City of Detroit to have their waste water treated at the City of Detroit's wastewater treatment plant. The communities served by the City of Detroit filed suit to reduce the rates they were charged by the City of Detroit. These communities alleged, in part, that the rates were excessive, unfair, and not in compliance with the terms of the contracts in force between the City and its suburban customers.

The case was assigned to Judge John Feikens, U.S. District Judge of the Eastern District of Michigan. With agreement of the attorney's representing all parties in the rate litigation, Judge Feikens appointed a panel of three Special Masters[*] to conduct a trial and make recommendations to the Court regarding means to settle the rate litigation and the conflicts between the suburbs and the City of Detroit which had arisen in the mid-to-late 1970s.

The Special Masters spent two months in preliminary hearings and then conducted a trial which took ten (10) days. The trial was held during February and March of 1978. The trial generated over 1300 pages of Testimony. The Report of the Masters was submitted to the Court on May 1, 1978. Two (2) primary issues which emerged from the trial as being the focal points of the conflict were as follows:

1. The sewage treatment rates calculated by the City of Detroit were based upon grossly inflated projections of revenue requirements.

2. The method of apportioning rates between the customers within the City of Detroit and the customers in the seventy-eight (78) suburban communities is unreasonable--whatever the actual revenue requirements may be.

All parties agreed that the suburban customers are properly charged with the costs of facilities which are specific to providing service to the suburban customers. Such specific facilities would include interceptors and pumping stations in the suburban area. All parties further agreed that where the

---

[*]Panel of Special Masters:
David Ragone, Chief Master (then Dean of Engineering, University of Michigan); Edward Cooper, Master (Professor of Law, University of Michigan); Jonathan Bulkley, Master (Professor of Civil Engineering, Professor of Natural Resources, University of Michigan)

wastes from the City and those from the Suburbs were
sharing common facilities, such as the wastewater
treatment plant, the costs should be apportioned
according to the flow volume from the City and flow
volume from the Suburbs.

During the trial, the following facts were
developed regarding the projected revenue requirements: (All figures are in million dollars).

	77-78	78-79	7/79-12/79
1977 Rate Study	43.5	57.9	35.0
1978 Revision	35.9	54.6	32.8
Difference	7.6	3.3	2.2

The sum of these differences totalled over 13
million dollars and represented excess revenue
collected versus revenue actually needed. The City
proposed to use these excess funds to reduce the debt
financing requirement for a system whose past practice
and current policy called for a maximum of debt
financing to pay for capital improvements to the
system. If the City were to be successful in this
proposal, it would mean a very significant change from
established practice.

The second major area of conflict had to do with
the rate setting procedures adopted by the City of
Detroit. In general, one may either use the cash
basis to determine revenue requirements and to set the
rates to raise the necessary revenues or one may use
the utility basis to accomplish this task. However,
the utility basis is primarily used with a private
utility. Under the utility basis, there is a
depreciation account which is utilized in the
estimation of the revenue requirement. Furthermore,
there is a depreciation charge and a rate of return
utilized to raise a portion of the necessary revenue
requirements.

The City of Detroit used the cash basis to
determine the revenue requirements and then utilized
the utility basis to set the rates. In doing so, the
City included both a depreciation charge and a rate-
of-return charge in the rates to raise the revenues.
The depreciation charges were calculated for the
common plant without reducing its book value to
reflect amounts contributed by grants from the United
States or the State of Michigan. The rate base was
determined by deducting the amount of such

contributions and accrued depreciation from book value. The City then made a judgment that it was proper to charge its suburban customers a seven (7) percent rate of return against the common facilities in the rate base which were there to treat suburban flows. If there were unmet revenue requirements, customers in the City of Detroit would be charged a rate-of-return of sufficient magnitude to generate the needed funds. It should be noted that all of these differential rates for the suburban customers were being implemented in the face of contracts between the City and the Suburbs that specified the portion of rates for treatment shall be uniform throughout the entire system.

The findings and recommendations of the panel of Special Masters included the following: (1) It is not reasonable to depart from the assumptions on which the 1977 rate study was based (Maximum Debt Financing). It is not reasonable to seek to justify current user charges by shifting to substantial financing of long-term capital expenditures out of current user charges. It is unreasonable to impose very large proportional increases in current user charges over a brief period of time for the purpose of financing long-term capital improvements which will benefit future generations of users over a period of many years. It is recommended that this condition be corrected by an addition to working capital and by refunds; (2) The method of charging depreciation utilized by the City is improper. They do not subtract grant funded contributions before making the depreciation charges. Also, there is no justification in charging a rate-of-return to customers since the plant and facilities have not been funded from general fund revenues. All of the facilities have been paid by the user fees and grants. Finally, suburban customers should be treated in the same fashion as Detroit customers except to the extent that a reasonable basis can be found for identifying costs attributed specifically to suburban customers or to Detroit customers.

Observation

In this case, a trial to determine facts was held by a panel of three Special Masters appointed by the U.S. District Judge. The Masters submitted a report to the Court with Findings and Recommendations. The conflict resolution process in this situation assumed that all parties had a full and complete opportunity to illuminate the problem and present the facts of the matter. The trial procedures provided a framework for full disclosure and full discussion of the different viewpoints and perspectives. The strength of the process is shown by the fact that the Master's Report continues to serve as a basis for the rate setting process and procedure within the Detroit wastewater treatment and collection system.

The Westway Project: Conflicts over Impacts/Permits[**]

The Westway Project had been conceived as a replacement of the West Side Highway for the lower West Side of Manhattan in New York City. It called for landfilling more than 200 acres in the Hudson River and would include the building of a 4.2 mile segment of interstate highway in this section of Manhattan. The estimated cost of this project was more than two billion dollars with 90 percent of the funding coming from the Federal Government through the Federal Highway Administration (FHWA) of the U.S. Department of Transportation. The New York State Department of Transportation, and the New York Department of Environmental Conservation were involved from the State level. The U.S. Army Corps of Engineers had the responsibility to issue the permits for landfilling under the provisions of the federal Clean Water Act. As a major federal project, the Westway Project needed to conform to federal requirements for the preparation of an Environmental Impact Statement (EIS) in accord with the provisions of the National Environmental Protection Act (NEPA) of 1969. In addition, the Corps of Engineers was required by its own regulations and other federal regulations to consult with other federal agencies including U.S. Environmental Protection Agency (EPA), the Fish and Wildlife Service (FWS), and the National Marine Fisheries Service (NMFS) to seek their opinions on the impacts of the proposed project on the aquatic resources of the Hudson River.

The final Environmental Impact Statement (EIS) was issued in January 1977 and the FHWA approved the location and design of the Westway Project despite protests from Federal resource agencies that the final EIS (January 1977) had not dealt adequately with the potential impact of the landfill on both the water quality and the fishery resources of the Hudson River. The Corps of Engineers subsequently granted a landfill permit in March 1981, nearly two and one half years after the original application for the permit had been

---

[**]See Special References in Reference List.

filed by the New York State Department of Transportation. This permit issuance caused the Sierra Club to file suit against the Corps of Engineers for failure to conform both to NEPA and to Section 404 of the Clean Water Act. A separate action by Action for Rational Transit (ART) was brought against the Westway Project. All of its allegations were dismissed except that related to NEPA. The two cases were combined and proceeded under the Sierra Club Suit (81 CIV. 3000).

United States District Judge Thomas P. Griesa of the Southern District of New York conducted the Sierra Club trial from January 19 to February 1, 1982. The Court on April 14, 1982 vacated (set aside) the Corps of Engineers permit for Westway. If the state of New York reapplied for a landfill permit, the Court directed that the Corps of Engineers would conduct the analysis of the Permit Application in accordance with NEPA and Section 404 of the Clean Water Act. Further the Court directed that the Corps of Engineers should prepare an adequate Supplementary Environmental Impact Statement (SEIS) dealing with the impact of Westway on the Hudson River fishery resources, including striped bass, and also dealing with current information on such non-fishery subjects as current cost estimates, current plans for the use of the landfill area, new information regarding alternatives, and any new information regarding the relation of Westway to the development of the West Side. The Court further directed that the Corps of Engineers to independently evaluate all of the existing fisheries data; and after consultation with U.S. EPA, FWS, and NMFS, determine what additional studies should be carried out. Finally, the Court directed the Corps of Engineers to record all activities, deliberations, and communications regarding its consideration of a landfill permit for Westway.

In July 1982 Judge Griesa directed that all prior actions taken by the FHWA in approving the design, location, and federal funding for Westway were vacated. FHWA was prohibited from granting any such approvals for Westway until a proper SEIS had been issued and reconsidered. It is clear from the action of the Court that the conflicts between the requirements of the federal laws especially the NEPA and the Clean Water Act and the substance of the information provided by both the Corps of Engineers and the Federal Highway Administration needed to be resolved by further study and a more complete and full consideration of the anticipated environmental impacts.

On January 24, 1985, after 2 1/2 years, the Corps of Engineers again decided to grant a landfill permit for the Westway Project. This permit was issued on February 25, 1985. On March 18, 1985, the FHWA decided to approve federal funding for the Westway Project. The New York State Department of Transportation then moved to have the injunctions previously imposed by the Court vacated since the agencies had fully complied with the federal law. The Sierra Club opposed contending that the procedures of the federal agencies had been legally deficient and the purported permits/approvals were invalid. An extensive trial was held to resolve these conflicting issues. The trial took 30 days in the period from May 20, 1985 to July 12, 1985.

The facts established during the trial included the following:

1. The SEIS issued on November 24, 1984 and signed by both the FHWA and the Corps of Engineers stated that the primary purpose of the Westway Project was Transportation. This is an important point in order to qualify for 90 percent federal funding of the two billion dollar project.

2. In the decision of the District Engineer in granting the landfill permit on January 24, 1985, it was stated that Westway is better termed a redevelopment project rather than a highway endeavor.

3. The District Engineer testified in Court that Westway is <u>not</u> needed as a transportation project; landfill is not needed for the purposes of transportation. The transportation needs could be satisfied by a 50 million dollar highway design which would not require any landfill. The District Engineer admitted he could not approve the landfill permit as a transportation project (since a non-landfill alternative existed) but he approved it as a redevelopment project since no alternatives existed and it offered great benefits. This information differed in a very fundamental way from what had been presented in the SEIS which characterized the project as primarily related to transportation needs. Because of these and other deficiencies, the SEIS

did not comply with the requirements of NEPA or the 1982 Court orders.

4.   In the Draft SEIS issued in May 1984, the Corps of Engineers found that the proposed landfill would have a significant adverse impact on the aquatic environmental--especially the striped bass fishery.   In the final SEIS issued on November 27, 1984 the Corps reversed itself and concluded the impact on the fishery would be minor.   No reasoned basis for this change has been established.   The Corps took the position that there was no change in its basic position. The Court found this position incredible--there was a fundamental change from the DSEIS to the FSEIS.   The Court found the conclusion of the FSEIS as to minor impact to be arbitrary and a violation of NEPA and the 1982 Court Orders.

5.   In carrying out its fishery analysis, the Corps of Engineers relied on a theory that was later repudiated by its author.   The study performed by the Corps did not generate data to support the theory and conclusions forwarded by the Corps.

As a consequence of the failure of the Corps of Engineers to comply with NEPA and the previous Court Orders, Judge Griesa found that the decision of the Corps to grant a landfill permit was based upon an inadequate FSEIS, and thus was arbitrary, in violation of the NEPA, the Clean Water Act, and the 1982 Court Orders.   Furthermore, since FHWA based its decision to grant federal funding on an inadequate FSEIS, the decision is in violation of NEPA and the 1982 Court Orders.   Judge Greisa then denied the State's motion to vacate the 1982 injunctions.   He further issued a permanent injunction which: (1) prohibited the granting of a landfill permit for Westway by the Corps of Engineers, (2) prohibited federal funding for Westway by FHWA and (3) prohibited the construction of Westway by the State of New York.

Observation

In this case the conflicts arose between different federal agencies as well as between an outside environmental organization and the U.S. Army Corps of Engineers.   The Court provided critical leadership and direction to assure that federal laws would be obeyed prior to the building of a major project with federal funds.   As a consequence of the full illumination of the issue and problem as required

by the Court Proceedings, the Court determined that
even after being ordered to carry out the letter and
spirit of the federal law, the responsible agencies
failed to perform the mandated tasks.   The Court
resolved the conflicts by entering a permanent
injunction to assure that the Westway project could
not be implemented since the responsible federal
agencies failed to meet the requirements of NEPA, the
Clean Water Act, and the Previous Court Judgements.

Instream Water Rights

A recently completed a doctoral dissertation
(McKinney, 1989) focuses upon the problems associated
with implementing instream flow programs in the
Western portion of the United States.   The basic
conflict arises out of the limited water resources of
the West and the institutional incentive which prompts
water users to <u>divert</u> water from the streams for
beneficial use.   Nearly eight-six (86) percent of the
total fresh water withdrawn in the West is consumed--
i.e. not returned to the river for downstream users.
This withdrawal and consumptive use places great
stress on instream water uses including recreation,
fish and wildlife, and hydropower production.
McKinney outlines a model program to promote Instream
Flow Programs in the West.   There are five major
components he has identified. All of these components
are designed to come together to reduce the conflicts
between off-stream uses and instream flow values.   The
elements include the following: (1) Establish a
Coordinating Committee which represents all of the
instream/off-stream uses for a particular river.
(2) Define the Program Goals and Objectives--i.e. to
maintain and enhance instream flow values.
(3) Review and Develop Instream Flow Management
Techniques.   This involves techniques for maintaining
existing (unappropriated) flows and developing
techniques for increasing flows in dewatered streams.
(4) Identify Priority Stream Reaches and Instream
Values. Specific instream resource values at specific
stream reaches need to be identified and the quantity
of flow necessary to maintain these flows estimated.
(5) The final component is to Monitor, Enforce, and
Evaluate Instream Water rights.   (McKinney, 1989).

Observation

Whether or not the proposed model developed by
McKinney will function effectively to reduce conflicts
is yet to be tested. He has performed very thorough
research and proposed a new set of instional

arrangements to mitigate this important class of water conflicts. It will be of great importance for more Western states to explicitly recognize values associated with instream flows and provide for the maintenance of instream flows.

Longterm Distributed Costs: Environmental Contamination

A very thoughtful study has investigated the impact of PCB contamination in the Hudson River (Wells, 1989). The conflict here is between the industry that caused the pollution impact and the costs of this pollution both in terms of the clean-up and the environmental impact of the pollutant on other natural resources. The research study indicates that the industrial contribution to the PCB clean-up has been on the order of $6.4 million while State and Federal contributions have exceeded $46 million to date. Furthermore, as a consequence of elevated PCB levels in the fish in the Hudson River there are estimated losses (past and future) to the recreational fishery alone in excess of $382 million. Furthermore, commercial fishing losses both past and future have been estimated in excess of $145 million.

Observation

The presence of distributed costs of this magnitude raises important issues of who pays for clean-up and how should those adversely impacted be compensated for their losses. Effective conflict resolution in the case of Distributed Costs will require new techniques to be undertaken before the fact to determine the adverse impacts of toxics if released into the aquatic environment. Those responsible for the pollution impact need to be liable for compensation as well as clean-up of such toxic pollutants.

Indian Water Rights

The conflicts associated with Indian Water Rights have been brought into sharp focus (McCool, 1987). The potential for tragedy is exceedingly high in this conflict situation. "In effect the government has given the water away twice: once through the states (non-Indians) and once through the federal courts (Indian Water Rights). More water has been legally allocated than is available." (McCool, p. 254) It is exceedingly difficult to envision the ultimate

resolution of this extreme conflict situation in the
Western portion of our country.

Observation

The history of the treatment of Indians with
regard to land and water is not a history of which we
can take comfort. As McCool observes, "to bring
justice to all concerned the government must provide
water or somehow compensate those who have been
injured by the lack of water . . . the solution will
be expensive. It will require more than just pork
barrel water policies. And it will test our
commitment to justice." (McCool, p. 255)

Conclusion

The cases presented in this paper illustrate the
importance of conflict as a component of the decision-
processes associated with water management issues. On
one end of the spectrum of conflict resolution
processes lies the arena of traditional litigation.
The Westway Project was handled by this mechanism.
Moving away from traditional litigation is the use of
Special Masters/Monitors and while it is closely
related to traditional Court procedures it provides an
innovative means for the Court to isolate complex
issues and utilize one or more persons with special
training to assist the conflict resolution process.
The Detroit Rate Case represents the use of Special
Masters.

If one continues to move along the conflict
resolution spectrum away from the traditional
litigation procedure, one would first encounter
negotiation, then mediation, and finally joint problem
solving. In terms of the cases presented, the
instream flow conflict and the model system proposed
by McKinney would represent joint problem solving.
The Indian Water Rights issue historically has been
handled by the federal courts. In the future, it will
need to use joint problem solving together with
mediation, negotiation and the Courts. The
Distributed Cost example points to the need for
negotiation and mediation to assure that full
environmental costs are recognized and required of the
responsible parties.

The role of the engineer in all of these examples
emerges as a key one in which appropriate quantitative
information is gathered and displayed for the benefit
of the decision-maker. The engineer has a special

professional responsibility to assure that a thorough and complete analysis is undertaken and the results effectively communicated.

References

Coser, Lewis, 1956. <u>The Functions of Social Conflict</u>, The Free Press, New York.

Dahl, Robert, 1965. <u>Modern Political Analysis</u>, Prentice Hall, Englewood Cliffs, New Jersey.

Easton, David, 1965. <u>A Systems Analysis of Political Life</u>, John Wiley & Sons, New York.

McCool, Daniel, 1987. <u>Command of the Waters</u>, University of California Press, Berkeley.

McKinney, Matthew J. 1989. "Implementing Western State Instream Flow Programs: A Comparative Assessment." A dissertation submitted in partial fulfillment of the requirement for the degree of Doctor of Philosophy (Natural Resources), the University of Michigan, 1989.

Vaillant, George E., 1977. <u>Adaptation to Life</u>, Little Brown, Boston. 396 pp.

Wells, Judith R., 1989. "Longterm Distributed Costs of Environmental Contamination." Research Paper: Water Science Program, University of Michigan.

Special References: "The Westway Project: A Study of Failure in Federal/State Relations."

Sixty-sixth Report by the
Committee on Government Operations

House Report 98-1166

November 1, 1984

U.S. Government Printing Office
Washington, D.C.

Also: The following opinions:

United States District Court
Southern District of New York
81 CIV-3000
Opinion: Dated: March 31, 1982
Opinion: Dated: June 30, 1982
Opinion: Dated: July 23, 1982
Opinion: Dated: August 7, 1985

A SOCIAL SCIENTIST'S VIEWPOINT ON CONFLICT MANAGEMENT

Madge O. Ertel[1]

Abstract: Social scientists can bring to the conflict-management process objective, reliable information needed to resolve increasingly complex issues. Engineers need basic training in the principles of the social sciences and in strategies for public involvement. All scientists need to be sure that that the information they provide is unbiased by their own value judgments and that fair standards and open procedures govern its use.

Not long ago, but before I was asked to make this presentation from the perspective of a social scientist, another participant in this conference, Frank Gregg, made a comment to me that came back to mind as I started to prepare it. In speaking about an interdisciplinary research project in which he is involved, he commented, "The trouble with the social scientists is that they're content to define a problem; they don't feel any obligation to solve it." I would submit that as a generalization that comment might be too harsh, but that there is a degree of truth in it that is useful in examining the engineer's role in conflict management.

If the social scientist tends to emphasize problem definition, then it could be said that the physical scientist or engineer similarly tends to concentrate on problem solution. The perception of the solution-oriented role of the engineer, in particular, has been a natural one because, historically, our society's goals have been oriented to construction and development. Now those goals are changing to an emphasis on stewardship and conservation-oriented management. These new goals are much

---
[1]Interagency Liaison Specialist, U.S. Geological Survey, 417 National Center, Reston, VA 22092.

more complex, and require a much broader mix of skills and disciplines for both problem definition and resolution. Now, too, workable solutions must be economically, politically, and socially acceptable, meaning that the disciplines of the social sciences must be added to those of the physical sciences as the engineer attempts to manage conflict in situations where there are differing objectives, not just different technologies for achieving an objective. The social scientists, by virtue of their training, can contribute information on such things as values, beliefs, and personal and organizational behavior that will not be evident to the physical scientists. I would submit, then, that an important role of the engineer in conflict management is to accept and incorporate this kind of information into the process.

The difficulty in merging these disciplinary perceptions comes about because of the inherent differences in the kind of data each brings to a problem, i.e., "soft" or "hard", as they are often characterized. "Soft" data are too often assumed to be subject to differences in opinion, while "hard" data are considered "real" facts. While acknowledging that social science findings can be more subject to various interpretations than can, say, physical measurements, it is equally true that to ignore them for this reason will mean that information essential to problem resolution will not be brought to a bargaining table or a drafting board.

The important obligation of the social scientists in addressing this dilemma is to gather, organize, analyze, and present their data in as scientifically rigorous a fashion as possible. The methods that have been developed by the behavioral sciences in, for example, conducting surveys and creating models of institutional behavior, make this rigor possible. The physical scientists have the right and responsibility to judge the validity of the methodologies used, but they cannot do this if they have no training in the basic principles of social science. Such training should be incorporated into the education of the physical scientists and engineers so that they can at least assure themselves of the validity of the procedures by which social science data has been generated. Once so assured, there is then a concomitant obligation to use the information as objective input into the decision-making process.

The need for objectivity is not limited to information gathering and use. In their book stemming from the Harvard Negotiation Project, "Getting to Yes: Negotiating Agreement without Giving In," Fisher and Ury (1981) make an important case for developing objective criteria as a basis for conflict resolution. This means reaching agreement, not on differing positions, but first on independent standards against which those positions can be measured. Among the examples they cite of such criteria are market value, scientific judgment, professional standards, precedent, and moral and legal standards. Agreement on objective criteria, they say, leads to principled as opposed to positional bargaining:

> The difference between seeking agreement on
> the appropriate principles for deciding a
> matter and using principles simply as
> arguments to support positions is sometimes
> subtle, but always significant. A principled
> negotiator is open to reasoned persuasion on
> the merits; a positional bargainer is not. It
> is the combination of openness to reason with
> insistence on a solution based on objective
> criteria that makes principled negotiation so
> persuasive and so effective at getting the
> other side to play.

Fisher and Ury also emphasize the importance of fair procedures, as well as fair standards, in producing an outcome independent of opposing parties' wills. "Consider," they say, "for example, the age-old way to divide a piece of cake between two children: one cuts and the other chooses. Neither can complain about an unfair decision." Even the kind of complex issues of public policy and investment that are being considered by this conference can be amenable to such a simple procedure. It was used, according to Fisher and Ury, in the Law of the Sea negotiations, one of the most complex negotiations ever undertaken:

> At one point, the issue of how to allocate
> mining sites in the deep seabed deadlocked the
> negotiations. Under the terms of the draft
> agreement, half the sites were to be mined by
> private companies, the other half by the

Enterprise, a mining organization to be owned by the United Nations. Since the private mining companies from the rich nations had the technology and the expertise to choose the sites, the poorer nations feared the less knowledgeable Enterprise would receive a bad bargain. The solution devised was to agree that a private company seeking to mine the seabed would present the Enterprise with two proposed mining sites. The Enterprise would pick one site for itself and grant the company a license to mine the other. Since the company would not know which site it would get, it would have an incentive to make both sites as promising as possible. This simple procedure thus harnessed the company's superior expertise for mutual gain.

I am sure that by this point in this conference, the usual procedures for resolution of conflict, such as facilitation, mediation, and arbitration, will have been discussed and documented. I will, instead, mention another now-conventional strategy to which social science literature, my own (Ertel, 1979) included, has contributed. That is the widespread incorporation of public participation into the decision-making framework. I say "now-conventional" because when social scientists started examining both the theory and practice of the field, it was because it was a new phenomenon of research interest. Now, I would hold, it is an accepted fact of life in most public-policy arenas, including water-resources planning, and often goes beyond the traditional public meeting to use conflict-management strategies. Active and structured public involvement does not resolve conflict, per se. Sometimes it even seems to engender it! But it has come to be seen as a necessary part of the engineer's arsenal of planning tools because it brings to the process the attributes of adequacy of information and fairness of procedure that I have already stressed. Effective design and conduct of public participation programs, however, depend on the use of skills and abilities that are not naturally possessed by all who have the responsibility. In 1980 I wrote of the need for the incorporation of training in public participation strategies into graduate-planning curricula, and I suggest here that training in basic public communications skills, democratic decision-making strategies, and human behavior should be part of an engineer's professional training.

One final point, which applies to both the social and the physical sciences, is the importance of consistent, reliable, and unbiased data as the foundation for any decision-making process. The public acceptance of U.S. Geological Survey data as unbiased stems not just from the agency's high standards for consistency and reliability. A major factor contributing to this reliance on the objectivity of the Survey's products is that the scientists who make up the Survey have a "third party" role in the decision-making process. That is, their professional roles as scientists are kept distinct from their private roles as participants in the democratic process. All scientists, as professionals, should present data and information for problem definition and solution, but should avoid involvement in value determinations that are the ultimate deciding factors in the political decision-making process.

REFERENCES

Ertel, Madge O., 1979, A survey evaluation of public participation techniques: Water Resources Research, v. 15, no. 4, pp.757-762.

_____1980, Identification of training needs for public participation responsibilities: Water Resources Bulletin, v. 16, no. 2, pp.300-304.

Fisher, Roger and Ury, William, 1981, Getting to yes: negotiating agreement without giving in, New York, Penguin Books.

INSTITUTIONAL STRUCTURES WORKING GROUP REPORT

The working group on institutional structures consisted of: William Lord (Chairman), Ann Bleed (Reporter),
William Cox, Frank Gregg, Merle Lefkoff, and Michael
Nolen. The product of this working group, in a very real
sense, would not have been possible if the group had not
practiced a number of alternative dispute resolution
techniques. The participants in the group represented
teachers, engineers, economists, mediators, writers, and
administrators. During the beginning discussions, different backgrounds, vocabularies and concepts combined to
create misunderstanding and conflict. In the end, per-
sistence and the determination to understand each other
led to a product which we feel has meaning and utility.

Guidelines for Institutional Structures

The framework for this paper comes from Gregg's key-
note paper, "Institutional Aspects of Managing
Conflicts", and Lord's short working group paper, "Institutional Aspects of Water Dispute Resolution". In these
papers environmental and water management problems are
classified into two types: symmetric problems, in which
causation is multidirectional and all actors who are
causal agents also suffer from resultant impacts, and
asymmetric problems, which are unidirectional, in that
one actor causes a problem for another, but not vice-
versa. Asymmetric problems can be further divided in a
number of ways. Of importance in this discussion is the
difference between spatial externalities, in which the
producer of the (usually adverse) impact is spatially
separated from the recipient, and temporal externalities,
in which they are separated in time. Symmetric problems
are easier to solve than asymmetric ones because all of
the actors share a common interest in doing so.

In their papers Gregg and Lord define an institution
as a set of written or unwritten rules that shape human
action or orders relationships among actors in a network
that functions over time as an arena for the pursuit of
diverse interests in a defined set of values. They
suggest that institutions be thought of as composed of
seven kinds of rules, those defining positions, boundaries, scopes, authorities, aggregation, information, and
payoffs. Definitions of these seven kinds of rules are
found in Lord's paper.

Based on our combined experiences and discussion at this conference, our working group developed criteria that these rules should meet if a stable resolution of a conflict is to be achieved and implemented. These criteria are:

1) the position rules must be sufficiently comprehensive to provide a position for each relatively homogeneous group of stakeholders.

2) the boundary rules must permit stakeholders to enter these positions.

3) the scope rules must encompass a range of outcomes which is broad enough to include stable solutions to the conflict.

4) The authority rules must permit occupants of positions to take those actions which will lead to stable solutions and forbid those actions which may block solution or render it unstable.

5) the aggregation rules must successfully integrate the actions of occupants of positions so that their joint actions produce the desired outcomes.

6) the information rules must ensure that information is sufficient and shared by all positions.

7) the payoff rules must conform to society's norms of fairness and equity.

To achieve a better understanding of how these rules operate, we applied them to an imaginary but realistic water problem found in western states, the allocation of water on Multiuse River, U.S.A. The strategic aspects of the physical environment are that the resource base is capable of supporting multiple uses, surface and groundwater systems are hydrologically connected, downstream users are vulnerable to withdrawals upstream (but not vice-versa), and past diversions have changed the physical shape and ecology of the river. In essence the problem is an asymmetric one, involving both spatial and temporal externalities.

The institutions allocating the use of water on this river have changed through time, in part because they were poorly adapted to the physical environment, in part in response to changes in the physical environment, and in part in response to changes in social values. The earliest water allocation institution, the riparian rights system, which fails to resolve water scarcity problems typical of the arid and semi-arid states, was very quickly replaced by the appropriative rights sytem. The rules of the doctrine of prior appropriation state that the first to divert water for a beneficial use has a right superior to those of later diverters, and that in times of shortage the senior right holder may divert water up to the limits of the right even though a junior right holder may be completely deprived of water. A water right can only be granted if the water is physically diverted from the stream. Each state has developed its own version of this institution and is responsible for implementing it. This system has governed western water use for close to a century.

In the 1970's, however, society's values changed and environmental interests sought the right to maintain flow in the stream. States sought to accommodate the new demands by establishing a new type of water right, the instream flow right, within the appropriative rights sys tem. No longer did water have to be diverted to constitute a beneficial use. Now one could attain a right to keep water in the stream for fish and wildlife or other instream uses.

At the same time, the federal government and some states established a new set of rules to accommodate environmental interests. These rules are exemplifed by the National Environmental Policy Act (NEPA) and the Endangered Species Act. NEPA requires the development of an environmental impact statement that analyzes the impacts of an action and its alternatives on the environment. This analysis and the whole decision making process is to be available for public scrutiny. The ESA prohibits any action that would be detrimental to an endangered species. This act also requires all governmental agencies to consult with the U.S. Fish and Wildlife Service whenever a proposed action might impact an endangered species. Table 1 briefly describes how well these three institutions, or rule sets, fare when evaluated through the use of the criteria developed by our working group. Continued conflict can be expected in those cases where the rules do not satisfy the criteria.

Table 1. Compliance of Rules for Water Allocation With Criteria for Successful and Stable Conflict Resolution

Appropriative Rights No Instream Rights	Appropriative Rights Instream Rights	Overlay of Federal Environmental Laws
POSITION		
1) Senior right holders	1) Same	1) Same
2) Junior right holders	2) Same	2) Same
		3) Impact anlyst
		4) Public participant
BOUNDARY		
RULES:		
1) Divert water for beneficial use	1) Same	1) Same
2) Same	2) Same	2) Same
		3) Appointment
		4) Open
EVALUATION:		
Fails to admit environmental interests	Fails to admit public good users	Fails to admit non-ESA environmental interests
SCOPE		
RULES:		
Allocates up to full flow of river to consumptive uses.	Allocates up to full flow of river to consumptive and instream uses	Same, but also to protect endangered species
EVALUATION:		
Fails to cover instream flows	OK	Good
AUTHORITY		
RULES:		
1) Divert water	1) Same	1) Same
2) Divert water after seniors	2) Same	2) Same
		3) Report impacts
		4) Request changes from decision makers
EVALUATION:		
Compliance	Compliance	Partial compliance

Table 1 - continued

	Appropriative Rights No Instream Rights	Appropriative Rights Instream Rights	Overlay of Federal Environmental Laws
AGGREGATION RULES:	Priority	Priority	Priority, plus endangered species constraint and potential political redress, following NEPA
EVALUATION:	Non-compliance	Non-compliance	Non-compliance
INFORMATION RULES:	Date & amount of right	Date & amount of right	Date & amount of right - incl. ESA
EVALUATION:	Compliance	Compliance	Uncertain compliance
PAYOFF RULES:	Inequitable to juniors but predictable	Inequitable to juniors but predictable	Inequitable to juniors potentially unfair to diverters Unpredictable
EVALUATION:	Partial Compliance	Partial Compliance	Non-compliance

SUMMARY - Ability To Reduce Or Avoid Conflict

Worked well until environmental interests appeared	Doesn't work very well	Doesn't work very well

The appropriative rights system met the criteria fairly well until environmental interests demanded that their objectives be recognized and accommodated. Conflicts were quickly and lastingly resolved, in spite of what some currently held values might suggest was a lack of fairness and equity.

Modifying the appropriative rights system slightly to accommodate the new environmental interests, by recognizing instream uses as beneficial ones, did not meet the criteria. It modified the boundary rules to admit instream users to the position of right holder, but it did not provide them with the authorities necessary to safeguard their interests in times of low flows. The newly obtained rights were very junior, and thus were preempted by more senior rights just when they were needed most. This problem is especially acute on over-appropriated streams where a junior instream flow right may be virtually worthless.

The federal and state NEPA and ESA laws have also opened positions to environmental interests, but without successfully resolving the conflicts. The major problem with these laws is that they have been superimposed on, but not integrated with, the states' appropriative rights rules. As a result, the authority to implement these laws is not clearly defined. States argue with federal agencies over who has the right to allocate water. The aggregation rules are defective.

In addition, the payoff rules for compensating those who must give up the right to water to accommodate environmental interests are perceived to be unfair. Many current water right holders adamantly oppose the granting of instream flow rights because they fear that they will not be fairly compensated for any losses they may suffer. Without substantial rule changes, continued conflict may be anticipated.

The Role of the Engineer

This attempt to delineate institutions as rules and show how they can be applied to determine potential sources of conflict may be an interesting exercise. It may even have utility for social scientists or conflict mediators. But, what does such a discussion have to offer an engineer: does the engineer have to be concerned with such issues? After all the major role of the engineer is to provide technical information about the physical system. An engineer cannot also be expected to be a social scientist.

At the outset we want to be clear that we are not suggesting that engineers take over the role of the social scientist. However, as technical analysts and providers of technical information, engineers often find themselves in policy making, policy implementation,or negotiating settings. Engineers are called upon to help write or review water policy statements and laws. Engineers are often the ones to implement water laws. In this role the engineers may be the only people involved in the decision making process. And, finally, engineers do get involved in decision making groups where negotiation is necessary. In many of these instances the best technical solution may be worthless because the political will or institution to implement it is lacking. Engineers must be aware that the solutions to water problems are often more political than technical. Understanding institutions will help engineers spot which solutions have a chance of implementation.

In addition, when working in these arenas engineers are often in a position to influence how institutional rules are formulated. Engineers who can focus on the decision making process and implementing institutions and who can identify where the process is inhibiting or con straining a solution may be able to change the rules or look beyond the constraint to find a workable solution.

The engineer may also be able to spot potential sources of conflict and seek ways to cope with or avoid this conflict. In some situations the engineer may be able to cope with this conflict alone. In others, a trained facilitator or mediator might be necessary. At the very least, an engineer needs to know when the help of a social scientist is indicated.

For these reasons, some understanding of institutions and how they operate can be extremely helpful to those practicing engineers who are likely to be involved in policy formulation and implementation. It is hoped that this brief description of the application of institutions and guidelines for their success can help the engineer to cope with potential conflict situations and achieve better solutions.

ANALYTICAL AIDS

THE ROLE OF THE ENGINEER IN DEVELOPING, IMPLEMENTING, APPLYING AND ANALYZING RESULTS FROM ANALYTICAL AIDS IN CONFLICT MANAGEMENT IN WATER RESOURCES

INTRODUCTION

The work group on analytical aids consisted of: Jonathan Bulkley; Jack Day; Walter Grayman, Reporter; James Heaney, Co-chairman; Rick Kattelmann; Charles Lancaster; Pete Loucks, Co-chairman; and Robert McGarry. The purpose of this workshop was to focus on the use of analytical aids in the area of conflict management in water resources with primary emphasis on the role of the engineer. Participants addressed the type of analytical aids that could be used; the characteristics, limitations and potential dangers of the use of such aids; and the engineers' role in the development and application of analytical aids.

Though the group was composed primarily of engineers (other members were a hydrologist and an attorney specializing in the environmental area), the initial views that were presented in the discussions of analytical aids were far from homogeneous. Views differed in terms of how analytical aids should be used; in terminology used in describing analytical aids; and in how broad the engineers' role should be in conflict management. The views expressed in this paper reflect synthesis and consensus of these sometimes disparate ideas.

A HYPOTHETICAL APPLICATION OF ANALYTICAL AIDS

The engineer sits facing the two color video screens that are part of the powerful workstation computer. Behind her, the facilitator and ten stakeholders are seated around a table. On one screen, a diagram shows the streams and major features of the watershed that the group is studying. In response to one of the stakeholders, the engineer has 'grabbed' a small symbol representing a dam and has placed it on the stream. A stage-volume curve appears on the other screen and when the engineer points at an elevation on the curve, the resulting extent of the reservoir automatically appears on the stream map. Other stakeholders contribute other suggestions - some relating to the operation of the dam, others relating to the cost sharing provisions for this alternative, and still others reflecting different projected growth and industrial development. Each of these is entered into the computer through the use of symbols and graphical techniques. Finally, after the stakeholders are satisfied with the parameters of the alternative, the engineer 'points' at the green button that is part of a 'traffic light' on the screen and the computer goes into action evaluating the alternative. Using large data bases containing hydrologic data, economic projections, spatially based descriptions of the watershed, and sophisticated hydrologic, economic and eco system models, billions of 0's and 1's are manipulated in the computer to evaluate the alternative.

After many millions of nanoseconds, the computer screen indicates that the analysis is complete. Several 'windows' appear on the screens showing economic information: capital and operating costs, and graphs showing how these costs could be distributed among the groups represented by the stakeholders and how they compare to previous alternatives; hydrologic plots showing the inflow and outflow hydrographs for the proposed reservoir design over a multi year period; another plot showing the projected impacts on the valued endangered species located in the fragile eco system located downstream of the proposed reservoir. In response to a request of a stakeholder, the engineer pops open another widow and explains a diagram displaying the degree of uncertainty that the computer has associated with the prediction techniques.

After further viewing of the results and explanations by the engineer, the stakeholders suggest further refinements and additional alternatives are explored. Finally, using various nominal group processes and computerized analytical aids which measure and weight the preferences of the stakeholders, a consensus position is reached.

A scenario approaching this hypothetical situation could be played out using hardware and software that is available today. Many of these techniques have been used in decision making situations throughout the world (da Costa and Loucks, 1989). In a few years, given the direction of current research in the computer area, a scenario of this type could be fully implemented as a 'decision support system' for facilitation / negotiation cases. Is this what we truly want? Will it contribute to the success of facilitation and negotiation? What is the role of the engineer in such a system? What are the dangers and limitations of such a system? These issues were addressed by our work group and the results of the discussions are summarized herein.

ANALYTICAL AIDS

Analytical aids are mathematically based, frequently computerized, methods for providing information for use in a wide range of social and technical pursuits including conflict management in water resources. Such aids cover a wide range of topics as shown in Figure 1.

COLLECTIVE CHOICE ANALYSES   SOCIO ECONOMIC ANALYSES   PHYSICAL SYSTEM ANALYSES

Figure 1 General categories of analytical aids used in conflict management

The jagged lines separating the categories of aids indicate the ambiguity and overlap between the model types. Starting from the right, aids for physical system analyses include models and data handling techniques for physically based information. Geographical information systems (GIS), hydraulic flow models, eco system representations, and reservoir operation simulations are examples of this type of aid. Aids for socio economic analyses include a wide range of tools that can be used to manipulate social and economic information for use in conflict management. Demand prediction models and optimization techniques are frequently used techniques that are in this category. In many cases, a specific aid may include components that relate to both the physical and the socio economic system. At the left end of the figure are collective choice analyses. This category includes a wide range of techniques that are used to combine the preferences of stakeholders to help reach a decision. In the broadest sense such techniques can include voting, the facilitation / negotiation process itself, nominal group techniques, and formal mathematical techniques for weighting and combining factors to select the 'best' alternative solution.

Examples of Analytical Aids

Several case studies were presented at this conference that have used analytical aids in the conflict management area. Other case studies were presented where analytical aids were not used but potentially could have been used to improve the decision making process. A review of the use of analytical aids in some of these case studies is presented below.

Potomac River Basin - In the water supply study for the Potomac River Basin, the Metropolitan Task Force used both a physical system model and an economic forecasting model (McGarry, 1989). The physical system model developed by Dan Sheer used historical river flows, operational characteristics of the three utilities involved in the study, and storage characteristics of the local and Potomac River reservoirs to study the adequacy of the system under drought conditions. Operational plans and centrally directed reservoir releases were simulated on a daily basis to test the response under historical Potomac River drought sequences. The engineer/managers analyzed the assumptions and the operational plans and accepted the conclusions that the existing reservoirs were adequate if the three utilities were operated to optimize the regional response. The economic modeling was performed by John Boland in response to the Citizen Advisory Committee's (CAC) concern with water use projections. Boland analyzed the water demand using computer models considering both the impacts of pricing policies and water conservation plans. He developed scenarios incorporating the risk of various levels of water use restrictions which were evaluated by the CAC and elected officials in terms of acceptable social and economic results. The complex issue of risk management / drought management was presented in a comprehensible manner (e.g. medium risk [8% probability] of moderate restrictions but a very low probability [1%] of severe restrictions) that led to acceptance by the group.

Pecos River Study - Analytical aids were an important part of the litigation between New Mexico and Texas regarding water allocation of the Pecos River (DuMars, 1989). The wording of the interstate compact required that a water budget be developed and that gains or losses along the river be attributed to natural or man made causes. Because of the protracted duration of the litigation, the final water budget model was a hybrid reflecting a series of judgments regarding the hydrology of the area. These relationships between input and output were based on statistical curve fitting techniques rather than modern process modeling approaches. In this case, the appropriate analytical aids needed to be simple and very easy to comprehend. The engineers' role was to develop technically defensible models that could conform to several judicial precedents on the hydrology that were based on a limited data set. Thus, the primary challenge was the development of a model that was constrained by historical views and was acceptable to both states.

Platte River Study - A wide range of analytical aids were used in the Platte River study (Bleed, 1989). Included in this study were a screening model designed to eliminate inferior alternatives used in tandem with a multi objective optimization model (Bleed, 1986). The optimization model maximized two non commensurate objectives, the present value of net benefits and the quality of wildlife habitat, subject to flow and capital constraints. Both of these models combined aspects of physical system and socio economic modeling. The study also included the use of GIS technology to analyze channel and vegetation changes. GIS provides a means of overlaying spatially based data and incorporating such data in both physical system and socio economic analyses.

Fox River/Green Bay Study - Day (1989) reported on the preparation of a Remedial Action Plan (RAP) for the Fox River/Green Bay, Wisconsin area. No formal analytical aids were used in this study. However, various physical system analysis aids could have beneficially been applied including a graphic display based on a GIS portraying the portions of the Bay presently affected by algae blooms during summer low flow and high temperature conditions to be used in conjunction with a model predicting the impacts of a cleanup of upstream non point sources. Such aids would have helped to inform local groups of the potential for improvements and would have stimulated a more extensive effort to identify alternative solutions and costs.

Bulkley (1989) reported on five cases in conflict management that are in various stages of resolution. In all of these cases, minimal or no formal analytical aids were used though their use could have assisted in their resolution. For example, in the case involving apportionment of the cost of the improvements to the Detroit Wastewater Treatment Plant between the City of Detroit and 78 suburbs, analytical aids for calculating and displaying the implications of various apportionment methods could have resulted in an improved process. In the Westway case, the Corps of Engineers were required to prepare a supplemental Environmental Impact Statement which focused on the impact of landfilling on both water quality and fishery resources in the lower Hudson River. Had the Corps actually proceeded with this study, it is clear that a variety of analytical techniques for assessing the physical and biological system would have been useful. Similarly, a variety of socio economic and physical system models could have been beneficially applied in the resolution of the other cases.

Application of Analytical Aids

As was illustrated in the introduction to this paper, if properly applied, analytical aids can serve a useful role in conflict management. However, the possibilities for abuse are also quite real and, thus, care must be taken in the selection and application of these tools. Some of the factors that should be considered in the use of analytical aids are discussed below:

- Appropriateness - Foremost in the process, the analytical aids must be appropriate to the situation. An inappropriate model can introduce incorrect information into the decision making process leading to a solution which may not fulfill the needs and expectations of the stakeholders.

- Communication - The analytical aids and the persons using and interpreting the results of the analytical aids must communicate the information generated by the analytical aids to the stakeholders. Frequently, this information may be quite complex and voluminous and to be useful, must be displayed in a meaningful manner.

- Packaging - The 'packaging' of the analytical aids is important in both establishing the credibility of the tool and in communicating information to the stakeholders. Packaging for the sake of dazzling the stakeholders with 'glitz' should be avoided since such a strategy can mask inadequacies of the analytical aid. This factor will become more important as the complexity of the models increase and the potential for abuse increases due to improvements in the visual packaging of computer based tools.

- Sound data and basis - It is essential that analytical aids be based on sound technical grounds and use a sound data base. Risks associated with uncertainty in the methodologies or data should be clearly delineated and communicated to the stakeholders. Techniques such as 'sensitivity analysis' should be employed to demonstrate the response of the model to variability in parameters and to direct areas for further field level analyses.

- Understandable methods - Many of the analytical aids are based on highly complex mathematical representations of the real world. These techniques frequently provide better information which can lead to more successful conflict resolution. Though the aids may be complex, it is essential that they are understandable to the stakeholders. This does not mean that the stakeholders must understand the technical details of the aids, but they must understand the aims and limitations of the methods.

THE ROLE OF THE ENGINEER

The engineer frequently serves in many roles in the conflict management area: as analytical expert/advisor, as a member of a interdisciplinary facilitation team (stakeholder), as the facilitator, and even as the decision maker. In each of these roles, the engineer can bring an an analytical, problem solving background to the process. However, in studying the role of the engineer with respect to the involvement of analytical aids, the most common role is as the analytical expert and advisor. In this role, the engineer may develop, select, implement and apply analytical aids, and analyze and communicate the results of the application of these aids.

Within the conflict management area, this role of the engineer as the analytical expert/advisor may be depicted schematically by the following diagram.

Figure 2 Schematic representation of role of engineer as analytical expert / advisor

In real world conflict management cases, the engineer may not actually sit in a room with the stakeholders and with his/her computer and directly interact with the stakeholders in a real time exchange. However, the role of the engineer is to help develop and evaluate alternatives and provide this information to stakeholders and/or decision makers. Typically, the involvement of the engineer differs depending upon the category of analytic aid that is being used. As shown in Figure 3, aids used to assist in physical system analysis are generally considered to be the primary responsibility of the engineer (or other scientists). Input by the stakeholders is relatively minor for these type of aids. The engineer may also have some responsibility for socio economic aids but the contributions and responsibilities are shared with the stakeholders. The primary responsibility for collective choice aids lies primarily with the stakeholders. Though the engineer may actually develop, select, implement and apply each of these aids, the responsibility for the parameterization of the collective choice models lies primarily with the stakeholders while the responsibility for parameterization of the physical system models lie primarily with the engineer.

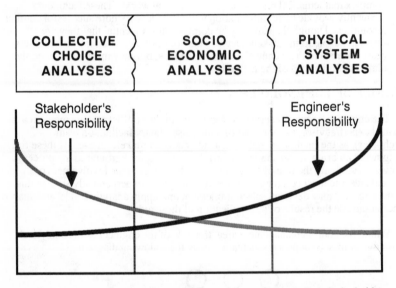

Figure 3 Degree of responsibility for parameterization of analytical aids

In this role, the engineer must exhibit certain qualities in addition to possessing the required technical capabilities, specifically: credibility, respect, and integrity . The need for these characteristics is magnified by the complexity of the analytical aids and technical processes which requires a trusted person to communicate the results to the stakeholders. Thus, communication skills and skills associated with working with people and groups become additional requirements for the engineer to effectively work in the conflict management area.

CONCLUSIONS

It is clear from our discussions that the use of analytical aids within the area of conflict management is an expanding one. As these aids become more complex, their speed and interaction` increase, and 'packaging' becomes more visually attractive, it is essential that the integrity must remain. The engineer can and should continue to serve multiple roles of developing and applying such aids, and analyzing and communicating the results of the application of the aids to the stakeholders and decision makers. The skills required by the engineer to perform these multiple roles should be fostered by the engineering educational field.

APPENDIX

References:

Bleed, A.S., 1989, "Platte River Conflict Resolution", Engineering Foundation Conf. on Managing Water-Related Conflicts: The Engineer's Role, Santa Barbara, CA

Bleed, A.S., 1986, "Platte River Nebraska, Water Allocation", Engineering Foundation Conf. on Social and Environmental Objectives in Water Resources Planning and Management, Santa Barbara, CA

Bulkley, J.W., 1989, "Viewpoint - The Engineer's Role in Conflict Management", Engineering Foundation Conf. on Managing Water-Related Conflicts: The Engineer's Role, Santa Barbara, CA

da Costa, J.R. and Loucks, D.P. (1989), "Computer-Aided Planning and Decision Support", Proceedings, Water Resources Planning and Management Conference, ASCE, Sacramento, CA

Day, H.J., 1989, "Viewpoint - The Engineer's Role in Conflict Management", Engineering Foundation Conf. on Managing Water-Related Conflicts: The Engineer's Role, Santa Barbara, CA

DuMars, C.T., 1989, "Interstate Water Transfer Conflicts: The Case of New Mexico and Texas", Engineering Foundation Conf. on Managing Water-Related Conflicts: The Engineer's Role, Santa Barbara, CA

McGarry, R.S., 1989, "Water Management in the Potomac River Basin", Engineering Foundation Conf. on Managing Water-Related Conflicts: The Engineer's Role, Santa Barbara, CA

Managing Water Related Conflicts Using Negotiation - Work Group Report

The work group consisted of Suzanne Orenstein, Conservation Foundation; Gregory Bourne, Georgia Institute of Technology; Curtis Brown, U.S. Bureau of Reclamation; Madge Ertel, U.S. Geological Survey; Timer Powers, South Florida Water Management District; Kyle Schilling, U.S. Army Corps of Engineers; Ernest Smerdon, University of Arizona; and, Claire Welty, Drexel University. The work group focused on the roles of engineers in public policy decision-making processes and, more specifically, in dispute resolution processes. The work of the group addressed three major areas: the role of the engineer in public policy decision-making, particularly as it pertains to conflict management; designing a conflict management process; and, recognizing the new dimensions of engineers in public policy decision-making and conflict management. A wide variety of dispute resolution and conflict management techniques have been used to resolve public policy issues. The work group commends the texts listed at the end of this paper as references to those techniques.

A. The Role of the Engineer in Public Policy Decision-Making and Dispute Resolution

The traditional role of the engineer in public policy related issues has been that of problem-solver and technical expert. Engineers play critical roles in a variety of water-related issues assessing feasibility and design options for dams, stormwater detention, sewage treatment, waste treatment facilities (effects on groundwater), water diversions, among others. Every community deals with some combination of these issues. Since they affect the ability of a community to grow, they are essential elements of public policy. Increasingly, water-related issues are at the heart of growth management related disputes.

Given the conflicts that can arise in this environment, is it important for the engineer to play additional roles to that of problem solver and technical expert? At least five other roles have been identified in which engineers may find themselves. These roles include negotiator/advocate, mediator, convener, neutral fact-finder and conflict evaluator. While the engineer may have occasion to play each of these roles, most members of the work group believe all remain secondary to the role of problem solver. The extent to which an engineer serves in any of these capacities depends on the situation. For example, if serving in an administrative capacity, the ability to perform these expanded roles may be paramount to the successful completion of responsibilities. On the other hand, if serving as a project engineer, the opportunities to engage in some of these roles (eg. convene a conflict management process) may be limited. Even under such conditions, however, some other roles will still be appropriate (eg. intra-organizational mediation concerning project objectives). As such, the organizational and project responsibilities of the engineer will largely dictate which of the roles are appropriate and important to fill.

Two premises are worthy to note. The first is that engineers are increasingly finding themselves in positions where unilateral technical decisions can not be implemented. Teamwork with other parties, including public sector interests, is often required. This requires the engineer to develop new strategies and new contexts for decision-making. Engaging in negotiations involves advocating particular approaches, assumptions or solutions. Beyond this, however, a process open to negotiation suggests dialogue, understanding the concerns of parties affected by a particular decision, and perhaps even consensus-building. Therefore, building the capacity of engineers to fill the various roles identified is important, along with identifying the potential pitfalls which can be encountered in attempting to serve in these other capacities.

The second important premise of this paper is that, in general, projects involving public policy issues will benefit from open dialogue. This premise is important to understand for two reasons. First, many still have negative perceptions about open decision-making processes. Many of these perceptions stem from experiences of public meetings for which preparation and organization were often not adequate. What we mean by open processes is discussed more in section 2 of this paper. Second, the reality of today's decision-making environment is that if interest groups are adequately organized and focused (which increasing numbers are), decisions can be effectively forestalled at the decision-making or implementation phases of a project. This reality needs to be effectively addressed if projects are to be approved and implemented in a timely fashion.

Given these two premises, realization of the new and various roles of engineers in decision-making takes on added significance. Three of the roles identified above, in particular, contain potential pitfalls in practice; as such, the work group focused on these three roles in greater depth.

Problem-solver/technical expert. The work group focused on two major aspects of the engineers role as problem solver and technical expert. First, is the need to understand the balance between political and technical forces as they affect decisions. Understanding that balance assists the engineer in clarifying his/her role in the overall decision-making framework. The following figure helps define the spectrum:

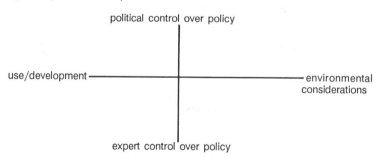

(Freemuth - Adapted)
Some decisions are dominated by political policy whereas others are driven more by the determination of technical solutions by experts. Without getting into the wide-range of implications associated with this spectrum, understanding the primary influences on decision-making can assist the engineer make more informed decisions about his/her role in the process. For example, a project to carry out a policy decision to emphasize use/development of resources over preservation may have significantly different characteristics from a policy decision to implement the best technical solution that can be derived to solve an issue

of environmental impact. The role of engineer as problem solver could be significantly different under these two scenarios.

The underlying importance of this to the engineer involved in public policy decision-making processes rests in the political paradox. Some observers believe that technically oriented people need to expand their perceptions about decision-making to account for the political realities. At the same time, political processes are not precise and to a large extent will be driven by technical information. As such, the engineer should have an appreciation for the factors affecting the decision-making process since most public policy decisions integrate both political and technical elements.

This discussion of the political and technical aspects of decision-making leads to the second major point; whether the engineer should be concerned with the process of decision-making. Given the increasing complexities of public policy decision-making, and implementation of projects that fulfill those policies, the work group strongly suggests that engineers think more proactively about the processes which support decision-making. The design, analysis, evaluation and implementation phases of problem solving can each be significantly affected by *how* decisions are made.

With increasing frequency, interest groups and parties affected by particular decisions act to challenge, delay and stop projects and their implementation. On the other hand, open, deliberative, consensus-building processes have in many instances helped resolve conflicts of interest and arrive at sound policy choices. Therefore, it behooves the engineer and those responsible for generating public policy options to understand how interested parties are involved in the decision-making process and to provide technical information that informs as many of the parties as possible. Engineers should objectively assist the multiple parties involved in decision-making to understand more thoroughly the technical choices they face. Since many engineers do not correlate the process of decision-making with their role as technical problem-solver, it is important for engineers to re-visit their perspectives on this inter-relationship.

Negotiator/advocate. Often times, engineers may find themselves in a position of advocating a particular outcome which reflects the bias of their organization or their personal bias. In and of itself, this is not detrimental, particularly if those bias' are understood. The problems emerge when the engineer is advocating a solution under the presumption of neutrality when in fact that presumption is incorrect. It is totally appropriate for the engineer to act as an advocate as long as confusion about neutrality is avoided.

Another aspect of advocacy should also be considered. Depending on the selection criteria, a variety of options might exist to solve a particular problem. One solution may be the least cost alternative, another may be the most environmentally sensitive and yet another may be the safest. As problem solver and technical expert, the engineer is called upon to develop and analyze the range of possible options given certain policy directives. This brings us to the second potential pitfall concerning advocacy: the need to distinguish between technical analysis and policy choices. Conflict can occur when engineers mix these two and suggest which option should be selected based on the best technical solution. For example, balancing acceptable risk factors in dam design and associated costs, which ultimately may dictate which solution is optimal (or realistic) for a specific situation, should be addressed explicitly in the decision-making process, rather than the engineer advocating a decision based on technical information alone. The two should be fully integrated into the decision-making process.

As has been observed, certain pitfalls exist for the engineer in the role of advocate. In the broader context, however, negotiation implies an openness to considering a variety of options and has several other positive attributes. Negotiation is not always advocacy as discussed above. Negotiation also provides a process to allow engineers to understand the preferences and interests of individuals and institutions who have a stake in the outcome.

A question which often arises, however, concerns when it is appropriate to initiate negotiations. How does one determine when an issue or outcome should be negotiated? In general, negotiations may be useful when:

1) inter-related decisions require coordination of design, evaluation or implementation of projects
2) broad, multi-interest support is needed to reach an agreement or implement a project
3) resources must be pooled to accomplish objectives
4) others are needed to voluntarily implement a solution or improve implementation
5) other decision-making approaches will likely provide an inferior outcome and/or negotiation offers the opportunity for a superior outcome.

Although the potential benefits of negotiation processes are great, the limitations of negotiation as practiced by many needs to be recognized. Typical problems encountered in negotiations include:

o   positional bargaining (bargaining about positions taken by various sides instead of the interests underlying those positions),
o   dueling experts (each side brings in their own expert to present information to support their position and refute the others expert, which tends to undermine the credibility of technical analysis and creates confusion among decision-makers), and
o   power politics (where a party who in perception or reality is dominant and attempts to influence the decision-making process at the expense of sound, rational decision-making based on the substance of the issues).

Effective models of negotiation are based on understanding the real and legitimate interests of the stakeholders. The substance of the issues are addressed based on the merits of the issues, where evaluation criteria are jointly developed, options are developed focused on meeting the concerns and interests of the major stakeholders, and decisions are based on objective criteria. These ideas form the basis of principled negotiation (Fisher and Ury) which stresses holding firm to ones objectives in a negotiation, but being flexible on how those objectives are obtained (Pruitt and Rubin).

Mediator - in most cases, engineers will not serve as mediators of major, multi-party, public policy issues. Nonetheless, engineers can serve an important mediation role in three areas. First, engineers can be an advocate for an open process to deal with differing viewpoints concerning a particular project. Often times, those involved in conducting a controversial project act to avoid conflict. Rather than encountering differences as they emerge and seeking to resolve those differences, efforts are often undertaken to disavow that such differences exist. With public policy issues, however, experience indicates that such efforts typically backfire causing even greater problems, such as project delay, distrust and perhaps even litigation. Therefore, project engineers have reason to advocate an open process.

Second, engineers can be an advocate for interest-based problem solving. By having a greater understanding of the interests of stakeholders, the engineering and problem-solving process can be made more effective and responsive. Furthermore, the objections which would likely result from certain alternatives can be addressed explicitly by the process or by technical analyses.

Third, engineers can work within organizations or project teams to mediate intra-organizational decision-making. Different factions of an organization or project team often bring differing views which affect the project design or development of alternatives. With the development of sound negotiation and mediation skills, engineers can serve in an important capacity which will help improve products, build support for decisions and improve working relationships.

The importance of the other three potential roles of the engineer should not be overlooked in a discussion of the engineer as problem-solver, negotiator and mediator. As **convener**, the engineer can serve to initiate open, consensus-building processes by bringing together crucial stakeholders and those responsible for decision-making. While this most likely will occur within an organization or project team, awareness of the possibilities will be helpful to larger decision-making processes. In consensus-building processes, the role of engineer as **neutral factfinder** emerges. In this setting, the engineer is requested to serve as a neutral expert whom each party feels is both an expert on the subject and relatively objective. If an engineer has a stake in the outcome, it is unlikely that he/she will be asked to serve in such a capacity. Most likely, engineers who do not have a stake in the decision and who are broadly perceived to be both knowledgeable and objective will be asked to serve in this role. This is a role that can be nurtured by engineers since joint factfinding is an integral part of consensus-building processes. The final role identified is that of **conflict evaluator**. The concept behind this role is one of awareness and anticipation. Many engineering professors are stressing the importance of increasing the awareness and sensitivity of engineers to potential conflicts likely to arise in engineering projects prior to their actual emergence. By so doing, the engineer is better prepared to deal with the potentially controversial elements of a project and support proactive conflict management and problem-solving processes.

B. Designing Public Involvement and Conflict Management Processes

One of the main constraints to the use of negotiation and consensus-building processes for controversial or complex public policy issues is awareness and education. Many planners, policy-makers and engineers are not knowledgeable of the options and tools which have been developed for managing public conflicts. In part this is due to the relatively recent expansion of demands on decision-making processes and those involved in such processes, including engineers. Many traditional means for dealing with public concerns lack either sufficient flexibility or theoretical underpinnings to achieve the resolution of conflict.

One way to assist the engineer in dealing with the increased demands encountered, is to understand more thoroughly the major causes and responses to conflict. The recommended readings list contains many thorough discussions of the social psychology underlying multi-party conflict. Another way to assist the engineer is to provide guidance on how to map conflicts and how best to deal with conflicts given the various stages of intensity. While more sophisticated "maps" exist, the following should provide some basic fundamentals for understanding how best to proceed with public policy conflicts.

| agreement | emerging disagreements | adversarial attitudes developing | polarization of issues and relationships | intractable conflict |

Dispute Spectrum

Primarily, conflict management processes are designed for the middle three stages of conflict. The process applied, and the intensity of the process, depends on the dynamics of the conflict. A variety of tools exist to address varying levels or intensities of conflict. These are represented in the following process spectrum.

| avoidance | public involvement (communication) | negotiation | mediation and joint fact-finding | adjudication - litigation, arbitration and administrative hearings |

Process Spectrum

The active stages of the process spectrum range from group communication and feedback processes, to direct engagement of stakeholders in negotiations, to assistance of a third-party (mediator) to help stakeholders reach agreement, to invoking a third-party's decision on the stakeholders. Negotiation and mediation offer the advantages of allowing major stakeholders to have direct involvement in decision making, rather than requiring a third party to dictate a decision.

Once the determination has been made that a dispute resolution process is required, how does one proceed? In general, it is helpful to break dispute resolution processes into three phases: conflict assessment/pre-negotiation, negotiation and joint factfinding, and implementation. The following tasks are associated with each of the three phases:

Conflict Assessment.
* clarify major issues
* identify individuals and organizations with a stake in the outcome
* identify individuals and organizations who can block agreements or implementation
* identify underlying interests of the major stakeholders
* obtain stakeholders and decision-makers acceptance of a process to resolve identified conflicts

Negotiation and Joint Factfinding.
* initiate the dispute resolution process
* agree on objectives of the process
* clarify differences among parties
* clarify interests of the stakeholders
* document existing conditions associated with the identified problems
* conduct joint factfinding/data collection as necessary

* generate alternatives to meet each parties interests
* establish evaluation criteria
* evaluate alternatives based on criteria established
* select options which maximize benefits to each party and meet process objectives

Implementation.
* identify tasks necessary to implement agreements
* identify who will conduct specific tasks
* establish a timeframe for conducting and completing tasks
* establish an advisory group (or similar mechanism) to oversee activities
* meet after a pre-designated period of time to evaluate agreements.

Often, the negotiation phase of the process is given the most attention. In fact, the negotiation phase is less likely to succeed if an equal or greater amount of time is not spent on the other phases. The value of adequate preparation before entering into negotiations or other dispute resolution processes can not be overstated. Likewise, systematically developing an implementation plan is crucial to the success of any negotiated agreements.

These guidelines are helpful regardless of the type of conflict management process employed. An appropriate time and place exists for each of the various types of conflict management processes available. In some cases, good two-way communication through well-designed public involvement programs is sufficient. On other occasions, direct negotiations may be necessary. These might be conducted directly or with the aid of a mediator. On other occasions, negotiations might be conducted in the context of a mini-trial. By becoming more aware of the available conflict management tools, and more comfortable with their use, engineers will be better able to respond to the demands encountered in controversial projects.

C. New Dimensions of the Engineer in Decision-Making and Dispute Resolution

As has been alluded to throughout this paper and others presented at the conference, the engineer is increasingly being cast into new roles or working in new environments. An example of the latter is the emerging use of project teams which include people without "technical" expertise. Project teams might combine engineers with economists, sociologists, biologists, etc. Project teams might also include representatives of interest groups and government. As such, engineers must be able to communicate effectively with people of varied backgrounds who have the skills and experience requisite to the successful completion of a project.

Many engineers have been working in such environments for many years. Even so, the role of the engineer may be shifting from that of primary problem solver and technical expert to that of team member. For some, this is a difficult transition. Yet under such conditions the engineer more than ever must be adaptable to maintain his/her effectiveness. While the need to adapt to the role of team member might not occur on every project, sensitivity to the need and conditions will be helpful when those conditions arise.

Given the expanding complexity of problems and demands on engineers, how can engineers create adaptive strategies for maintaining their effectiveness. Three mechanisms are suggested; education, training and development of new methods for engaging in decision-making processes.

Education. Sentiment is growing among professional educators and engineers for expanded curricula to build the capacity of new engineers to understand and respond effectively to conflict. Many university-based engineering programs which focus on public works and other forms of engineering with public policy implications, place little emphasis on the political and sociological dimensions of the decision-making environment. It is strongly recommended that engineering curricula be expanded to provide greater exposure for developing engineers to the multiplicity of interests they will encounter. This is a critical step to help new engineers be effective in multi-disciplinary environments. Specifically, curricula should be developed concerning the engineers role in public decision-making and conflict management processes.

Training. In addition to educating new engineers, a clear need exists to build the capabilities of experienced engineers in these areas as well. Continuing education programs should be stressed for engineers who work on projects of public interest, who deal directly with the public and who are often involved on inter-disciplinary project teams. Courses should focus on effective public involvement techniques, communication skills and negotiation skills.

Develop new methods for engaging in decision-making processes. Concern exists among some engineers that the mechanisms for engineers to interact in decision-making processes is often limited. Development of new approaches to participation in decision-making processes would enhance the effectiveness of engineers. This problem is characterized in part by the dilemmas encountered in presenting technical information to the public. Too often, inadequate attention is given to helping the public understand the technical aspects of projects. Public uncertainty about data collection and interpretation, analytical analysis, the basis of assumptions used in analytical design, and technical evaluation criteria have been fostered to a large extent by decision-makers assuming a lack of public interest in or ability to understand the issues. While this presumption may have some validity, it also creates conflicts. Therefore, the development of new attitudes and capabilities for sharing and explaining technical information and assumptions may greatly reduce conflicts caused by uncertainty, misperceptions and distrust.

Clearly, the increased complexity of many public policy issues and the increased demands of various constituencies on public leaders has changed the decision-making environment. Engineers involved with issues of public interest are directly affected by these dynamics. As such, many engineers are required to adapt and develop new dimensions. This paper is intended to assist engineers better understand the decision-making climate in which they work and to explore new tools and adaptive strategies for working in this climate. By becoming more comfortable with expanded or different roles, and associated new perspectives, engineers will enhance their standing and effectiveness.

REFERENCES

Roger Fisher and William Ury. Getting to Yes. New York: Penguin Books, 1981. ?

John Freemuth, "The National Parks: Political Versus Professional Determinants of Policy". Public Administration Review. May/June 1989.

Dean Pruitt and Jeffrey Rubin. Social Conflict. New York: Random House, 1986.

OTHER SUGGESTED READINGS

Lawrence Bacow and Michael Wheeler. Environmental Dispute Resolution. New York: Plenum Press, 1984.

Gail Bingham. Resolving Environmental Disputes. Washington, D.C.: The Conservation Foundation, 1986.

Susan Carpenter and William Kennedy. Managing Public Disputes. San Francisco: Jossey-Bass, 1988.

John Folk-Williams, Susan Fry and Lucy Hilgendorf. Water in the West. Covelo, CA: Island Press and Sante Fe, NM: Western Network, 1985.

David Lax and James Sebenius. The Manager as Negotiator, New York: The Free Press, 1984.

Christopher Moore. The Mediation Process. San Francisco: Jossey-Bass, 1986.

Lawrence Susskind and Jeffrey Cruikshank. Breaking the Impasse. New York: Basic Books, 1987.

Engineering Foundation Conferences

<u>Managing Water Related Conflicts: The Engineer's Role</u>

Sheraton Santa Barbara Hotel
Santa Barbara,

PARTICIPANT'S LIST

Bleed, Ann S., State Hydrologist
    Nebraska Dept of Water Res.

Bourne, R. G., Executive Director
    Georgia Institute of Tech.

Brown, Curtis, Chief, Decision Analysis Sect.
    U.S. Bureau of Reclamation

Bulkley, Jonathan W., Professor
    University of Michigan

Cox, William E., Professor
    Virginia Tech

Day, Harold J., Professor
    University of Wisconsin

Delli Priscoli, Jerome, Senior Analyst
    U.S. Army Corps of Engineers

Dumars, Charles T., Professor
    University of New Mexico

Ertel, Madge O., State Liaison Specialist
    U.S. Geological Survey

Grayman, Walter M., President
    Consulting Engineer

Gregg, Frank, Professor
    University of Arizona

Heaney, James P., Professor
    University of Florida

Kattelmann, Richard C., Hydrologist
    Computer Systems Lab

Lancaster, Charles L., Assistant Program Mgr.
    U.S. Army Corps of Engineers

Lefkoff, Merle S., President
    ARS Publica

PARTICIPANT'S LIST

Lord, William B., Professor
    University of Arizona

Loucks, Daniel P., Professor
    Cornell University

McArdle, Donna Marie
    Engineering Foundation

McGarry, Robert S., Director
    Montgomery County,Dept Trans.

Moore, Christopher W., Partner
    CDR Associates

Nolan, Michael F., Supv. Civil Engineer
    U.S. Army Corps of Engineers

Orenstein, Suzanne G., Senior Associate
    The Conservation Foundation

Powers, Timer
    South FL Water Mgmt. District

Schilling, Kyle E., Chief, Policy Studies Div
    U.S. Army Corps of Engineers

Smerdon, Ernest T., Dean
    University of Arizona

Viessman, Jr., Warren, Professor
    University of Florida

Welty, Claire, Asst. Professor
    Drexel University

Yribar, Daniel R., Chief Water Resource & Op
    U.S. Bureau of Reclamation

SUBJECT INDEX
Page number refers to first page of paper.

Analysis, 23
Analytical techniques, 233

Bureau of Reclamation, 223

Case reports, 156
Civil engineers, 238
Claims, 70
Colorado, 156
Compensation, 94
Computer applications, 233
Conflict, 1, 15, 23, 38, 54, 70, 94, 110, 131, 156, 170, 180, 194, 208, 223, 233, 238, 245, 261, 280
Contract terms, 116
Contracts, 70

Dam safety, 223
Decision making, 131, 223, 280
Droughts, 15

Earthquake loads, 223
Engineers, 54, 116, 131, 170, 194, 233, 280
Environmental issues, 23, 208
Expert systems, 141

Federal government, 116
Floods, 15
Florida, 141

Guidelines, 266

Hydrology, 15

Information, 261
Information management, 180
Institutional constraints, 1, 110, 266
Institutions, 266

Litigation, 54

Methodology, 261
Models, 23, 141, 180

Native Americans, 180
Negotiations, 38, 94, 116, 131, 156, 194, 208

Planning, 141
Political factors, 94, 245
Problem solving, 194, 208, 223, 233, 238, 261, 266, 280
Professional role, 54, 131, 170, 194, 233, 238, 280
Public participation, 261
Public policy, 280

Risk management, 116
River regulation, 131
Rural areas, 238

Safety analysis, 223
Social values, 245
State government, 170
State planning, 170
Streams, 156
Structural analysis, 223

Urban areas, 238
U.S. Army Corps of Engineers, 70, 156, 194

Water allocation policy, 38, 131, 245
Water management, 110, 131, 170
Water policy, 1
Water resources, 15, 23, 38, 54, 70, 110, 156, 208, 233, 245
Water resources management, 1, 141, 238
Water rights, 38, 180
Water supply, 116, 141
Water transfer, 94
Water use, 94, 245
Watershed management, 238
Watersheds, 238
Wyoming, 223

AUTHOR INDEX

Page number refers to first page of paper.

Analytical Aids Work Group, 233

Bingham, Gail, 38
Bleed, Ann Salomon, 131
Brown, Curtis A., 223
Bulkley, Jonathan W., 245

Cox, William E., 94

Day, Harold J., 238
DuMars, Charles T., 170

Ertel, Madge O., 261

Grayman, Walter M., 15
Gregg, Frank, 1

Heaney, James P., 141

Institutional Structures Working
Group, 266

Lancaster, Charles L., 194
Lefkoff, Merle S., 156
Lord, William B., 110, 180
Loucks, Daniel P., 23

McGarry, Robert S., 116
Managing Water Related Conflicts
Using Negotiation Work Group,
280
Moore, Christopher W., 208

Orenstein, Suzanne Goulet, 38

Priscoli, Jerome Delli, 70

Shabman, Leonard A., 94
Shillito, Rose M., 180
Smerdon, Ernest T., 54

Wallace, Mary G., 180